Stephen Potter

Alan Jenkins

Stephen Potter
Inventor of Gamesmanship

Weidenfeld and Nicolson
London

© Alan Jenkins

George Weidenfeld and Nicolson Ltd
91 Clapham High Street, London sw4

ISBN 0 297 77817 x

Printed and bound in Great Britain by
Morrison & Gibb Ltd, London and Edinburgh

Contents

Illustrations

The author and publishers would like to thank the following for permission to use pictures: Andrew and Julian Potter, 1, 2, 3, 4, 5, 6, 8, 9; BBC Hulton Picture Library, 10, 11, 13; Lady Meynell, 14; Cadbury Schweppes Ltd, 15; Heather Jenner, 16; and Captain Jack Broome, 17.

Chapter 1
A man so various

The Potter *oeuvre*

'The conceit of making FACETIOUS FORMATIONS by treating -*manship* as the suffix was invented by Stephen Potter in his *Gamesmanship*, *Lifemanship* and *One-Upmanship*, and he has had many imitators: *brinkmanship* is said to have been coined by Adlai Stevenson.'

Fowler's *Modern English Usage* (2nd edn, revised by Sir Ernest Gowers)

'*One-Upmanship*, one of the shaping books of its time.'

Sir Francis Meynell

'He created a world in which he could move easily, and he created an audience that moved easily with him.'

John Stewart Collis

Potter on Potter

'I'm a Twenties man. . . . I belong to the Age of Wireless.'

in a newspaper interview

'Failed academic lecturer, failed novelist, failed literary biographer, reasonable compiler, reasonable educational pamphleteer, failed editor, failed book critic, failed rowing blue. . . . Invented Gamesmanship and Lifemanship in a final attempt to restore the situation.'

from the jacket of his penultimate book

'I don't think there were many young men of my education in London earning quite so little as I was at 30, certainly not married ones. But I was very, very happy.'

'I always hoped my fifties would be the time when I really started writing. . . . I am bursting with ungleaned and undigested material, mostly autobiographical.'

in letters to Rupert Hart-Davis

'A long worm of ash messily drooping from his cigarette.'

self-description in a broadcast

'I was always a last-minute man.'

'Walter Mitty? Why, he's exactly like *me*!'

People on Potter

'He was like a big, overgrown boy, with a great deal of charm.'

Rupert Hart-Davis

'A substantial, honourable and enduring man.'

Bernard Levin

'Long walks with Stephen, talking about books – that was when I grew up.'

Lionel Millard

'His alert eyes were set in laughter wrinkles, his hair always looked as if he had been running his hands through it – as he usually had. He walked about quickly and restlessly.'

John Arlott

'I always see him, cigarette dangling, head on one side, eyes screwed up against the smoke.'

Joe Bryan III

'Such a gifted man – if only he'd discipline himself.'

Herbert Farjeon

'Radio was made for him, and he for radio.'

Joyce Grenfell

'I became very tired of the second-class adolescent mind, the boasting, above all the frenzied collecting of literary lions.'

a BBC colleague

'Stephen, how do you manage to get ash on the back of your collar?'

a bewildered hostess

'A catalyst.'
Robert Gittings

'Wine and music were among the lifelong interests of this most lovable man. While his talk about the former was often loaded with those hidden stratagems one associates with Gamesmanship, music was much too serious a matter for frolics of that kind.'
Lord Horder

'The gentle art of *not* making enemies.'
J.S.Collis

'Quick changes of mood which gave him a multiple personality.'
Sir Francis Meynell

'A rather *dashing* driver.'
Elizabeth Jane Howard

'A hopeless driver!'
Alistair Cooke

'He couldn't get on without praise.'
Mary (Att) Potter

'A bendy, smiling, funny, huggable man!'
Shelagh Metcalf

'We teased each other for 25 years without a moment of malice.'
John Metcalf

'A tall, gangling, untidy, ash-strewn figure . . . with thinning, fairish hair, peering around like some alternately genial and irritable bird of the crane family.'
J.W.Lambert

'Conscious disarray . . . playing the role of genius.'
Rupert Hart-Davis

'Like a good-looking sailor, in elegant turtle-necked sweaters – the sort of Englishman you used to see in bars in Portofino.'
Lady Marley

'Looks like a benign Malcolm Muggeridge.'
Daily Express, 10 April 1959

'He had something of the ham in him . . . there was something very special about his trousers.'
Roy Plomley

'Stephen's contribution to radio was intellectual gaiety.'
Douglas Cleverdon

'. . . a very open mind. It was not comprehensive in understanding
. . . no clear vision or really philosophical feelings, nothing
passionate in the way of intellectual conviction.'
J.S.Collis

'He loved life and lived it bravely.'
Heather James

'. . . our long talks about golf – on which he could be grave and
gay, absurd and endlessly shrewd.'
Alistair Cooke

'His affected amateurism. . . .'
Betty Hardy

'His clown's face. . . .'
Joyce Grenfell

'His pudding-basin haircut. . . .'
Mary Hope Allen

'As soon as he entered a room you knew he was *different*.'
Capt. Jack Broome, DSC

'He was that rare thing, an educated wit.'
Wynford Vaughan-Thomas

'A college oar hung over the mantelshelf of his study. I always
wondered whether this was a piece of One-upmanship.'
John Arlott

'A *laughing* man. . . . Even if he beat you at a game he made you
feel it was a privilege.'
Judge Cyril Conner

'If I am to blame, forgive me over glorious golf.'
S.Potter, mending a quarrel with J.S.Collis

'A tremendous love of life and an enormous variety of interests.
. . . He once told me that what he really would like to do above all
was to produce a work of such etymological importance that he
would be remembered for all time.'
Andrew Potter

'An instant expert . . . he always held that almost any subject was accessible to the layman and was only obscured by a barrier of technical jargon.'

Julian Potter

'He was wonderful at saying the salving thing.'

Lionel Millard

'He had a *cold* streak.'

Lord Horder

'For me, he could do no wrong – I'm blind to any faults he may have had.'

Joe Bryan III

'A fair-haired man with a high forehead and pronounced rear-head, a very English-gentleman face, voice and manner, with a first-rate smile.'

S.Potter at nineteen, described by J.S.Collis

'A great *discoverer*.'

Jack Hargreaves

'Senior undergraduate or junior don.'

Roy Plomley

'The funniest man I've ever met. . . . No, I can't remember anything he actually *said*. . . .'

several informants

'Not to speak anthropophagously, he was a *delicious* man.'

Joe Bryan III

'His talk was better than anything he wrote. . . . He was, to the end of his life, a character he had invented called Stephen Potter.'

John Metcalf

'I still miss him very much – one of the originals who are never replaced.'

Alistair Cooke

Chapter 2
8 June 1931

Nineteen thirty-one has come down in history as a year of financial disaster narrowly averted by a National Government and the abandonment of the Gold Standard, the emergence of Ramsay MacDonald as a national hero ('Thank God for him!' was the headline over J.L.Garvin's editorial in the *Observer*), a naval mutiny at Invergordon, and a tearfully patriotic, spectacular musical play by Noël Coward at Drury Lane called *Cavalcade*.

But for our present purposes the outstanding event of that watershed year was a lawn-tennis match, played at the Greenford, Middlesex, recreation grounds of Birkbeck College, a branch of London University. It was a doubles match in which two lecturers of the College were playing two undergraduates. The identity of the undergraduates is unknown – we can refer to them only as Smith and Brown. (If either of them recognizes himself in this context, let him please come forward and claim the historical recognition which is his due.)

Monday, 8 June, was historically unremarkable. Mr Lloyd George had just made a speech on Free Trade. Parties of MPs had just visited war graves in Flanders. Dean Inge of St Paul's had given a lecture on 'England 1000 Years Hence' in which he saw no hope for peace unless the population could somehow be reduced to twenty million. In Germany there were boring political brawls between communists and Nazis. Miss Texas Guinan, the New York nightclub queen, and her troupe of dancers were trying to land at Le Havre without labour permits. Professor Piccard, at Augsburg, had risen in a balloon to a height of 15,500 metres. Experiments with traffic lights were being carried out all along Oxford Street.

A seemingly more important tennis match, the Davis Cup semifinal, had, during the weekend, been played off at Devonshire Park, Eastbourne: Britain, represented by Bunny Austin and Fred Perry, had beaten South Africa. But there was no portent, no prodigy, no two-headed calf or lion in the Capitol, to forewarn the world of the imminent birth of Gamesmanship. Yet stay – had there not been an earthquake tremor across the whole country just after midnight, its epicentre in the North Sea, causing a burst water-main in Shoreditch? The Eagle Star rushed out a new earthquake insurance policy, and *The Times* correspondence columns were filled for weeks with letters from readers whose memories went back to the terrible quake of 1884.

The two lecturers made an odd pair. One, the hero of this book, was Stephen Meredith Potter, aged thirty-one, lecturer in English, whose hair was 'golden' or 'grubby fair', according to whether he was being described by a girl or a man, and whether he had washed it during the last few weeks. A thin, wiry man of 6ft 1in., gangling-athletic, he tended to take refuge, when things were going badly, in such apologetic phrases as 'Of course, tennis isn't really my game'. He had published a baffling first novel, and a pioneering critical book on D.H.Lawrence which had made, he was entitled to claim, and did, 'quite a splash'. He would one day be famous, famous (in his view) for the wrong reason, as the inventor of Gamesmanship, Lifemanship and all that developed therefrom; a professional funny man who was expected to be witty and whimsical wherever he went.

The other lecturer almost defies description. Smaller, fatter, with a goatish greying beard, he wore dark baggy trousers hitched up by an old tie, or possibly string. He played tennis with an all-metal racquet, then regarded as totally caddish. Dr Cyril Edwin Mitchenson Joad, DLitt, then forty, had been appointed Professor of Philosophy at Birkbeck the previous year, was educated at Blundell's and Balliol, and had been a John Locke Scholar in Moral Philosophy. He pronounced the word 'fee-lotho-fee', having an extraordinary voice with guttural r's and a lisp which sounded German-Jewish but may have been a speech impediment. This voice would one day be nationally famous, as famous as his gales of squealing laughter, like the sound of armchairs on unlubricated castors being pushed briskly about a room, as he took part in, and often dominated, a popular and sometimes hilarious question-and-answer radio programme, 'The Brains Trust'. He was particularly noted for parrying almost every question to which he could not supply an immediate answer with 'It depends what you mean by . . .'. He dabbled in all sorts of esoteric matters, such as the teaching of the fashionable guru Radhakrishnan, who sought to combine the practical energy of the West with the passive inner peace of the East.

Two years after this historic tennis match he earned equal measures of admiration and obloquy for speaking, at the notorious Oxford Union debate, for the motion 'that this House will not fight for King and Country'. His total of books, mostly popular-educational, would exceed fifty. Some of them had been written during his twelve years as a civil servant at the Board of Trade and the Ministry of Labour; colleagues of his have told me that the service was not altogether sorry to lose him as he tended to use Government stationery for his philosophical works.

Joad, a conscientious objector to all manner of things, could seldom see a notice saying 'Trespassers will be Prosecuted' without climbing a barbed-wire fence or a padlocked gate to have the pleasure of defying private property, safe in the certainty that 'you can't prosecute for trespass unless you can prove damage'. As a conscientious objector to conventional morality he was a great seducer of earnest left-wing girls at Fabian Summer Schools. A great proponent of co-education, indeed co-everything, he loved to organize mixed hockey matches near his home on Hampstead Heath, at which few rules were unbroken and no holds barred.

A firm friend of Harry Price, the psychical researcher who investigated Borley Rectory, Joad took part, in 1932, in Price's celebrated black-magic experiment known as the Blocksberg Tryst. On the top of the Brocken, in the Harz Mountains, an 'unspotted maid' would be introduced to a white goat which, after magic ceremonies, would be transformed into 'a youth of surpassing beauty'. Before the gathered press of all Europe precisely nothing happened.

Towards the end of Joad's life he was apprehended for travelling without a valid railway ticket. He had, in fact, been doing this sort of thing for years and his friends tell of the lengths he would go to indulge this gesture of rebellion. Travelling from Paddington to Penzance he would nip out of the train at Bodmin Road and buy a ticket for the last fifty miles of a 300-mile journey.

If Joad has monopolized our attention for the last few paragraphs it is because he was an important influence on Stephen Potter (but not, we hasten to add, in the matter of railway tickets); the kind of

Bohemian larger-than-life character that fascinates a young man raised conventionally in the suburbs of south London. On 8 June 1931 Joad was playing his usual rather sweaty game of tennis, the kind of game he always enjoyed at the Essex home of his friend, H.G.Wells. The game was not going well for the two lecturers. Let Potter himself explain:

'Our opponents were . . . competing against us not only with the advantage of age but also with a decisive advantage in style. They would throw the service ball very high in the modern manner. . . .' It was clear, from the preliminary knock-up, that Potter and Joad were going to be beaten by two 'particularly tall and athletic young men' who played back-hands, not from the navel but, in the new Wimbledon manner, at arm's length across the body. Joad seemed paralysed; even by grasping his racquet with both hands he was unable to touch the younger men's smash services. The score was forty-love for the younger men when Joad produced what, in the history of Gamesmanship, was to be known as Joad's Gambit. Smith was halfway across the court, about to serve to Potter when Joad, standing close to the net, suddenly rapped out: 'Kindly say clearly, please, whether the ball was in or out.'

To a couple of students, 'both in the highest degree charming, well-mannered young men, perfect in their sportsmanship and behaviour', this was completely off-putting. Smith consulted Brown, and both apologized unnecessarily. Brown added: 'Do let's have it again.' Joad, unsmiling, said: 'No, I don't want to have it again. I only want you to say clearly, if you will, whether the ball is in or out.' An atmosphere of awkwardness had been created. The young undergraduates felt, though it had never been expressed, that their sportsmanship was in question. Smith's next two services were double faults. Potter and Joad won the game.

Thinking things over afterwards, amid 'the damp roller-towels of the changing-room', Potter conceived the first outline of the Games/Lifemanship science, the twin arts of 'winning games without actually cheating' and making your opponent 'feel that something has gone wrong, however slightly'. And yet, as he himself admitted, something of the kind had been practised by him and his friends for the past decade or more. The Farjeons at Forest Hill, London SE, and afterwards at St John's Wood, NW; the Meynells in London and Essex and Suffolk, even when playing so innocuous a game as ping-pong – they had all, unashamedly and against the nice traditions of their upper-middle-class and public-school upbringings, played to *win*.

The idea of fair play, anyway, is a little less than a hundred years old and probably dates from the Christian foundations of such schools as Rugby, in particular from Dr Arnold. Somewhere in the archives of the Lifemanship Correspondence College at Station Road, Yeovil, there is no doubt a suppressed thesis, based on an Ancient Greek philosopher who shall be nameless, which comes right out with it, and says, 'If at first you don't succeed, *cheat*.'

This would have shocked nobody in the Ancient World. There may be a word for 'gentleman' in various foreign languages, but there is no word for 'fair play', and only approximations for the expression 'good loser'. Duplicity was a Greek virtue and Odysseus was 'many-wiled'. It was normal in chariot races to interfere with your opponents' wheels, and Professor Peter McIntosh, in his *Fair Play: Ethics in Sport and Education* (Heinemann 1979) quotes 'one race of 40 chariots – [in which] only one survived'. The 'all-seeing eye' of Zeus was supposed to ensure justice; but, if you lost, your own mother wouldn't speak to you. Pythagoras alone seemed to hold that sport was a good thing provided every competitor refused to win, and Aristotle thought sportsmen were 'useless to society'. Pythagoras, but not Potter, would have understood the American tennis star, Chris Evert, who 'corrected the umpire when he had given a point in her favour' and 'lost the point, the match and the championship'. How merciful that Potter did not live to witness the crude Gamesmanship of Nastase at Wimbledon, clowning to upset his opponent and complaining to the referee.

Gamesmanship, Lifemanship and One-upmanship have taken their place among the cults and keywords of the last thirty years, alongside Mitford and Ross's U and non-U, Parkinson's Law, Priestley's Admass, Macmillan's Wind of Change, Churchill's Iron Curtain, De Bono's Lateral Thinking, Orwell's Newspeak and Doublethink, Searle's St Trinian's; perhaps they even rank with the effect on fashionable speech, in their lifetimes, of Wodehouse and Sir Alan Herbert. All have altered, in varying degrees, our language and thought. Under the heading 'Brinkmanship', Fowler's *Modern English Usage* acknowledges our language's debt to Potter. The deciding factor was the use of the word in a *Times* leading article – 'American brinkmanship has not led to British panic'. In *The Oxford Dictionary of Quotations* he is unrepresented, although the editors see fit to include the anonymous copywriter for Beecham's Pills – 'worth a guinea a box'. He comes more into his own with *The Penguin Dictionary of Quotations*, which gives six quotations from Potter, one each of Professor Ross and Nancy Mitford, six of A.P.Herbert, eight of James Thurber and twelve from George Orwell. As for *Roget's Thesaurus*, Lifemanship, Gamesmanship and One-Upmanship are noted as coinages and classified under Conduct, Cunning (subsection Imagination) and Amusement, but their inventor is shamefully unacknowledged.

The mock-scholarship, with appendices, footnotes and the solemn citing of fictitious or real authorities, should have made it clear that the whole thing is a joke; yet, in touring America and Canada, Potter found his slender output catalogued in libraries under psychology as well as sport (but seldom under humour). In certain American universities they were actually 'set books' for a psychology course; while the Simon Fraser University at Vancouver seemed to take them seriously as blueprints for winning games. And Dr Eric Berne, in *Games People Play : the Psychology of Human Relationships* (André Deutsch 1966) ends a mighty classification of games with a note on 'games that lead to psychiatric disabilities', apparently the subject of intensive seminars at San Francisco, and adds, almost with a sigh of relief, 'due credit should be given to Stephen Potter for his perceptive, humorous discussions of manoeuvres, or "ploys", in everyday social situations'.

There are those who deny that Potter invented the *-manship* joke at all, and that it arose from a form of banter, led by Francis Meynell and Joad, peculiar to members of the Savile Club, to which he belonged for more than thirty years. But we shall probe deeper than that. We see no reason to doubt Potter's claim that he invented the *word* Gamesmanship, and that it was first used in a letter to Sir Francis Meynell in March 1933 when discussing the tactics to be used in 'a forthcoming lawn tennis match against two difficult opponents'. We shall try to show that the concept of Gamesmanship had its origin in Lifemanship (not, as may appear from Potter's publications, the other way round), and that Lifemanship can be traced back to a mode, or code, of behaviour and speech found in the Oxford of 1919 and developed during the lifelong, self-confessed 'immaturity' and social insecurity of Potter himself. For Stephen Potter was his own Lifeman, and as his 'ploys' became known to his friends (and he was not without enemies), he was outmanoeuvred or

'one-upped' at least as often as he 'one-upped' others. His widow
says: 'Stephen fought his way through life as if he were an underdog
– he did it naturally.' Success turned bitter in his mouth because he
succeeded where he did not particularly want to succeed, and failed
at the impossible targets he set himself in other directions. Most of
the critically important events in his life, rough-hew it how he
would, happened to him by accident. 'Can you learn to be a social
success?' he asked, in a radio interview quoted by Joyce Grenfell in
her BBC memorial programme for him. And he concluded: 'It's a
matter of continuous warfare.'

Chapter 3
11 February 1947

We now leapfrog the thirties and the Second World War, and find ourselves shivering in the great Fuel Crisis of the winter of 1946–7. Stephen Potter, not yet internationally known, was at the peak of his success as a writer-producer for radio. Throughout the war years he had been turning out feature programmes at the rate of one, occasionally two, a week. He had given radio its first sophisticated humour, and he had been allowed to do it amid the solemn hunks of culture on the Third Programme.

What we know today as Radio Three had begun on 29 September 1946. Its advance publicity had said nothing about humour or satire, although the stifling regimes of Admiral Carpendale and Sir John Reith had now given place to the Director-Generalship, since 1944, of a newspaperman, Sir William Haley. The Third Programme, listeners were warned, taking its place beside the workaday Home Service and the frankly low-brow Light Programme, was for 'selective not casual listeners' who were 'attentive and critical'. Words like 'enjoyment' were not used. The Third Programme's first evening included the first performance of Benjamin Britten's *Festival Overture*; Bach's *Goldberg Variations*; talks by Field-Marshal Smuts, Sir Max Beerbohm and Sir William Haley; and something called 'How to Listen'. Well, it was by Stephen Potter and Joyce Grenfell, who had been doing wonderfully funny 'How' programmes ever since the middle of the War; surely the Third Programme would not open with anything funny? Looking at the small print of the subtitle, 'how not to, how they used to, and how you must', people began, incredulously, to realize that it would; and that the *Daily Express* had judged too soon in deriding it, in advance, as 'the Heavy Programme'. Lord Briggs, historian of the BBC, looking back on that evening, says: 'Stephen Potter's broadcasts – his broadcast script on the very first evening pointed the way – were to be one of the few real attempts to initiate explorations, and they soon influenced broadcasting as a whole.'

The War had done much to liberate broadcasting from the drawing-room-on-Sunday atmosphere of the old BBC. There was a determined thrust among younger reporters like Richard Dimbleby, Chester Wilmot, Stanley Maxted, Frank Gillard and Wynford Vaughan-Thomas to make radio lively, even more immediate than daily journalism; to let radio do what it could then do better than any other medium, in the days before mass television – bring the world into everyone's home. Stephen Potter was part of this movement and led one column of it – the documentary radio feature. To this he added something unique – a capacity for self-mockery. Hence 'How to Listen' – a spoof to open the weighty Third Programme.

Seeing that the Third Programme occasionally could be allowed to be funny, and watching the listening figure with some misgiving (by 1949, when Stephen Potter was no longer on the BBC staff, it had fallen to 0.3 per cent of the population, a mere 100,000 people who were said to be 28 per cent upper-middle class, 37 per cent lower-middle class, and 35 per cent working class), other BBC writers and producers began to agitate for more humour and satire on the Third. Edward Sackville-West (himself a radio writer-producer) claimed, in *Picture Post*, that the Third Programme was 'the greatest educative and civilizing force England has known since the secularization of the theatre in the sixteenth century'. As its listeners had to be civilized first in order to understand it, his argument is not easy to follow. Alan Pryce-Jones, writing in the *BBC Quarterly*, supported the case for more humour: 'Is it too much to hope that to all the other pleasures of the intelligence may be added, during the next five years, a more frequent experience of the intelligent chuckle?' Perhaps the Third Programme's greatest victory was over Evelyn Waugh who had hitherto regarded radio as the opium of the people. Yielding to Max Beerbohm's enthusiastic advocacy he bought – or rather, he ordered his wife to buy – his first wireless set.

It seemed that Stephen Potter, regularly employed by the BBC since 1938, was set for the life of a BBC trusty. He would one day perhaps be head of Features, he would retire full of honour at sixty, he would . . . Well, perhaps not, he was not what you would call an administrator. One of the questions the BBC interview board used to ask aspiring executives was: 'Do you keep a tidy desk?', meaning a desk with nothing but a blotting pad and a pen-stand on top of it. We shall see that Stephen was never like this.

The atmosphere of broadcasting at this time must be imagined against a background of the immediate post-war years. Shells of bombed buildings still waited for demolition. Rubble and weeds filled open spaces. Food rationing was worse than it had been during the War. And the winter of 1946–7 was the coldest for fifty-three years. 'Sixteen degrees of frost were recorded in London,' says an historian of those days. 'Icebergs were observed off the coast of Norfolk. In Lancashire a man borrowed a pneumatic drill to dig up his parsnips. . . . There were fourteen-foot snowdrifts. . . . The stoker of an early-morning steam train from Huddersfield to Bradford put his head out of the cab and was seriously injured by a huge icicle hanging from a bridge.' All transport froze where it was. A vicious circle – no coal, because no transport, so no coal to feed power-stations and gasworks, because no transport.

By 11 February 1947 there was only six days' stock of coal in the country. People went shopping by candlelight. All periodicals were ordered to stop publication until further notice. The *Radio Times* with its five million circulation went on publishing until the wrath of Fleet Street suppressed it. The Home and Light Programmes continued, for the sake of public morale, but the Third was suspended.

From Broadcasting House the order went out to underemployed staff, including almost everyone working on the Third Programme: 'Go home. There is nothing for you to do. We'll let you know when we need you.' Stephen at this time was reviewing books for the *News Chronicle* and, intermittently, drama for the *New Statesman*, in a determined attempt to augment his £800 BBC salary. But even these activities ceased as the fuel crisis deepened. No gas, no electricity, no light. Fortunately Stephen, wiry and obsessively fit, never demanded comfort and seldom felt the cold. How should he pass the time? The weather was far too cold for golf.

He had not written a book for ten years: his last, published before he joined the BBC, had been an attack on the way English literature was taught in universities, called *The Muse in Chains*. What should he write now? The crisis could hardly last for the time it takes – say, about six months – to write a book of the average length of 80,000 words. The need for laughter, for cheering up, was intense. What had given him and his friends the most fun, looking back over the years? Games, yes; but more than that . . . What about that idea he had so often discussed with friends like Ronald Simpson the actor, Bertie Farjeon the revue-writer, and Francis Meynell the typographer–designer? That same idea he had noted down in the changing-room after the afternoon of Joad's Gambit in June 1931?

Orderly writers (they are few) compose in orderly exercise books or on orderly typewriters with orderly reams of typing-paper. This was never the Potter way. Seizing any scrap of paper that lay to hand (and this was justifiable, since there was a paper shortage), be it the backs of old scripts, pages torn from partly filled exercise books, or – as one witness swears – the superior sort of toilet paper, he began to write, huddled in an armchair, chain-smoking cigarettes whose butts, aimed at an ash-tray, did not always land on target. A carpet pitted with burns always betrayed the recent presence of Potter, and many carpet-burns grouped round an armchair indicated Potter in literary gestation. What emerged from this was a handwritten – dare one call it manuscript? – which only Potter could read. Since, all his life long, he needed reassurance in the form of praise, he would read bits of the book to his wife Att (Mary), to visiting friends, and ultimately to his publisher.

There is a story, which we are disinclined to believe, that the first publisher to see *Gamesmanship* was the late Sir William Collins, to whom it was allegedly sent because of his well-known passion for games, and that he returned it sharply, saying he did not think it at all funny. This is indignantly denied by Sir Rupert Hart-Davis who claims that he was certainly the first publisher ever to be approached. The most compelling evidence in his favour is that nobody who did not already know Potter would have allowed him to read his masterpiece aloud rather than submit it in orderly typescript. Joyce Grenfell, who had known Rupert since childhood, claimed that she was among the very first of Stephen's friends to hear about *Gamesmanship*, and that she was the bridge between Stephen and Hart-Davis who had not met for some time. As so often in Stephen's life there is a splendid old-boy amateurism about the whole thing.

Yet Rupert was indeed an old friend. His publishing career had begun at William Heinemann, in 1929, where his duties were, he says, those of an office boy. He had then, at twenty-five, become manager of the Book Society and a director of Jonathan Cape, who had published Stephen's first few books. Jonathan Cape himself was happy to hand over some of his authors to Rupert who, for all his editorial toughness, took infinite pains with them. Another editor had dealt with Stephen's first and only novel, *The Young Man*, and his book, *D.H.Lawrence*. Rupert and Stephen met and collaborated during 1933 on Stephen's *Coleridge and S.T.C.*

Rupert's publishing company was about a year old when the sixteen-day Fuel Crisis hit Britain. He was established in 'a basement in Bayswater' at 53 Connaught Place. His list, gentle-manly in the extreme, did not yet contain anything that could be called a best-seller. He had published *Fourteen Stories* by Henry James; Rupert Brooke's *Democracy and the Arts*; the same in a limited edition; Eric Linklater's *Sealskin Trousers*; and a topical critique of the Labour Government by the economist Roy Harrod, *Are These Hardships Really Necessary?* This last had been a source of great irritation to Rupert who hated 'economist's jargon'. 'Why on earth must you say "the increasing overall level of unemploy-ment" when you simply mean "more men out of work"?'

Gamesmanship did not alter the general trend of Hart-Davis's publishing but it gave him his first best-seller. Stephen's diary for 20 March 1947:

Most charmingly enthusiastic telephone from Rupert Hart-Davis asking to see *Gamesmanship*. . . . I taxi down to Connaught Street to find them all in a basement. ('Mind your head' shouts Rupert to me.) 'All' includes Rupert, Bunny (David) Garnett, more sleepily amused and genially slow than ever now that his hair has gone early white. Also his son, another Richard (?19), who helped me pay for my taxi. Then I (having looked forward to this moment all the way) explain to an audience (who I expected beforehand to be appreciative) with brief extracts and acted bits, the point of gamesmanship. How I like doing this to a small virgin audience!

'Stephen had scribbled it all down on messy little bits of paper,' says Rupert Hart-Davis, 'which he kept fishing out of first one pocket, then another. As he read it to us, he had us rolling on the floor. I said yes at once. It was a terrific gamble – remember, we had paper rationing in those days. I risked printing 25,000 copies!' Rupert does not actually *say* that some of it was written on toilet paper but, in the climate of 1947, it would have surprised nobody.

There is evidence that Rupert contributed some ideas to the

book, especially on a subject close to his heart. On 15 May Stephen wrote to him: 'More superb cricket material! *Thank you*. I am considering now what to do about this enormous subject. . . . Writing about cricket in *Gamesmanship* is like those splendid men who write monographs on the occurrence of the word "the" in Shakespeare.' *Gamesmanship* was one of the first books to exploit the comic possibilities of indexes as well as footnotes and this, too, yields evidence of more than one mind at work.

How to illustrate this kind of book? The normal way would be to send the script to Nicolas Bentley or one of the *Punch* artists and give him his head. But few things were normal about *Gamesmanship* and its successors. The casual old-boy net went to work again, this time around the village of Nettlebed in Oxfordshire where various friends and friends of friends of Potter used to foregather after Henley Regatta. The process produced a retired colonel, turned King's Messenger, who had served in South-East Asia during the War with Col. Peter Fleming (husband of the actress Celia Johnson), travel-author, writer of *Times* fourth leaders 'which my readers are conditioned to think funny', and a considerable landowner in those parts. This retired colonel drew military uniforms with expert knowledge. He signed his work 'F. Wilson, Lt. Col.'. It was considered that this signature looked too insignificant. Could he not call himself by his full name, Frank Wilson? It was then that Potter and Hart-Davis, alive to the comic side of all colonels, decided on 'Illustrated by Lt. Col. Frank Wilson'. Wilson had one great advantage over Nicolas Bentley and the established illustrators: he was less expensive and he could be bullied into redrawing his pictures again and again until both author and publisher were satisfied. He turned out to be a minor genius of deadpan farce, inspired by the solemnity of all manuals whose helpful illustrations are numbered 'Fig. 1.', 'Fig. 2.', etc.

By now, most of Stephen's friends knew that not only was *Gamesmanship* going to be published in the 1947 Christmas list, but that most of them were going to be in it. (If you have 100 friends and put them all in a book you are certain of having 100 readers.) Moreover Stephen was ever prone, seeking approval, to show his friends what he had written.

Sir Francis Meynell had recently bought Cobbolds Mill near Bildeston in Suffolk. It had been a working cornmill until 1938 and parts of it were many centuries old. A stream where kingfishers play ran right under the house, which is a combination of watermill and miller's residence. Here the Meynells gave endless weekend parties at which everybody had to play games, some of them of Meynell's own invention. It was only right that *Gamesmanship* should be dedicated to Meynell as 'Gamesman No. 1'.

One weekend, in the spring of 1947, Stephen and his wife, Att, arrived with a typescript which Stephen immediately thrust into Meynell's hands: 'Please read it at once and tell me what you think of it.' The Potters then modestly left the room. Meynell and his wife Dame Alix Kilroy, known as 'Bay', read chapter one and, says Meynell, 'laughed and laughed again'. 'Find Stephen and tell him how funny it is,' said Bay. 'He was not hard to find,' Meynell says, 'for there he was, kneeling on the other side of our door with his ear to the keyhole: "I wanted to hear if it made you laugh!" ' The subtitle of *Gamesmanship* was, at this stage, 'How to Win Games without Cheating'. Meynell's contribution to the book, in addition to a proportion of the ideas in it, was the insertion of the word 'Actually' before 'Cheating'.

The book appeared in November 1947 in nice time for Christmas. It was reviewed by all the critics who mattered, including several friends of Stephen's, some of them with inside knowledge of the Savile Club mafia who had contributed ideas to it. Over the next thirteen years it was to go into fourteen impressions. It was reviewed in *The Times* by Ian Fleming who had not yet created James Bond; in the *Daily Herald* by John Betjeman, not yet within spitting distance of the Poet Laureateship; and in the *New Statesman* (but not until the New Year) by C.E.M.Joad who treated the book as if it were a profound psycho-philosophical study and appeared mystified by the part played in it by 'an apocryphal character, C.Joad'.

The would-be literary and dramatic critic, the scholar manqué, was now willy-nilly propelled along the path of full-time professional authorship, of international lionization as a wit, known and labelled for one joke. He was forty-seven, the same age as the century. It is time to look back at that century, to see how Lifeman came into being, and what he actually did with his life.

Chapter 4
The world of no. 36

36 Old Park Avenue,
Feb 1, 1900

My dear Mrs Reynolds,

I am sure you will be rejoiced to hear the news in my telegram. Our son arrived soon after midnight this morning. Lilla was taken ill about 10 o'clock, so that, though sharp, it was a short affair. Of course, being unexpected, the nurse was not here, and I had to drive over to Barnes to fetch her, but she had gone to Wiltshire that afternoon. However, after two or three hours' hunting I got a very satisfactory nurse at a nursing institution at Balham and she arrived in time to wash and dress the baby, which Doctor Oram was glad not to have to do. As there was no nurse his friend Mr Twigg came in to help him so he got on all right.

I am glad to say both seem to be doing well this morning. I am now waiting for the Doctor to call before going up to town. . . . With usual love to Captain Reynolds and yourself,

Your affectionate son-in-law Frank.

Frank Potter, an accountant in the firm of Bird & Potter, recently promoted to partner, was forty-one, his wife, Elizabeth Mary Jubilee, known as Lilla, thirty-six. They already had a daughter Muriel who was now six. Six years is just enough difference in age to turn Big Sister into Second Mother. Young Stephen, having made his entry into the world on a bitter snowy night with uncharacteristic punctuality, was destined to grow up with two mothers. He would become, in more than one sense, a spoilt child; for the expression can also mean 'child of an older parent', and there was a tradition of this in the family. One of Stephen's grandmothers was born in 1806, a fact to send anyone furiously calculating.

Just as Bird & Potter never called each other anything but Mr

Bird and Mr Potter, so Frank never called his parents-in-law anything but Captain and Mrs Reynolds.

Old Park Avenue is a short, narrow, almost semicircular road leading off Nightingale Lane near Clapham Common, south-west London. Its houses were mostly built in the 1890s in one of the speculative building operations that, since 1880, had transformed the west side of Clapham Common and the village of Wandsworth into – not a residential sprawl so much as a gridded arrangement of terrace upon terrace of identical houses, all with lace curtains dyed in tea and pot plants, generally aspidistras.

Clapham Common, where Stephen played as a boy (and learnt to row on the pond that was once painted by Turner) has had a mixed reputation. The Steinie Morrison murder in 1911 did it the same kind of harm that the poisoning of Charles Bravo did to Balham. Some Georgian houses on the south side, and others on the north side, tell of a time before the stockbroker invasion of the fashionable 1840s, before which it was still possible to talk of Clapham (as Thackeray did) as 'a pretty little suburb', indeed a separate village. In two world wars Clapham Common has known the presence of artillery: it was used as a firing range from 1914–18, and for naval guns used in a desperate anti-aircraft role from 1940–4. Julian Symons, in a fragment of autobiography, notes that in *his* boyhood in the 1920s prostitutes gathered near the bandstand and the fountain, and there was a local music-hall joke: 'Have you heard the one about the nine-year-old boy who started to walk across Clapham Common one dark night and came out the other side a married man with three children?'

But in Stephen's boyhood there was cricket and tennis and girls and endless things to watch, such as dogs straining to contribute a drop of urine to a staging-post where other dogs had gone before; a sight which in later years caused him to remember the Common as smelling of 'stale dog'.

The 'Captain Reynolds' of Frank Potter's letter was the father of nine surviving children, of whom Lilla, Stephen's mother, was the prettiest daughter. There is a perennial tendency for anyone with the surname Reynolds to be nicknamed 'Josh', after Sir Joshua the painter, and indeed some of the Reynoldses claimed a tenuous descent from him. The Captain had walked out of his bullying father's house at the age of seventeen to enlist in the Guards. The Crimean War had already begun and the Coldstream Guards promised a home as well as glory. Joining as a private he worked his way up to regimental sergeant-major. Normally this would have ended his promotion for one could not, in those days, be commissioned from the ranks unless one was a quartermaster. Josh was indeed a quartermaster and so he became Lieutenant and finally Captain Reynolds. When on duty at St James's Palace he had received a 'Good morning, Josh!' from the Prince of Wales; he and the Guards were the reasons why Stephen's mother could claim that she had been 'born in the Tower of London'.

The Reynoldses lived at Court Lodge, near Caterham Barracks. Here this large family formed the Court Lodge Orchestral and Dramatic Society, producing the home-made musical entertainments that were so necessary in the days before gramophones, wireless and television. Lilla, second daughter of the family, played the piano, sang and acted and would one day win a scholarship to the Royal Academy of Music where one of her fellow students was Marie Tempest. Miss Tempest was considered 'fast' because she used geranium petals as rouge.

Lilla's favourite brother was Willie, known as 'young Josh' and to Stephen eventually as 'Uncle Josh'. Uncle Josh was to become a considerable influence on his life.

His father's family was less glamorous to young Stephen. They came from Belvedere, then a riverside village in Kent, midway between Plumstead and Erith. The unforgettable uncle on this side of the family was James, nine years older than Frank. He had studied French and German at Lausanne and Nuremberg and was secretary to Lord Brassey the railway king at whose stately home he had actually dined, played tennis and been waited on by footmen.

Frank lived in lodgings in Wandsworth. Lilla too was sharing a small house nearby with her brother Walter. Wandsworth was then – in the 1880s – a country village about to become a suburb. Frank, playing the violin in the Wandsworth Common Orchestral Society, and Lilla, singing contralto in *The Messiah* at the local church, were bound to meet eventually. They took the same trains to and from London every day. They went to the same church. They both took part in the Handel Festival at the Crystal Palace. They both belonged to the Allfarthing Lane Lawn Tennis Club. Frank's first words at their introduction were: 'Do you play tennis, Miss Reynolds?' Her reply: 'No, but I'd like to, thank you very much!' He proposed to her in 1885, they were married in 1889, honeymooned in Venice, and moved into 36 Old Park Avenue. Frank Potter at last got his partnership in the firm and was well on the way to his FCA. The only cloud on the horizon was Frank's investments which steadily lost money. Stephen, in his auto-biography, blames the family weakness common to both Potters and Reynoldses – 'financial haemophilia'. That weakness included a lack of skill at buying solid houses, for no. 36 turned out to be 'jerry built'. (It looks solid enough today and has been converted into three flats.)

Stephen's first five years contain little of historic interest. Big sister Muriel, then eleven and at Clapham High School, was asked to write an essay on her little brother. The exercise book, according to immemorial tradition, is superscribed: 'Muriel Lucy Potter, 36 Old Park Avenue, Nightingale Lane, Balham, London, S.W., England, the World'. Doting sister, who will one day be his sternest critic, both literary and moral, writes thus:

A sweet loveable little pickle. . . . If one asked him what his name was, he would certainly reply, 'Stephen Merrydif Potter', but he has a great many nicknames and pet-names as well . . . Stephen, Steve, Stevie, Step-hen, Step, Chick, Kinny, His Lordship, the Junior Member and the Fat One. . . . At different times Stephen becomes different men whom he admires for their bravery or their skill. At one time his ambition is to be a lifeboat-man. Then he has to be addressed as 'George' (why I don't know). I am his 'girl', Mother his 'wife'. He then collects boats of every kind and floats them in his bath. Bed-time is a joyous hour, when he can revel in storms and splashing the bathroom taps. The tubbing over, he trots up to bed, flushed with the honour of saving several (imaginary) persons from the terrible 'storm'.

We are further told that he has a scarlet dressing-gown, the colour chosen because it is 'soldier-like', and that he loves to wear his mother's dressing-gown when he plays at being a lady. Like Christopher Robin he accepted his first 'grown-up braces' as a symbol of manhood, 'took them to bed with him and cuddled them all night'. The essay got full marks and a 'V.G.'

We shall not attempt to read anything Freudian into this but simply note that Stephen at five exhibits a mixture of vanity, precocity, and Walter Mitty-ism entirely proper to his years.

Poor Muriel. Emotional, vulnerable, she will be proud, be-wildered and sometimes disappointed in him when he grows up. But now he is six, the age from which he actually remembers things.

It was considered safe, in those days, for a child of six, dressed in a sailor suit with HMS *Indomitable* on his hat, to walk alone across the Common to school. School was the junior section of Clapham High School for girls, where they took boys in mixed forms up to the age of ten. A place, Stephen afterwards recalled, of 'indoorness and sit-stillness'. Muriel was already in an upper form of Clapham High which was one of the new, up-to-date, Froebel-trained schools of the Girls' Public Day School Trust.

Stephen was in Upper II, the most senior class to which boys were admitted. He is remembered, by a girl seven years older, who found herself in the same form for half a term, as 'a thin pale child with bright golden hair' who was inclined to be 'very angry that anyone should show any signs of intelligence greater than his'. At six he was being taught to handle fir-cones and acorns in what was called botany, which he did not like (years later he would conceive a passion for botany which could even distract him from golf when looking for a ball in the rough). He was also taking part in school concerts, playing piano duets with one of the mistresses and being reproved for unnecessary showmanship, such as smiling sideways at the audience to show how easy it was. Not, one feels, the right school for Stephen. There is something here of the precocious exhibitionism of his contemporary prodigy, Master Noël Coward, born just six weeks before Stephen.

Stephen's reading during these years shows nothing very unusual. Father's study was full of old *Vanity Fairs* and *Spheres* (but apparently no *Strands*?), theatre and concert programmes, Conan Doyle's *History of the South African War* – Frank never threw anything away. There were Kenneth Grahame and E. Nesbitt books as well as the *Just So Stories* – but every middle-class Edwardian child was reading these. *Puck* led on to the *Boy's Own Paper*. A touch of originality: Stephen preferred *Gulliver's Travels* to *Robinson Crusoe*. The great discovery, at the age of about nine, was that books were written by *people*, people who lived lives of their own. The edition of *Gulliver* had a life of Swift at the beginning which Stephen mistook for one of the stories. This was reinforced by Muriel reading aloud the song in the *Just So Stories*: '. . . comes Tegumai alone to find The daughter that was all to him'. Muriel explained that Kipling's own daughter had died just before he wrote the story. Stephen could not now read it without wanting to cry. *The author's life was as important as what he wrote. . . .*

The happy ordinariness of life went on. Like every child who grew up near Clapham Common before 1939 Stephen bowled iron hoops along those flagged pavements; later, he roller-skated at five times the speed until the liberating mobility conferred by his first bicycle, a BSA costing the enormous sum of £11. Even making allowance for the greater simplicity of life seventy years ago, the rarity of treats such as tram-rides to the Army & Navy Stores in London, the first films, the four theatres a year and summer day-trips to the coast by the London, Brighton & South Coast Railway, allowing too for the fact that in the euphoria of being young almost everything is enjoyable, it has to be admitted that life for the Potters was lacking in unusualness.

Holidays, for instance: Bird & Potter were kind to Frank Potter, who after all worked at his office from 9 till 7 and often brought work home as well; they gave him six weeks' holiday a year, two at Easter and four in August. Stephen seems to have shown no such rebellion as Lupin Pooter's contempt for 'good old Broadstairs'. The normal pattern was Worthing for Easter and Swanage for August. Both, in those days, were still small seaside towns with plenty of late eighteenth and early nineteenth century left in them. Teignmouth, Bude, Whitby, right up in Yorkshire – the Potters tried each of these resorts as they became fashionable but always returned to Swanage and Worthing. Only Uncle Josh went abroad for his holidays to Belgium and Normandy. Stephen's conservatism about travel would last most of his life: never a linguist, never keen on Abroad, he would in adulthood judge places by their golf-courses.

Frank was a churchwarden at St Luke's and so there was regular church-going on Sundays. Only the music meant anything to Stephen. The only hope of escape on Sunday was to get Uncle Jim to take him to Warlingham where certain cousins and an aunt and an uncle lived. Uncle Jim, a sad, rather deaf man whose wife had died young, was the Potters' lodger. He had been taken in 'temporarily' after his wife's funeral. He stayed for twenty-nine years. But he helped to balance the family budget; also to pay for Stephen's schooling. At Warlingham, then a country village, Uncle Herbert, a do-it-yourselfer, had a workshop. He was an amateur archaeologist. He also had an Edison Bell phonograph with a cylinder which played Harry Lauder singing 'I Love a Lassie'. The boys had such luxuries as a Bassett-Lowke model railway. It was all much, much better than church. Church made him feel *good*, but that was all.

Stephen, the younger child, the only son, described his position in the family as that of 'Crown Prince of No. 36'. He was, like Master Noël Coward (then living in another part of the Borough of Battersea), Mother's Boy. But he was also Uncle's favourite, Uncle being Young Josh, his mother's brother. Josh (or Willie) was manager of Drummond's Bank in Trafalgar Square, a splendid vantage point from which to see processions such as George V's at his Coronation. Drummond's became part of the Royal Bank of Scotland where all Potters and many of their friends would bank. Josh was the sort of uncle who did conjuring tricks with half crowns which he afterwards gave to delighted children. He made Stephen feel grown up by calling him Step. He was glamorous with his rakish summer straw boater and his long gold cigarette case. He was a theatrical, Dickensian, declamatory character. He knew artists and actors, especially two famous *Punch* illustrators, Shepperson and Townsend – how? Because he belonged to something unimaginably glamorous called the Savile Club, for which he would, one day in the future, put Stephen up for membership. He bullied the family about their investments. He owned the first car in the family, a bull-nosed Morris. He produced and acted in amateur theatricals and took the family to Drury Lane pantomimes. And he sang the 'Indian Love Lyrics'.

Meanwhile, being now too old for Clapham High School, Stephen had been moved to a boys' preparatory school in Rillo Road, Wandsworth. Here he learnt to avoid bullying by a system of bribery: by suitable gifts one could buy immunity for a week. His only friend was a boy of whose accent Stephen's mother disapproved. Apart from a mild interest in football he showed no aptitude for games.

The year 1914 meant two main events for 36 Old Park Avenue: Stephen was sent to Westminster School as a day boy and a new maid arrived to join the crowded household. The first event happened in February, the second in May. The new maid, Minnie Elms, was seventeen: she was to stay with Stephen's mother for thirty-six years. Minnie, now eighty-three, remembers the Potter clan as 'large, very happy and united', with enormous family gatherings at Christmas. If she had one collective criticism of them it was that 'they never thought that other people might be as clever as they were – people like me just didn't have the money'. Stephen at fourteen she found 'rather snobby – he never talked to me'. When you are a boy of fourteen it can be a disturbing thing to have a girl in the house who is only three years older.

Muriel was now in her second year at St Hugh's College, Oxford, to which she had won a scholarship. She was well on the way to a first-class degree; later, she would be one of the youngest headmistresses in the country. She had taken up Liberal politics, a fairly radical thing to do in 1912, especially for a girl. All this was the kind of success that the family hoped Stephen would attain. But there were few signs of it at present.

He did, however, begin to keep a diary. He was to keep it almost continuously for the rest of his life. Acute observation and literary content do not play much part at first; his detailed diaries do not begin until his thirty-fifth year. Among the first entries (7 May 1914) is: 'Minnie Elms, our new servant, came for the first time. I like her. I think she is jolly decent.' Starting the habit of a lifetime he sticks press cuttings among his written entries, choosing the most sensational headlines: 'Germans Still Fondly Dreaming of Zeppelin Attack on London: Relying On It for a Chance to Satiate Their Bitter Hatred.'

We learn that St Luke's Church Hall is full of Belgian refugees. The Potters take each other to the theatre more frequently than most families: '23.9.14 – Saw *Mr. Wu* from the pit at the Savoy Theatre. Most thrilling play I have ever seen. About China. Saw airship over Strand.' On Boxing Day: 'Pantomime awfully good. Sissie and Ma and Pa and Uncle Willie and I go. Frightfully funny donkey. Teach Uncle Willie "Pounce Patience" in evening.' Two days later: 'School report comes. Rather feeble. Nevertheless 2/6 each from Ma and Pa. Why I know not.' Yet another treat on 2 January: 'F.R.Benson in *Henry V*. 1st Shakespeare play I have ever seen. Have read it twice and know most of the 1st Act by heart. Like it awfully.' Suddenly a sick man appears at the door: 'Uncle Percy home from France. He has trench feet.' (Uncle Percy, returning to France, will get trench fever as well and die within the year in a base hospital in Rouen.)

By 1916 he is beginning to think about the War: 'Two Zeppelins brought down – official. Cheers! But *think of the dead*' – and on his seventeenth birthday he reflects: '17 (sweet 17) is too near 18 to be pleasant. If the war doesn't end soon I shall have to join the beastly Army and lay down my blooming life for my blinking country.' By July 1917 an air-raid produces a profundity: 'N.B. The amount of cowardice in a man = the vividness of his imagination. Cowardice should rarely be despised – unless it is selfish cowardice.' And a family argument plants an ethical problem in his mind: 'I don't see how two people can be unselfish to each other simultaneously.'

For once, the next decision about Stephen's education had been taken by his father not his mother. How the family finances were manipulated to make public school possible is not clear; probably Uncles James and Willie lent a hand. Westminster was a weekly boarding-school with a lot of London-dwelling day boys and the only difficulty was getting there. This depended largely on Minnie. Minnie worked a fifteen-hour day, from 7 am to 10 pm. It took her from 8.30 to 8.45 or later to wake him up. 'Saints' Days were the worst,' Minnie remembers. 'Last-momenting', so much a part of his whole life, had begun early. So had the corresponding talent for desperate speed. It was his boast that he could get up, wash, dress, eat breakfast (three minutes), bicycle to Wandsworth Common station, collect Westminster topper and tail-coat from ticket-office, put them on, catch train, learn ten lines of Virgil in ten minutes to Victoria, and catch the no. 11 bus up Victoria Street to Westminster Abbey (which is the Westminster School chapel) – all in thirty-four minutes flat. All his life Stephen was to derive a heady excitement from being late. Punishment for being late for chapel was a 'penal drill', a new kind of punishment which, during the War, was becoming popular among schoolmasters and would linger for a few years afterwards.

Scholastically, and indeed in other ways, Stephen was not a great success at Westminster. Mother and Frank took an optimistic view of his middling reports: they *knew* he was brilliant; it was just that he was 'outgrowing his strength'. In later years he was to blame the school for its obsession with Latin and Greek, its mechanical ways of teaching, its neglect of poetry and things of the imagination, its sterile house loyalties (his house was Ashburnham). . . . But were not all public schools like that in those days? All masters seemed old because all the younger ones were away fighting. There is no evidence that Stephen worked very hard and there is almost no record of him in the school archives. He blamed the teaching for his lack of progress, especially his own badness at speaking French. He seems never to have realized – strange for one who was later to appear to others as a flamboyant personality – that the speaking of a foreign language is an histrionic performance.

Geometry (the beautiful reasoning of Euclid) attracted him; so did science, but there wasn't enough of it. He even accused Westminster of stunting his natural enthusiasm for games. Games? But he surely meant team games. Stephen was never a team games boy or man. Why not fives, then, or rackets? Was it the fear of not winning? And yet – sport was the only key to social success at school.

Other minor talents showed themselves, drawing for instance. A crayon sketch of a red poppy had been shown, with 12,000 other schoolchildren's drawings, at an exhibition at the White City; and he was already, at twelve, illustrating letters to friends with caricatures. A love of maps was another manifestation of drawing. And the family all agreed that his letters were so amusing. In later years he was to learn that his style, condemned by Fowler's *Modern English Usage,* was one he shared with Dickens, 'polysyllabic humour', such as writing 'in the vicinity of his abode' when you mean 'near his home'.

It is extraordinary how many authors have become authors because, filled with the vague consciousness of being different from, or superior or inferior to, other people, they have said to themselves: I am going to be a Great Author. Nobody ever says to himself, I am going to be a Little Author, grinding out books or stories to earn a living. George Meredith was Father's favourite novelist, and Mother was reading Meredith when she was pregnant with Stephen, and so Stephen's middle name was Meredith. This was a heavy responsibility. If you are named after a writer, do you not have to become a writer? The Potters were a bookish family and Father sometimes read aloud to the family on Sunday evenings until overcome by paroxysms of coughing due to chain-smoking, a vice his son was to inherit. Father read Ruskin, with whose beautiful prose no one else at no. 36 had much patience. It was Uncle Jim who guided Stephen towards Dickens. Dickens was Stephen's first idea of a Great Author.

But for the moment music was the chief outlet for Stephen's sensibilities. He was learning the piano. Frank, his father, played the violin and piano: he also composed operettas, in a style midway between Sullivan and Edward German, for the local church operatic society in aid of Christmas Parcels for the Troops. (We have to keep reminding ourselves that there was a world war going on all this time – a cataclysm of which south-west London saw little beyond the occasional silver Zeppelin caught in searchlights.) The producer, of course, was Uncle Willie.

One positive thing Westminster School gave Stephen was a sense of history. A lot of the school was impressively old. In the Shell was a bench with J. DRYDEN carved on it; also INIGO JONES. But the main influences were still family ones – Uncle Percy, his mother's youngest brother, who took Stephen to cricket matches, and Uncle Jim, who took him to Thurston's in Leicester Square to see first-class billiards (Gray, Reece and Inman). Uncle Percy, we have seen, was to die of trench fever in France. The Westminster attitude towards games only made Stephen want to excel at them outside the school atmosphere. To this end he secretly did dumb-bell exercises after the fashionable Sandow system.

The present archivist of Westminster School tells me there is absolutely no record of S.M.Potter in any school magazine or other document. Yet S.M.Potter did distinguish himself in his penultimate year and there is a photograph in the *Illustrated London News* of 28 February 1917 to prove it. On Shrove Tuesday every year, according to ancient and futile custom, a pancake is tossed before a large assembly of boys and their parents and the boy who grabs it intact is said to have won the 'greaze' and is given Maundy money (plus, in Stephen's time, a golden guinea). Stephen, representing his form, captured the pancake by falling on top of it so that all the other competitors fell on top of him. It was his first moment of glory at school. His mother kept the pancake until her death.

Somehow it gave him the courage to volunteer for the school rowing club, run by a boy called Brandon-Thomas whose distinction was that his father had written *Charley's Aunt*. He showed considerable promise at rowing and was picked to row no. 3 in the School Four. The boat had fixed seats which meant an agony of chafed and bleeding bottoms. This fact betrayed Stephen: in an important race on the Thames against a rival school he caught a crab, causing his crew to lose four lengths. And yet – was it a crab or a snag, an obstacle in the water which was nobody's fault? The *Daily Telegraph*'s rowing correspondent saved Stephen's face by writing: 'But for the excellent watermanship of no. 3 the boat might well have overturned.' Honour was further safeguarded by doctor's orders – no rowing for three months. But the sneaking feeling of failure in this race never left Stephen for the rest of his life. It was – in a phrase he invented some years later – a 'pillow-biting' humiliation (regretting in the small hours of the morning things you have done and said the previous night).

The War came a little nearer as lists of old boys, 'missing, believed killed', were posted on school notice-boards. Cadet Potter, in the Westminster officers' training corps, drilled one day a week and went to camp at Tidworth. As farm-workers were called up schoolboys volunteered for work on the land during holidays, camping in tents in the fields. Stephen had just discovered romantic poetry, a subject not, apparently, covered at Westminster, except for Tennyson and Milton and the great speeches of Shakespeare. After a day's potato picking, near Bovey Tracey on Dartmoor, Stephen earned suspicious glances from tent-mates as he pulled out a calf-bound edition of Keats. Of course, Potter was just showing off ... and yet he had caused general consternation by coming out with it, bare-faced: 'I *like* poetry.' A little later he capped it by what his friends interpreted as pure swank: he wanted to leave school at once and join the Army.

As others had done before him, and were to do again in the Second World War, he used the argument: 'If I volunteer now, I can choose my regiment and get a commission without going through the ranks.' Ah, but what regiment? Grandfather Josh's regiment had been the Coldstream Guards.... But cavalry was more dashing, and very fashionable. Typically, he gave himself a crash course by buying a book on horse management which did not, however, say anything about how to ride the beasts. Half-a-dozen lessons at a military riding school in Richmond Park, and some private lessons on Tooting Bec Common which ended in a fall, left him with the impression that horses were not his natural companions; and it was almost with relief that he heard from the 15th Hussars that they had not after all any vacancy for him.

Like many not very self-disciplined men Stephen found the Army 'placid' and free from responsibility. He was at an infantry training battalion, the Inns of Court regiment, at Berkhamsted, Hertfordshire. 'I liked the discipline,' Stephen wrote many years later, 'and throve on it.' He also gloried in the aggressive physical health the Army gave him: it was open air all the time, for they were under canvas, eight men to each bell-tent. Stephen drew self-confidence from the habit of barking commands and giving instructional talks. Here, in the Army, he had his first great, unqualified, total success: he passed out top of his company.

Grandfather Josh had died in the year of Stephen's birth but his influence lingered on. It helped to get Stephen into the Brigade of Guards whose headquarters was then at Bushey. He was met at the railway station by a man of unmilitary aspect with a gentle Irish accent and an unsmiling, deprecating humour: 'I'm sorry there is no actual drum to greet you.' Stephen had expected to be marched to his new barracks by a screaming NCO, but this Irishman simply *walked*. As he walked, he fantasized. Everybody at Bushey was given a hundred lashes before breakfast, but there were Turkish baths and many other luxuries to make up for it. . . . The gentle Irish voice went on, speaking in carefully modelled prose; you could almost hear the semicolons. For this was John Stewart Collis, the prose-poet of the three remarkable Collis brothers, destined to become a lifelong friend.

In his autobiography Jack Collis gives his own first impression of Stephen: 'A fair-haired man with a high forehead and pronounced rear-head, a very English-gentleman face, voice and manner, with a first-rate smile.' Collis had put his name down for the Enniskillen Dragoons – yes, cavalry was the romantic objective, as with Stephen. He had been in an OTC at Tidworth and had preceded Stephen by a few weeks at Berkhamsted. There was to be much shared laughter between them.

Bushey Hall had once been a Hydro and even the Army could not destroy its comforts. For a Guards OTC it now held a weird mixture of battle-scarred veterans, absolutely green recruits, aristocrats and nobodies, some of them as old as forty-five. One of the elderly was the actor-manager, Gerald du Maurier, who was useful as a plain-clothes spy, in wig and beard, on field-exercises. Du Maurier was a great asset to the mess: he could always be relied on for songs and recitations and there were some cadets who resented the indulgence of NCOs towards him.

Collis was Stephen's first talk-friend. He was much better-read, had resisted his public school (Rugby) far more effectively, and could quote the speeches of Macaulay, with orotund rhetorical emphasis, from memory. He was apt to do this in the middle of a game of golf: Bushey Golf Course was used for parades and tactical exercises, but it could still, at a pinch, be used for golf. 'Stephen could always beat me at golf,' Jack Collis remembers, 'and could talk about golf championships with facility: but I had no difficulty in dealing with him at tennis.'

In the evenings they played billiards at the club-house, and there was much laughter. It is probable that neither of them, certainly not Stephen, had yet heard of Surrealism, or Edith Sitwell, or James Joyce, or any writer who used words for their sound, not for their meanings. Together they invented a word-game – and Stephen was to play many word-games in his life – which had no name, but might as well be called Atrocious Juxtaposition: finding an adjective and a noun with absolutely no possible natural relationship and forcing them together: for example, 'washed Kodaks'. This can be excruciatingly funny for those playing the game, if for no one else, and they developed a system of awarding each other marks for outstanding audacities. The 'marks' system was to continue, in talk and correspondence, all Stephen's life.

There was a distinct possibility, at this time, that Stephen, having found appreciation and self-confidence in the questionless security of the Army, might have chosen to stay on as a regular officer. The future great Clubman, seeking refuge in the gang-companionship of club life, might have found it first in the mess. The mind slightly boggles: Potter as a colonel, on the North-West Frontier, military attaché in Washington, policing riots in India, emerging perhaps as a general in the Second World War. . . . But Jack Collis was removing any such possibility by feeding his mind and imagination. Feeding the imagination, as with *Hamlet*, could weaken the will to action.

Besides, the War was nearly over. The last great German offensive had been turned, a counter-offensive mounted, and the casualty lists were slightly less paralysing in their horror. On 11 November 1918 a special parade was called at Bushey and, in the scarcely raised voice cultivated in the Brigade for all communications except words of command, the Colonel announced the Armistice. Stephen and Jack went to Trafalgar Square to stand on one of the lions and watch London going mad as it had not done since Mafeking Night.

Stephen stayed at Bushey long enough to get his commission in the Coldstream Guards, a properly gazetted second-lieutenant. Jack Collis became an honorary lieutenant in the Irish Guards. When they parted they did not think they would ever see each other again. They would write, of course. Meanwhile Jack had a university place at Trinity College, Dublin, but had passed it up in favour of Balliol, Oxford, where the entrance examination had been made easier for the benefit of returning servicemen. Stephen collected his uniform and the splendid hat with gold on the peak and wore it around London for six weeks. He wore it to Westminster for the next Pancake Greaze – a mistake: uniforms were already out of fashion and several old boys he talked to had been shelled and gassed in the front line.

The uniform of a chartered accountant – dark suit, wing collar, bowler hat – had no glamour at all. This, since he had shown insufficient talent in any particular direction, seemed the natural future for Stephen, in Bird & Potter, of 28 Victoria Street, Westminster – far too near the old school. (The firm survives today as Bird, Potter, Winder & Lloyd, of Gloucester Place, NW.) The offices were stuffy and dark, the windows always shut. Though both breathed cigarette smoke as naturally as air there was a profound difference between father and son when sharing an office: Frank felt the cold and feared draughts which were held to be the cause of most illnesses; Stephen, who could hardly be persuaded to wear a vest, was a claustrophobic flinger-open of windows, and paced up and down like a captured racoon in any indoor situation.

Jack Collis was going to Balliol; sister Muriel had got a first at St Hugh's and was now teaching English at St Paul's Girls' School. . . . Concentrate, Potter: one day, perhaps, the firm will be called Bird, Potter & *Potter*.

Oxford. . . . Perhaps some family telepathy had been going on, or perhaps it was already clear that accountancy and round rulers for ruling columns were not the field in which genius could express itself. We do not know, and Stephen, in his fragment of autobiography *Steps to Immaturity*, does not try to guess, what reasoning went on in the Potter parents' discussions about his future. It meant a good deal of sacrifice, after Westminster fees, but here it was. He was offered the chance to go to Oxford.

Chapter 5
Schoolboys and warriors

Oxford in 1919 was not yet the Oxford of Evelyn Waugh, who would not go up until 1922, or of the aesthete Harold Acton, or of 'Oxford bags'. It *was* the Oxford of Beverley Nichols and a clique of fashionable young Liberals at the Union which would soon have Kenneth Lindsay as its first Labour President. It was not yet the Oxford of William Morris, the motor car manufacturer, who did not build a factory in the village of Cowley until 1922. There was an undergraduate population of only 3000. Nearly as many Oxford men had been killed in the War and the list of names on one college war memorial was said to be thirty feet long. It was an Oxford depleted of both undergraduates and dons. Some undergraduates had come back to complete studies begun in 1914; others, like Harold Macmillan of Balliol, badly wounded, unable to face a student community in which only one of his old friends had survived the holocaust, could not. The Dean of one college was subject to violent rages and drunken outbursts, which were said to be due to 'trench shock'. Not for another year would women students be part of the University.

The undergraduate population was divided fairly sharply into 'schoolboys' and 'warriors'. Stephen was technically a schoolboy, not having actually fought in France; yet he had by the skin of his teeth got a commission. How would he play this one? Which 'set' would he join? If he tried to be a warrior, would the warriors accept him? The warriors were older, in life-weariness as well as age. They were men who had been colonels and majors and captains, some before they were twenty; others were as old as twenty-five. They tended to refer to dinner in Hall as 'the Mess'. One or two of them were married. There were 'short courses' for ex-servicemen who needed a degree quickly. The warriors took life seriously, had little patience with Bolshevism or agnosticism, sometimes objected to Jews and Roman Catholics and were apt to register their dislike drastically by debagging and room-wrecking. As they had been wearing uniform a few months or weeks ago, so they now, with little variation, wore light-grey flannel trousers, Harris tweed jackets (Norfolk), college ties and scarves, with ragged academic gowns above. For dinner and all even faintly formal occasions evening dress was worn. Chapel was, if not absolutely compulsory, regularly attended.

It was snowing unseasonably when Stephen arrived at Merton College in May, full of good intentions. He felt he had 'muffed' school. At Oxford he *must* succeed. He had at last some inkling of the financial sacrifices his parents had made to send him to Westminster and were now making to send him to Oxford. The question of winning a scholarship had seemingly never arisen. Merton, he had heard, was a 'work college'. He would go in for sport only as much as was necessary for health. He could not be betrayed into excelling at it. Lucky he wasn't at Christ Church where there were so many Old Westminsters who would remember what he was like at school. Christ Church, anyway, was too socially stratified and money-conscious.

Merton was *old*, nearly as old as the University. 'It had', Stephen wrote in an autobiographical fragment, 'the most slow-walking, learnedly stooping and don-like dons, its quadrangles are the most historically contrasted in architectural period, its dining hall has the most highly polished tankards, the knobbiest old tables.' It had a bit of the old city wall containing a sleepy college garden, with the Meadows and the river beyond.

School had felt like prison, a place where you could not beat the system. University – he felt it at once – was going to treat him as an equal. Someone offered him whisky: he gulped it down neat because he felt it was the sophisticated thing to do. (Conformity had now become voluntary and thus much more powerful.) He had a 'scout' who called him 'Sir' and whom he shared with twenty other men. In Hall, as he dined, a portrait of Professor George Saintsbury hung behind him.

Freshmen, dining in Hall on the same bench for the first time, eye each other nervously, wondering whether or when to initiate a conversation. All are asking themselves: this man sitting opposite or beside me, will I get to know him, will he turn out to be a friend? Stephen noticed a 'whippy-looking young man' with very keen, clear eyes, a little older and more relaxed than himself, apparently imitating his own rather self-conscious way of looking furtively about him. This other man looked 'pleasantly officerish'. They introduced themselves.

'I am Second Lieutenant S.M.Potter.' (Wrong, Potter, wrong. One doesn't immediately mention the Army; one waits for the other fellow to press it out of one.)

'And I am Major G.B.W. Hamilton Gay.' Deadpan.

'Hyphenated?'

'Not exactly, but there is a definite atmosphere of hyphen,' said Gay. Two up to Gay: one for rank, one for witty remark.

Gordon Hamilton Gay had been on the stage before Army and Oxford. He came from a theatrical family and was half-brother to Harry Welchman, romantic lead in musical plays, who was at the moment rehearsing for *Afgar*, a new production at the London Pavilion. This at once made Gordon a glamorous figure. He had a musical-comedy trick of cupping his hand in his chin, leaning negligently on his elbow which then slid off the edge of the table.

English language and literature was then a new school at Oxford; to read it was as trendy as reading social anthropology today. It was distrusted by the classical establishment: Evelyn Waugh, coming up to Hertford College three years later, would say, 'English is no School for a gentleman.' It was modern, barely as old as the century, and sister Muriel had taken a first in it. Stephen was to have Tommy Seccombe as his tutor and he would share him with another freshman named Lionel Millard who had been in the Royal Artillery and just missed a commission.

Millard, fair-haired with a fine profile, wanted to be an actor but was opposed by his puritanically religious family. Stephen struck up acquaintance with him in a sparring argument at dinner in Hall.

'You fancy yourself as Hamlet, Lionel Millard,' said Stephen in the rasping voice he was always to use when winning arguments. Today, sixty years later, Millard remembers this moment clearly. 'It was his way of saying: "Will you be my friend?" ' It was also a victory for Stephen: Millard at that time had not read *Hamlet*. Stephen was afterwards to learn a great deal from Lionel who was far more widely read. Both Lionel and Gordon Hamilton Gay were to be Stephen's lifelong friends.

Merton was a strangely democratic college just after the War – certainly if you compared it with, say, Jesus or sober St Edmund Hall. Undergraduates were invited to dine at High Table to an extent which never happened in my own Oxford of some fourteen years later. For one thing, it enabled the dons to give freshmen rather too much to drink with the object of loosening their tongues. Millard's tongue was loosened to such an extent that next morning Stephen said to him: 'God, you made a fool of yourself last night!' It was, and would always be, a paramount anxiety in Stephen's life not to make a fool of himself. When he did it was what he called a 'pillow-biting' situation.

A tutorial with Tommy Seccombe was largely a matter of not going to sleep; for Seccombe spoke with eyes closed as if he were dropping off himself. He had spent the War teaching young gunner cadets at Woolwich Arsenal to add a little culture to their ballistics. He was a prolific contributor to *The Dictionary of National Biography* above the initials T.S. He implanted in his pupils the principle: 'Read the original before you read the criticism.' This principle is disobeyed by almost everyone cramming hurriedly for examinations. Seccombe mildly prefaced each remark with 'I suggest. . . .' 'I suggest you start by reading Spenser's *The Shepherd's Calendar.* . . .' It was strange being spoken to as an equal: quite unlike school.

Freshmen – first-year students – never change. Irreverence, running down people and institutions, is almost a duty. Deliberate lateness at lectures, reading to your tutor the identical essay that you read him three weeks ago, to see if he notices – and you never know whether he has twigged the joke because he says nothing. There are doubts about the value of lectures at all, since most lecturers are appointed because of their academic distinction, not because they are audible. Alone among the Merton dons of these years Geoffrey Mure, philosopher and much-decorated soldier, only a few years older than Stephen, took singing lessons in order to learn how to project his voice. Mure, once a classical scholar, was moving over to philosophy which was gradually replacing religion in his mind. He was a timid, gentle don. In just under thirty years' time he would be Warden of Merton.

Dons in those days were so donnish that you could hardly mistake them for anything else. It was unimaginable that one day dons would take part in radio and television panel-games. Dons were to be seen in Merton garden: F.H.Bradley, the philosopher, who had never been known to speak to an undergraduate, and who was eternally unpopular for having stopped the tolling of the Chapel bell at two o'clock on Fridays in memory of Walter de Merton, because it disturbed his after-lunch nap; H.W.Garrod, who always wore a hat, even indoors, to conceal his baldness (he was only forty-ish, but looked very old). Garrod not only talked freely to undergraduates but invited them to play tennis and bowls and liked them better if they were good at games. Sometimes – strange vision – dons were to be seen playing Dons' Tennis in Fellows' Quad, upon whose ancient lawn nobody below the rank of Master of Arts was allowed to tread.

Nobody knew what kind of voice the Warden had because no undergraduate ever saw him. Thomas Bowman, a mathematician, hated undergraduates, believing them to be irrelevant to the life of the University. He had been elected Warden in 1903 when he was already fifty-four. Regarded as a temporary appointment he somehow became permanent. Now, in 1919, at sixty-eight, he must surely retire soon? But no; he was ninety-four when he died in 1945. He seldom ventured outside the Warden's Lodge in term time. Drunken undergraduates on bump-supper nights and other festive occasions tried to produce some reaction from him by relieving themselves through his letter-box. Withal, this seeming recluse was heard to say that he hadn't much use for S.M.Potter, finding him 'frivolous and indecisive'.

Garrod, unsmiling with his thin gentle voice, inaudible unless you were in the front row at lectures, was a great leg-puller and something of a Lifeman. Another ex-classic who was specializing in English, he admired Stephen's brain and wanted him to be a don. He had Stephen's passion for winning arguments and would go to great lengths to do so, on more than one occasion snatching down a book from his shelves and 'reading' from it a fictitious paragraph in support of his case.

Very different was Professor H.C.Wyld, tutor in philology. He too saw Stephen as future don material though Stephen at this age showed no great talent for the science of words. (Philology was to become a ruling passion about twenty years later.) To successive generations of undergraduates philology has its funny side, especially the names of German practitioners of *Beowulf* textual criticism with names like Bopp and Bugge. Just as the great Sir Walter Raleigh defined the best English as 'the language spoken by an English lady in her drawing room', so Wyld (who came from a long line of Indian Army and civil servants) defined it as 'the English spoken by an officer in a good regiment'. Wyld, who cultivated the role of an English country gentleman, was the author of books on colloquial English and the past and future of pronunciation. One was called *The Best English, with Notes on Mr. Gladstone's Pronunciation.*

David Nichol Smith, Fellow of Merton, with his musical Edinburgh voice, was Goldsmith Reader in English. If you had him for your tutor he always started you on Pope, to his mind the greatest English poet. One of his pupils was Jack Stewart Collis, now at Balliol. Stephen had lost touch with him after Bushey Hall Cadet Battalion. Jack, it seemed, was tackling Oxford more forcefully than Stephen. He had instantly joined the Union and had already, in the very first debate of the term, made a speech – only two minutes, just before division time, but it was a start. Stephen, as so often, was jealous.

They fell to arguing about poetic diction, and how Wordsworth had (in the critical language of the time) 'swept away the dead wood of the eighteenth century' by using simple words like 'birds' and 'fish' instead of 'feathered choir' and 'finny tribe'. That week Stephen's essay for Tommy Seccombe contained one of those fearful generalizations to which we are prone in our first year: 'The 18th century wrote their verses in the study for a reader sitting in an armchair with a glass of vintage port at his elbow.'

Would Seccombe be shocked? No. All he said was: 'Mr Potter, there was no vintage port before 1836.'

Dons may be donnish but donnishness is infectious: it was fashionable, in the Merton College of 1919, to cultivate a scholar's stoop and slow walk after the years of marching and standing to attention. All Stephen's friends did this. Friends – another new experience. Stephen had made few friends at Westminster. Now, for three years certainly, perhaps forever, friendship was deeply important. Young men of unformed characters label each other with roles. Jack Collis labelled Stephen 'dreamy': vague, forgetful, liable to lose things. People who knew one at university go on remembering one as one was then, refusing to recognize any change. In a sense, they are right: the middle-aged man can be foreseen in the student.

What mattered in 1919, if one wanted popularity, was to be thought 'absolutely priceless'. All this little group of freshmen, Stephen afterwards wrote, were

with precisely similar backgrounds, public school, middle-class origins and homes, with happy family lives. . . . We all thought of ourselves as almost laughably different . . . we clung to our slight individual differences like rafts. We acted and re-enacted the pictures of ourselves seen by the eyes of our friends. Either you were 'absolutely priceless', i.e. true to your difference – or you were nothing.

Next to 'absolutely priceless', the highest compliment was 'how absolutely typical'. Later they would develop a system of 'marks' for outstanding pricelessness.

Throughout his Oxford life Stephen belonged to several 'sets'. He was a 'hearty', yet mocked the hearties; a learner-aesthete, yet avoiding any preciosity which might have disqualified him from other 'sets'. Unpolitical, he did not join the Union. Keenly interested in acting (but not very good at it) he joined the Merton dramatic society not the OUDS.

He had his main friendships with Lionel Millard and Jack Collis; yet he consorted with six other fellow-freshmen with whom he had far less in common. They would all, at one time or another, row in the Merton boat. They called themselves 'The Six', and for twenty years after going down they would write quarterly composite 'bulletin' letters, circulated to each in turn, chronicling what was happening to them all. This was, in a sense, Stephen's first club, not counting the Myrmidons, an exclusive dining club at Merton rather like Pop at Eton.

George Storey, an Irishman about six months younger than Stephen, slow, cautious and a very hard worker, was obviously going to get a first in his incomprehensible subject, chemistry. He would be killed in the Second World War. Herbert Wright, known as 'Root', had aged quickly for his years: he had joined up straight from school (Wellington), had two years in the trenches and sustained a wound over one eye, dangerously near the brain. An all-rounder, 6ft 4ins, he was the perfect public schoolmaster; and that is what he became. Tom Hamilton Baines, curly-haired and heavily built, was the son of a Midland bishop. His pricelessness consisted in extreme orderliness and not losing things; also in playing the double bass with which he liked to accompany gramophone records of Beethoven symphonies.

George Binney, a plump Etonian, also reading English, said to be ambitious for a title (he was eventually knighted in the Second World War), was locally famous, in the Oxford of 1919–22, for wearing plus-fours. Authorities such as Christopher Hollis maintain that Brian Howard, some three years later, pioneered them; but Stephen, all his life, was adamant that Binney not only was the first to wear them, he actually *invented* them. With his short academic gown on top they looked ludicrous. Binney would lead Arctic expeditions and write books about Eskimos.

Cyril Conner's pricelessness lay in the fact that he was the only really well-dressed undergraduate. He had been Captain of the School at Haileybury. He wore, not the standard tweed sports coat, but a blue blazer with brass buttons. Cyril Conner's trousers were pressed daily. His dressing-table was covered with splendid toiletries. His manners were impeccable. He played the piano, sang songs by modern composers such as Vaughan Williams, and was learning the 'cello. He worked hard on Stephen, trying to civilize him. 'He tried to plane me down a little,' Stephen remembered later. 'He stopped me chucking cigarettes in the fireplace so that they half missed it. He tried to get my shirt perfectly tucked into my trousers – I was still in the stage of hating my clothes, putting them on as if they were enemies.'

Cyril had a Norwegian mother, which meant that he had wonderful holidays in Norway, which meant that he spoke Norwegian fluently, and which meant that he could always attract Norwegian girls who were plentiful in Oxford. Stephen was transfixed with envy.

Cyril read law and was destined for high administrative jobs in the BBC and a judgeship. One of his daughters would become Penelope Gilliatt, the journalist and author.

The natural coxswain of the Merton boat was the light and 'whippy' Gordon Hamilton Gay. He and Stephen developed a song-and-dance act together, based on a 1919 musical show, *Tails Up*, starring Jack Buchanan and Phyllis Titmuss. The hit song was 'Wild Thyme':

She: 'I'm very fond of wild thyme.'
He: 'I've had a wild time too.'

For forty years afterwards, to the consternation of spectators who
had never seen it before, Stephen and Gordon broke into this dance
whenever they met. Gradually the song disappeared, leaving only
the dance which they called 'peardrops'. If they met in the street,
where there was not room to 'peardrop', they greeted each other
with a special whistle.

Jack Collis was always trying to make Stephen address himself
more seriously to life. Collis was now well set up at Balliol, 'a
scholar's paradise' where men took firsts in Greats and then
disappeared into the Treasury, perhaps never to be seen again. He
had Hilaire Belloc's old rooms overlooking the Martyrs' Memorial
in St Giles. He was working his way up, at the Union, to being a
'paper speaker'. It was, he said, all a question of catching the
'iceberg eye' of Beverley Nichols the President.

With Jack Collis Stephen devised a system of Life Scoring
(whose relevance to future Lifemanship will be apparent). It was
not entirely original: Christopher Hollis said it began in a coterie at
New College who awarded each other marks for 'bad breath, sex
attraction, ill-washed neck and the like'. It went with a fad of speech
which might be called 'understatement by double negative'. Collis
used it now, with an offer of eighty-five marks to Stephen for
coming to the Union to hear him speak: 'It might not be totally
unamusing for you.' A postcard from a really exotic foreign country
might rate as many as 200 marks. An invitation to tea with the
unpopular Warden, despite its extreme rarity, was worth only six.
Being asked to stay with a duke during the vacation was almost
incalculable. You could also lose marks – for saying the wrong
thing, for making a fool of yourself in a 'pillow-biting' way.

Jack was the first man Stephen had ever met whose childhood had
not been entirely happy. He came from a beautiful home at Killiney,
on the border between Co. Dublin and Co. Wicklow; but he
maintained that his mother hated him and loved his twin brother
Robert. . . . Stephen pondered this; it was a new idea, as new as the
idea, highlighted by the recent Russian Revolution, that there were
millions of people in the world who were miserable because they
were poor. Jack Collis eventually became Junior Treasurer of the
Union, speaking mainly on Irish questions; he also helped to form,
with Kenneth Lindsay, the Oxford University Labour Club of
which he became President. Both Collis and Lindsay tried to goad
Stephen into taking more interest in politics; while Stephen

probably voted Labour, he was never really committed. 'The only man who could make me vote Tory,' he said many years later, 'is Michael Foot.'

Stephen had vowed to himself that neither rowing nor any other time-consuming sport should be allowed to deflect him from work – work with the object of getting a first, nothing less. Then, one evening, Geoffrey Mure, the young philosophy don, knocked at his door: 'I wondered whether, next term, you'd take on the job of Merton Boats?'

Stephen was being offered the captaincy of the Boat Club. Why? Because university rowing was in a parlous condition since the War. Hardly anyone knew anything about rowing. Mure had heard that Stephen had rowed at Westminster. . . .

Striving to forget the bleeding bottom which had ruined his Westminster rowing career, Stephen mumbled: 'Well, if you think I would be any good. . . .' And so – S.M.Potter, Captain of Boats.

The summer vacation approached. It would of course be Swanage again for the Potters – or 'the South Dorset area' as Stephen preferred to call it in the presence of Mertonians who were going to far more fashionable and distant places like the Black Forest or the Italian Lakes. But there was a sudden change of plan. A friend from Westminster called 'Flap', who was maturing the more rapidly for not being at a university, had become an expert on motorcycles and was supplying them to friends. Would Stephen meet him at Exeter, collect a Norton and ride it with him to Land's End?

In 1919 nobody took driving tests and there was no Highway Code. If you could ride a push bike, you could ride a motorcycle: you just sat astride, engaged bottom gear, and hoped for the best. Flap was already an expert on girls, whereas Stephen, according to his diary, had only kissed one; so it was an easy *non sequitur* to suppose that he was also an expert on motorbikes. There is no record of how they got to Cornwall but the next scene is at the Sennen Cove Hotel.

Flap, the great provider of girls, was soon in conversation with two of them, both petite and very pretty. Flap concentrated on the blonde one who was the daughter of a prebendary in a cathedral city; that left the brunette, whose father was a professor of tropical diseases at London University, for Stephen. The two girls were henceforth known as Prebendary and Tropical. It is believed that

Tropical's real name was Dorothea; but Stephen's early diaries always clam up on the subject of falling in love. It is on the far more fascinating subject of falling *out* of love that he really goes into deep self-analysis.

Timid and gawky, Stephen contrived to encircle Tropical's waist while helping her up steep hills which are fortunately plentiful around Sennen. On the third day he held her hand. The physical attraction was quickly rationalized by 'tastes in common' – dogs, Dickens, Beethoven. Above all, Tropical was funny and laughed a lot. She made Stephen feel that all his conversation was brilliant.

'Obviously,' Stephen wrote afterwards, looking back on his nineteen-year-old self, 'this was love.' He would show Flap that he wasn't after all so backward with girls. On the fourth evening, after a magnificent sunset, followed by contemplation of the stars and the first long kiss, there seemed to be an understanding between himself and Tropical. The Potter family were on their usual summer holiday in Dorset. Stephen wrote to his mother telling her he was engaged.

The family took it surprisingly well; at least nobody *said* anything stronger than, 'That's nice, dear.' But the engagement was kept secret from his Oxford friends. Next term Pass Moderations, a preliminary examination involving classics which had to be got through before concentrating entirely on English, was looming up. And he was Captain of Boats. And there was Tropical who lived rather too far away for regular meetings. Tropical meant three letters a week and one telephone call from the porter's lodge.

The Boat Club was getting difficult. Stephen was captaining oarsmen, some of whom were far more experienced than himself: men like David Raikes, until recently known as 'the youngest Colonel in the Army', DSO, MC, a solid, serious oarsman from Radley who was all set for a Blue. He never became one of 'The Six' because he was incapable of seeing jokes. The only thing that made him laugh was *Sandford of Merton*, the famous parody of an Oxford novel, 'All rowed fast, but none so fast as stroke,' which he never realized was a joke. Raikes would eventually become President of the University Boat Club. The Merton Eight was also strengthened by Horsfall who would soon be stroking the Olympic Eight.

It was rowing versus Tropical: Stephen could not concentrate on both. She gave him dancing lessons at her parents' house with her mother popping round screens to make sure that Everything was

All Right. One day he forgot to arrange a meeting in London with Tropical because of a pressing rowing engagement. Useless to tell his coach that he had a date with his fiancée. The word was simply not understood. Tropical arrived in Oxford unannounced and watched the crew training. It was embarrassing. It was the beginning of the end.

Sister Muriel now took a diplomatic hand. To save Stephen from the awkwardness of having to spend his summer holiday with Tropical, and at the same time broaden his very limited knowledge of Abroad (a day trip to Boulogne and thirty-six hours in Paris, both with Uncle Jim), she stood him nine days in Paris, to be followed by a bicycle tour of Germany, Holland, Luxemburg and Belgium. Jack Collis jeered at this latter plan as a 'great British act of superficial travel'. He was right: Stephen retained extraordinarily little of these journeyings beyond a few Dutch pictures, to put in his memory beside the 'Laughing Cavalier' who hung above the umbrella stand at no. 36.

In his second year Stephen shared lodgings, at 15 Oriel Street, with Cyril Conner. It was a strange friendship, based partly on their being opposites, partly on music, for Cyril was Stephen's musical educator. The rooms were 'beamy with fifteenth-century effects'. Cyril was as meticulously neat as Stephen was untidy. Stephen's untidiness, which had now become part of his 'pricelessness' and thus his character fixed for life, was largely his mother's fault: 'She was well pleased to follow me round with dustpan and brush.' Cyril's patience must have been tried, yet today he says, 'Stephen was very easy to live with.'

Off Merton Street was that rare thing, a Real Tennis court consisting of a net and a sort of sloping roof at each side. The ball was heavier than the normal tennis ball and, no doubt with memories of *Henry V*, Act I, one had to remember the ancient names of sectors of the court – Grille, Dedans, Tambour. In his own rooms in college Stephen, who never much felt the cold, had had miserably small fires or no fires at all (a fact which filled his mother with anxiety so that she would come rushing up to Oxford with fresh supplies of woollen underwear). Now he had to get used to Cyril's grand scale of comfort. As you entered the living-room of 15 Oriel Street there was a big bowl of fruit on a table. Stephen was never known to enter or leave the room without eating a fistful of grapes. Cyril was a man of regular hours; Stephen would stay up all night and then sleep in till lunch or later. At Oriel College was another friend, Howard Marshall, one day to be known as a radio anchorman and sports commentator: it was a simple matter to rig up a rope between his own and Howard's rooms to act as a signal when one wished to talk out of the window to the other.

Stephen's mother might be eternally indulgent but Cyril's was not. Cyril, who lived at Eastbourne, invited him to stay during the vacation. Stephen arrived on his bicycle with a bursting briefcase containing, among other things, his only 'good' suit. Langley Cottage, Ashburnham Road, was a Tudor-type large villa with a big garden and a standard of comfort and luxury very different from no. 36. He had ridden some 120 miles from Dorset in just over seven hours. He was offered a bath before dinner in the most luxurious bathroom he had ever seen, full of several kinds of soaps, multicoloured towels and toilet waters and unlimited hot water straight from the tap, not, as at no. 36, from a geyser which never gave you a really full bath.

Coming down to dinner Stephen was attacked by Mrs Conner: 'Stephen, I've just spent twenty minutes cleaning up the bathroom. Do you always fill the bath to the top so that the water slops over? Cyril has spent weeks telling me how charming you are. Well, the charm isn't working yet.'

Stammered apologies; but Cyril's mother hadn't finished yet. She had had to use Vim and other abrasives to clean the bath: 'It wasn't a job I could possibly ask Ivy to do.'

Ivy, the maid, just under five feet high, was the cause of much suppressed laughter because she could not be trained to say, 'Is there anything more you require, Ma'am?' The idea that there was anything one could not ask a maid to do was new to Stephen. Cyril's mother set about training him in manners – lighting other people's cigarettes for them, opening doors for ladies – and even provided him with a child's rubber mat (with G.E. Studdy's Bonzo dog on it) under his plate because he ate so messily.

There were always Scandinavian girls at the Conners'. Stephen began to practise flirtation, the art of not getting too deeply involved, which was to last him through much of his life; for falling in love meant Responsibility – 'a word which often put me into a trance of inaction'.

The Conners and Eastbourne were 'posh'. They had a cook as well as a maid, and a chauffeur with the staggering Norman

Conquest name of Edgar de Bois Maison, called Mason for short. He drove an equally posh Chrysler. And there was Albert Sandler playing the violin, leading the famous Palm Court orchestra at the Grand Hotel. At Langley Cottage the Conners had the first really good gramophone Stephen had ever heard. He was, under Cyril's influence, introduced to string quartets, Ravel, Vaughan Williams, side by side with popular dancing hits like 'Dardanella' and 'Japanese Sandman'. Cyril, in Stephen's much later phrase, was his 'musical tin-opener'. Few new enthusiasms came unbidden to the young Potter; he must always persevere, aided by 'tin-openers'.

Back at Oxford Stephen felt he ought to join the Bach Choir which, although disliking Bach, he did. Rowing was becoming rather a chore. In a few years' time he would be saying airily to girls (and I quote from his 1947 radio satire, 'How to Blow Your Own Trumpet'), 'Yes, I'm afraid I was a galley slave at Oxford – chained to the oar – a waste of time, I suppose. . . .' And he was to display in his study, hanging from the picture rail, two of those varnished oars, one for winning the Visitors at Henley, the other for making seven bumps in Torpids. He didn't really love *rowing*, he began to realize; but he did love *winning*. And that would one day mean being a member of Leander, being able to wear the blazer at future Henley Regattas and the tie everywhere. Meanwhile an invitation to join a Trial Eight for the great Boat Race resulted in failure. Once again, as at Westminster, he felt he had 'muffed it'. He never rowed again.

Now Final Schools were approaching. Now he must concentrate on work. Was he getting bored already with Eng. Lit.: the annotations, the stock phrases of literary criticism, the lifelong dislike of an author which can be induced by studying him as a 'set book'. . . .? One day he would blow it all up in a puff of satire called *The Muse in Chains*. For the present, like the girl students he used to mock, he was taking the most voluminous lecture notes ever seen. He enjoyed, surprisingly, textual criticism: '. . . as brain-shaping as a crossword'. But having to express literary opinions was worrying: he took refuge in the idea that 'the writings of deep experience are fed to young men whose experience of life is only superficial'. And in those days nobody seemed to think a writer's life was relevant to his work.

Ah, but there were still distractions! Looking out of the window of 15 Oriel Street he saw a beautiful girl talking to a beautiful man. The man was Cecil Ramage, President of the OUDS (and also of the Oxford Union). The girl, a few years older, was Cathleen Nesbitt, the guest star, who had loved Rupert Brooke. She and Ramage had played opposite each other in the OUDS production of *Antony and Cleopatra*: it was believed that they were engaged. . . . They represented the unattainable life-outside-Oxford.

But, still, there was Shakespeare: study of Shakespeare, under the influence of the great Sir Walter Raleigh, was the lasting benefit of Eng. Lit. Raleigh, extremely tall with a fine voice, devoted much of his lectures to reading aloud from Shakespeare. Socially, he was famous for a verse starting, 'I wish I loved the human race,' and for his opinion of a 'good talker' who was said to be 'the life and soul of our common room'. 'In the midst of life,' intoned Raleigh, 'we are in death.'

Stephen, all his life, divided his friends into 'sets' and 'specialists'. Lionel Millard was his 'Shakespeare friend'; together they would engage in a long-term competition as to who would be the first to see performances of *all* the plays. But it was Jack Collis who invented the expression 'breath-catcher' – a poetic phrase or moment in a play which you would remember all your life: 'spanielled him at heels', 'a man thronged up with cold', 'prithee, undo this button'. These were variants of Stephen's own word, 'poetry-shock', which he first experienced when, in Keats, he found 'sunburnt mirth'.

He had seen less of Lionel while concentrating on rowing: Lionel had had a cruel stroke of bad luck. His father had lost money; Merton had kindly waived some of the fees but Lionel had been forced to move out three miles to very cheap lodgings in Cowley. Lionel was going to be either a Shakespeare scholar or a Shakespearean actor: it all depended on whether he would get a first. (He did, in the end, win the Shakespeare contest, helped by the Old Vic in London, Bridges Adams's company at Stratford-on-Avon and a chance discovery of a touring company in *Henry VI*, Part III, while motoring through Barnsley, Yorkshire.)

Stephen was now one of the favoured undergraduates who were invited quite often to dine at High Table and afterwards take port in the Senior Common Room. There was also a kind of One-upmanship Bowls in which Stephen was abetted by Geoffrey Mure. Not all High Table conversation was intellectual. The dons were gravely fascinated by Stephen's parlour trick of whistling a tune while simultaneously humming a contrapuntal harmony to it.

Nichol Smith, Raleigh and Wyld, three of the world's most important scholars, listened to Potter's rendering of the *Tannhäuser Overture*. It never failed. His chief sponsor was Professor Wyld, pupil of Henry Sweet (said to be the original of Shaw's Professor Higgins). Wyld played about with phonetics and 'future pronunciations', and was fond of pointing out, rather too often, that Alvescote, his village in the Cotswolds where he liked to play the part of a country gentleman, was correctly pronounced *Orlsc't*.

Alvescote was the scene of Stephen's theatrical debut. It was odd, perhaps, that Stephen had not joined the OUDS and taken part in the great revival of Oxford drama with undergraduate stars like Cecil Ramage and Robert Harris making great local names in Shakespeare and in experimental productions such as Hardy's *Dynasts*. Was he not too college-bound? Too late, in one's last term, to change that. But now Merton wanted him, with no experience of acting, to play the male lead in another version of the Cleopatra story – Dryden's *All for Love*, in Restoration dress. It would mean playing passionate love scenes with Joan Buckmaster, one of the great beauties of the contemporary stage. . . . Wyld was probably behind it all. Mercifully – it would almost certainly have been a 'pillow-biting' disaster – Stephen, with becoming modesty, refused. Lionel Millard played Serapino and the prologue was spoken by Cyril Conner. Geoffrey Mure and Lionel co-produced. For a college production it had a most distinguished audience. The lavatory facilities in colleges being limited there was a mixture of cast and audience in the men's urinal during the interval. Stephen and Lionel found themselves with W.B.Yeats, Herbert Henry Asquith and the Poet Laureate, Robert Bridges. They resolved thenceforth to keep a lifelong list of 'People I have Pissed with'.

Wyld persevered: would Stephen play Claudio in *Much Ado About Nothing*? It was to be produced by Wyld's daughter in the garden of a manor house near Alvescote. The daughter would also be playing Hero. Geoffrey Mure would be Benedick. The invited audience would consist mainly of people from the village. The play would be shortened, especially the scenes with Dogberry and Verges. (This was a mistake: the villagers would have loved them.) Stephen was a reasonable speaker of blank verse but had no idea what to do with hands and body. He also several times forgot his lines. The audience did not seem to notice; indeed they sat in stunned silence throughout the play until the church scene in Act

IV. As Stephen, playing Claudio, struck an attitude and declaimed, 'O Hero, what a Hero hadst thou been, If half thy outward graces . . .,' a gale of laughter swept the garden. A pun! To the village audience it was sheer relief, something they could understand.

Finals were now terrifyingly near. To get a first one had to offer a special subject. Stephen had chosen satire. But he had not read enough satire; had not read enough of anything. Well, Raleigh would be examining – he knew how to please Raleigh. Could he, by sitting up all night, mug up enough?

Raleigh, at that moment, was seriously ill with a fever after a long journey by air to the East as historian of the newly established Royal Air Force. One day students, attending a lecture on Pope by Professor Nichol Smith, found that the advertised subject had been abandoned. Nichol Smith stood before them with tears in his eyes. Raleigh was dead and Nichol Smith spoke only of him, quoting Ben Jonson on Shakespeare: 'I loved the man, and did honour his name on this side idolatry.'

Wyld would be examining in Middle English. That should not be too bad. Only Lionel had really done enough work. Jack Collis, who had openly cribbed in his Latin Unseen in Pass Moderations, had no chance of cribbing now. Only Lionel seemed to have a chance of a first. Much depended on the results of Finals. Both Lionel and Stephen were favourites of Wyld and Nichol Smith who could help them to get academic jobs after Oxford. As there was a shortage of undergraduates and rowing men, so there was a post-war all-European shortage of young dons. American universities were sending head-hunters, talent-scouts, over to Europe. Lionel Millard was already under surveillance for a possible lectureship in Ohio. Dons and examinees pointedly avoided each other until the results were known.

There was still the Viva Voce to be got through. Vivas are a chance to improve on the impression you have made in your written papers. You dress up in subfusc suit, white tie and mortar-board. Stephen, who had decided to present a devil-may-care front to the examiners, was nervous. Wyld was there and Nichol Smith and Brett-Smith, and a don called Simpson, and – surprise! – Quiller-Couch, borrowed from Cambridge.

Wyld (gently): 'You didn't seem quite at home in one of the language papers, Mr Potter.'

He asked a question about the fifteenth-century Paston letters –
and suddenly the name Paston eluded Stephen.

Simpson: 'We found it extremely difficult to read your writing, Mr
Potter.' Stephen's writing, all his life long, made no concessions to
the eyesight. 'You say that "everybody knows the words in which
Dryden praised Chaucer". Can you tell us what some of those
words are?' Some of them are 'veneration' and 'rough diamond',
but Stephen could remember no more. Lionel's Viva had been
better: Quiller-Couch said to him, 'You're the first undergraduate
I've ever met who has answered every single question on
Shakespeare!'

The results of Finals would not be out for ten more days. Stephen
and Lionel decided to break the tension by a bicycle tour of the
Cotswolds and the Shakespeare country; somehow Shakespeare
included Marlowe and at one point they found themselves at
Berkeley-on-Severn for its associations with *Edward II*. The high
spot of the tour was looking at the gravestones in Stratford
churchyard and seeing the names of characters in *Henry IV*. It
seemed that Shakespeare also included Gray's 'Elegy in a Country
Churchyard', for on the day the results of Finals were published
they were in Stoke Poges. They telephoned Merton College and
asked where they stood in the Class Lists. They had both got
seconds.

The news came as a relief at the time; but that second class would
rankle all Stephen's life – it would always debar him from a
top academic post. (And yet Sir Walter Raleigh, back in the nineteenth century, had somehow survived a second? Ah, but he had
published books of criticism. Perhaps that was a key to Stephen's
future.)

Degrees were less important then, of course. Monocled Rcbert
Harris the actor had handed in his papers after the statutory half-
hour and left the examination room. Christopher Isherwood at
Cambridge would do the same four years later. It was even rather
magnificent to go down without bothering to take your degree.
Oxford was, after all, a mainly social institution.

Jack Collis had got a fourth. He didn't seem to care. Stephen
wrote him one of his salving postcards: examinations were not to be
taken seriously, Jack's fourth was 'merely funny. . . . I should
imagine that either Simpson or Brett-Smith objected to your style.'

The card was written from Cyril Conner's house at Eastbourne where Stephen was having golf lessons.

Oxford was over. For Stephen, all hope was not yet lost. There was no hurry, plenty of time. 'I'm going to change my profession every five years,' he had bragged to Lionel. Imagine being the same thing, working for the same firm, all your life, like Father! Wyld obstinately believed that he ought to have got a first and recommended him to Otto Jespersen, the great Danish philologist, who knew of a lectureship vacancy at, of all places, Uppsala, Sweden. The salary – incredible wealth in 1922 – was £800 a year for five years. Stephen, unwilling to hang about while waiting for news, joined an Oxford party visiting European hospitals. He was not in the least interested in hospitals but it would enable him to visit five different countries at minimum expense. It would not be difficult to pose as a medical student. The only strong impression he retained was of Max Reinhardt's production of *Peer Gynt* in Berlin, which cost him 80,000 inflation-marks, or 1s 2d. Waiting for him in Berlin was a letter from Wyld telling him that the Uppsala job wasn't on after all – Stephen was six months too young. Was that the real reason – or was it his second-class degree? He would never know.

In 1922 a new, experimental thing called 'wireless broadcasting' was beginning. It was terribly amateurish – a bit of a joke really; it couldn't possibly last. Stephen, in common with many graduates of his age, seemed to think that he would automatically be offered a job. One knew someone who knew someone who was looking out for someone like oneself. One could pick and choose. It would have to be in London, of course – London was the centre of everything. Somehow Stephen got an interview with the new British Broadcasting Company (not yet Corporation), at Savoy Hill, and found himself facing the head of administration, Admiral Carpendale. They needed a talks producer at the new Birmingham studio. The salary was £8 a week. . . . In 1922 on £400 a year you could have a flat, a wife, two children and a car and still save a few pounds a year. But Birmingham! Not for another seventeen years would Stephen visit any provincial city; not for about that length of time, indeed, would he ever earn as much as £8 a week. He turned the job down. The man who would one day make his most solid reputation as a broadcaster turned his back on radio. He wanted vaguely, oh how vaguely, to be a writer. Nothing so practical as journalism seems to have occurred to him. The official Oxford view of the time was that journalism corrupts both style and intellect. What should he write about? There must, it seemed to his romantic mind, be a period of self-discovery, there must be Years of Wandering with, of course, plenty of golf and tennis.

Chapter 6
The wandering twenties

One of the dangerous results of the Honours School of English Language and Literature is that it causes young men to think they are going to be writers. In Stephen's case it confirmed a near-certainty that had been there since about his second Oxford year. For what else can you do with an English degree? You can be a teacher, as sister Muriel was (she was now senior English mistress at St Paul's Girls' School). You can take holy orders as Jack Collis was doing (though he would not stay long at a theological college). You could, of course, go on the stage – this was still Lionel Millard's obsession though he, too, would end up teaching. Or you can enter the Civil Service for which you must take one of two special examinations – Administrative for the top grade, Executive for such humble jobs as Inspector of Taxes. The English School, although liberating the imagination, tends to implant the idea that a nine-to-six office job is out of the question.

Stephen, at twenty-three, had most of the qualities required for a public- or grammar-school assistant master: good second, good public-school and university background, reasonable all-rounder at sport and just-missed-a-Blue. But he had left it rather late: his job applications should have been in immediately after coming down from Oxford. At home, no. 36, Uncle Willie was digging at him about a job in Bird & Potter: 'You know, Step, most young men would give their eyes and ears for a chance like that. . . .' Father, however, did not push him towards the family firm: Father, looking in wonder at the son who might yet lead the free, creative life he had never dared to follow, knew better. Some instinct in him recognized a late developer when he saw one.

I know I am a genius, but what am I a genius at? Writing – perhaps acting too? But what shall I write *about*? Satire and humour? *Punch*, perhaps? No good; can't get any ideas. . . . Stephen's reading at this time was dominated by Samuel Butler, Bernard Shaw and H.G.Wells. These were the Great Emancipators. Wells's *Outline of History* had come out two years before, in weekly parts: by some libraries, including the Oxford Union Library, it was banned.

Butler, whose *Way of All Flesh* was full of unhappy Victorian family life, had nothing in common with life at no. 36 Old Park Avenue. But he taught you not to take anything for granted: '. . . that parents know best, that school reports are fair and correct, that choosing a wife is something straightforward'. As with all his heroes Stephen fell for Butler completely, almost uncritically. With Wells, it was the optimistic certainty of Progress and the new idea that history is a lot of things happening at once all over the world, from *homo sapiens* onwards, that were so exciting. As for Shaw, it was *Pygmalion* that for the present dominated Stephen's thoughts and for a very odd reason. *Pygmalion* gave Stephen his first job.

Pygmalion is about turning a flower-girl into the social equal of a duchess by curing her of her Cockney accent. Professor Wyld, at Merton, had stressed the importance of preserving local dialects; but, with his love of phonetics (he had once phoneticized the London pronunciation of *railway* as *raiuwai*), Wyld would have agreed that Cockney is a social disqualification. 'Why shouldn't I, like Professor Higgins,' Stephen reasoned, 'turn Cockney voices into Received Standard?' So he put an advertisement in the personal columns of *The Times*: 'Cockney accents cured. Apply Box 1234.' To interview his pupils he had to hire a room in London. It did not seem to occur to him that to get a regular supply of clients it was necessary to advertise regularly, once a week if not daily. He had one applicant who came twice at ten shillings a time. 'Cost of room five shillings a time, advertisement four and six, net profit five and six,' Stephen wrote in one of the twopenny note-books that were the repository of his thoughts and experiences at the time.

What next? As so often in his life, doubts and decisions must be resolved – or perhaps escaped – by violent physical exercise. Golf or tennis were not enough: there must be a journey of self-discovery, a long journey, and it must be on foot. Now began a period which, if asked what he was doing during 1924 and part of 1925, he would refer to afterwards as 'Shakespeare's missing years – remind me to tell you about them sometime'. And if you reminded him he changed the subject.

The really long (500-mile) walk would not happen for another two years. Then he would set a target of forty miles a day; but for the present walk – mostly in Coleridge country – twenty-five would do. Would Jack Collis come too? No, Jack was too busy. Announcing his departure in a letter of July 1924 Stephen fell into the old 'marks' game: 'I have been marking the weather. Interesting point: Are marks given to the weather complimentary or not? Surely to Climate the uncomplimentary is complimentary.' Nearly all Stephen's letters, unless he used other people's stationery, were on leaves torn from exercise books, or on pencilled postcards. '*Nether Stowey, Monday*. 25 miles a day choked by wind, blinded by sun, flattened by rain, broken by mountains – rather good, also, to be able to decide to walk NE and move off in the exact opposite direction.'

Apart from giving him perfect physical health, the walk solved nothing.

He knew he was wasting time delightfully. There were days with Lionel Millard in the British Museum Reading Room, seeing who could find books on the most recondite subject – Peruvian Featherwork or Embryology. This was partly a genuine thirst for instruction: 'Stephen couldn't bear not to know things,' Lionel remembers. A more dangerous Reading Room game was to take out rare and almost priceless volumes, just for a dare – a Quarto Shakespeare or a Kelmscott Chaucer – and read them in a nearby cafe. Security was very slack in those days.

There was, too, a memorable holiday with Jack Collis at Killiney, on the border between Co. Dublin and Wicklow. The Collis home was on a slope that went down to the railway line which followed the edge of the bay. 'If the engine driver saw you running, he would stop for you.' There was Maurice, Jack's older brother (by eleven years), on leave from the Indian Civil Service which would soon send him to Burma to be a District Magistrate: he would become biographer, historian, novelist, painter and critic. There was Bob, Jack's twin, his mother's favourite, a doctor, soon to specialize in sick children in Nigeria, Dublin and London. There was Jack's strange mother, whom Stephen characterized as 'fatally retired into the private hell of her own egotism'. Above all, there was tennis, golf and billiards and Jack doing his wonderful imitation of Bernard

Shaw. What was there about Ireland that so appealed to Stephen? The country? The lack of responsibility? The holiday stayed in his memory all his life.

Jack, now escaped from his theological college (he realized in time that the pulpit had been only a target for his 'hankering after oratory') was full of new plans. He was now living in London and 'freelancing', whatever that meant. He had had an article accepted by the *Irish Times* and was actually writing a book on Shaw – with Shaw's encouragement! Of course things were a bit easier for Jack – he had that £150 a year allowance from his father and didn't frivol it away – but he was getting down to it, he was creating something. . . . Stephen was envious: now Jack was the leader of them both.

Jack Collis made him go to Fabian meetings to hear Shaw on Sidney Webb, St John Ervine on Shaw, Shaw on Shaw, Shaw on Christianity. . . . Cockney voice from the back of Battersea Town Hall: 'Yes, but what abaht the Immaculate Conception?' Shaw: 'My dear sir, *all* conceptions are immaculate.'

It was Jack Collis who first took Stephen to the 1917 Club, 'founded in honour of the Russian Revolution', which to intellectuals of the 1920s was the beginning of the liberation of all mankind – in the phrase of those days, 'the Russian Experiment'. Anyone could join and Stephen did. It was in Gerrard Street, Soho, next door to a brothel and opposite Mrs Kate Meyrick's notorious 43 nightclub which was always being raided for selling liquor after hours. One went to the 1917 Club mostly at lunch-time. The floors were uncarpeted, the teashop tables had grubby cloths on them. There were two main rooms adjoining, 'the windows impenetrable with steam, the air full of smoke and the smell of shepherd's pie and cabbage, noise and clatter . . .'. There were two waitresses: Gertie ('I'm coming as quick as I can') and Annie who never spoke, large with varicose veins.

The ground floor was taken up by the secretary's office and a cloakroom, and in the basement was a large ping-pong table where furious games were played after lunch. After all the left-wing food, the mashed potatoes and boiled puddings, you needed the exercise. More than twenty years later Stephen did a radio programme on this phase of his life. 'The whole dining-room, dim and soggy with steam, became bracing and electric for me. To be in the same room as H.G.Wells . . .!' True, his first conversation with Wells had not been very edifying.

Wells: 'What size hats do you take?'
Potter: 'Rather big. Nearly $7\frac{1}{2}$.'
Wells: 'All that bulge at the back of your head. It doesn't contain anything really. The sort of information you can get from a Baedeker. *I* take $5\frac{1}{2}$ in hats.'

The 1917 Club membership was truly awe-inspiring: Ramsay MacDonald, Arthur Henderson, Bacharach the music critic with his natty bow-tie; Francis and Vera Meynell – never heard of them, but he must be the poet Alice Meynell's son; George Lansbury and his son Edgar. . . . There was an exciting legend that the Lansburys and Meynell had smuggled the Russian crown jewels into the country to finance the *Daily Herald*. The jewels, hidden in a tobacco pouch, had been handed over in Copenhagen to Meynell by Litvinoff, Soviet representative in Britain. Meynell had then inserted them into soft chocolates and posted them to Cyril Joad in London. Herbert Farjeon, with his 'worn-away, hollowed-out intellectual face', was dramatic critic of the *Sunday Pictorial* (rather a low-brow paper, but Farjeon could write for all levels). He played ping-pong to *win*, groaning with effort. There was some kind of editor called Kingsley Martin; J.W.N. Sullivan – how could a man be both a scientist *and* an authority on Beethoven? Stephen was soon hopelessly beaten in a discussion on the Rasoumoffsky Quartets.

There was a weird-looking man in crumpled tweedy clothes with a beard and a speech impediment who laughed loudly at everything – Joad was his name – a top Civil Servant who also wrote books on philosophy.

Among stage personalities were Russell Thorndike and John Laurie from the Old Vic, Harold Scott and Elsa Lanchester (but their true milieu was the Cave of Harmony where they could sing Victorian music-hall songs like 'Please Don't Sell No More Drink to My Father'); Komisarjevsky the Russian producer and designer; and a beak-nosed comedienne called Betty Potter whose real name was Meinertzhagen. The theatrical connection was important to Lionel Millard who had also joined the 1917; for the 1917 was an unofficial theatrical agency and job exchange. If Peter Godfrey, founder of the Gate Theatre, was casting Gorky's *Lower Depths*, there might be a chance of a part at £2 a week, or at least ten bob a day and one meal for crowd work, or no pay at all just to be able to say one was not 'resting', especially for Sunday-night performances of very *avant-garde* plays.

'I am more certain than ever,' Stephen confided a little pompously to his diary, 'that what I write must have a political and social purpose.' Or again, rather nearer the mark: 'Perhaps what I write will be critical. . . . Perhaps I am a kind of Sitwell in embryo.' At Oxford Kenneth Lindsay had always chided him for his irresolution about politics. Even the Fabian Society lectures he had attended in much the same sort of spirit as he would have gone to an organ recital of Bach. It was Betty Meinertzhagen who relieved his mind by assuring him that it really wasn't necessary to be a card-carrying member of the Communist Party or the ILP to qualify for the 1917.

Stephen always had a passionate desire to conform, even if he kicked against conformity; he had to belong to a 'set'. The question of dress worried him. His Good Suit was obviously too good; that left his plus-fours which were his substitute for the flannel bags and tweed jacket at Oxford. But there were little coloured tabs at the top of the stockings: surely these were wrong for the 1917? They belonged to his 'golf and dancing' world; it did not occur to him that other 1917-ers might also play golf and dance. So the tabs were removed before he entered the Club.

At the 1917 Stephen met many of the people who were to be long-term friends and guide him through what he thought of as the world of sophistication. But he had to guard against saying the unsophisticated thing: 'pillow-biters' like, 'Yes, I do enjoy painting, but music means much more to me than anything else . . . in fact, sometimes I think it is the only thing.'

Soon he was playing tennis at Cyril Joad's house in East Heath Road, Hampstead, partnered by Francis Meynell. Joad at once scolded Stephen for being late – 'typical adolescence. The time soon comes when juvenile errors are no longer charming' – followed by the famous cackling laugh. Sometimes they played at Golders Green Club where the secretary would send them regular little notes: 'Tennis clothes should be plain white.' Back at East Heath Road there was what Stephen thought of as 'continental' food and much music, usually on Joad's pre-1914 pianola; and Joad's crystal-clear talk. 'I am not an original fee-lotho-fer,' he would say. 'A good boiler-down, call me.' No pillow-biting for Joad: he was candid about his own social gaffes – how he had been reprimanded by the

much older Professor Gilbert Murray for writing to him 'Dear
Murray'; how he had been rightly accused by Bertrand Russell
(whose precise voice he copied) of pinching his ideas without
acknowledgement.

There were to be many adventures in Joad's company. He took
Stephen to play golf at Tandridge, one of the grander Surrey
courses. After the first hole it began to rain. ('God micturating,'
Joad said.) They returned to the car but not to the clubhouse. The
secretary appeared: 'Have you gentlemen paid your green fee?'
They had not – and Joad was not a member. 'British officialdom,'
said Joad in disgust. On another occasion, playing the Brook course
in the New Forest, Joad broke off the game to bathe naked in a
stream. Stephen, many years later, told both these stories in *Golf
Gamesmanship*.

Jack Collis was now living romantically in Dockland on the south
bank of the Thames. He had a room at the back of a pub in
Rotherhithe, overlooking the river. He seemed to know exactly
what he was doing and where he was going. He had forsworn girls
and drink and would not let himself look out of the window at the
distracting, busy water-traffic. The book on Shaw was finished and
it was going to be published by Jonathan Cape, the daring man who
had recently reissued the complete works of Samuel Butler. Like
Stephen, Collis seemed to prefer living in total chaos. He had
recently got engaged for the second time to a girl from Barnet who
was known simply as Barnet; but it was already off, hence
the monastic discipline. There were galley-proofs from Cape
all over the bed. He showed Stephen a sheaf of letters from
Shaw.

Jack had a new friend whom he wanted Stephen to meet, Gerald
Edwards, G.B.Edwards, who liked to be called G.B. He had dark
hair and was Welsh-looking with unblinking frank eyes. He liked to
call artists by their first names: thus Van Gogh was always Vincent.
He was an apostle of D.H.Lawrence. Stephen risked a few
comments such as 'obsessed with sex'.

'Not obsessed – he *possesses* it. I think Lawrence might have a lot
for you.' Oh dear, another conversion: Lawrence, he was assured,
would give him a mystical experience. Some writers, like Aldous
Huxley, seemed to be saying No to life. Lawrence was saying Yes.
G.B. knew a bit about German philosophy, especially Nietzsche.
Well, why not? Bertie Farjeon and Francis Meynell actually *knew*

Lawrence: Francis had lent him a cottage, Lawrence had coached his niece through an examination, and they had only quarrelled for the usual reason – that Lawrence put the Meynells ungratefully and libellously into a novel. Stephen took G.B. home to no. 36 to have a bath because there was no bath in the bungalow on the edge of a wood near Eltham where G.B. lived with a wife and five children who wore no shoes.

How did G.B. live? Nobody seemed to know, but he occasionally had articles published in Middleton Murry's *Adelphi* review. Stephen found himself struggling with *Women in Love* and, as if it were the other side of the coin, *Fantasia of the Unconscious*. G.B. had become to Stephen 'my wonderful new friend', or 'my Lawrence friend'.

G.B. was 'un-Oxford', that was his attraction. It was also the reason why they would never see eye-to-eye. He was too solitary to have a lot of friends all speaking the same public-school university language with its private jokes. G.B. was also mad on Walt Whitman and Edward Carpenter. Stephen tried these too. G.B. had an infallible method of making him try new writers – he would say: 'Perhaps you're not ready for him yet.'

'The Twenties,' Stephen wrote many years later, 'were to float with the tide, first this way and that, and to enjoy it.' There had been his Aldous Huxley phase: he had found there his own aimless wandering world, described with horrible detachment, funny but in the long run depressing. He took *Those Barren Leaves* with him to the Oval, to read during the duller patches of the game when Hobbs was not batting and Tate was not bowling; he was embarrassed to meet G.B. there.

The Meinertzhagens cheered him up. 'Am I too solemn about things?' he asked Betty, whose stage surname, Potter, had been adopted from her aunt's maiden name: her aunt was Beatrice, Mrs Sidney Webb, of the Fabian Society.

'You have to have a bit of solemn,' she replied gravely.

'We are not starved of sex,' Stephen went on, 'we are starved of chastity!'

Betty was ten years older than Stephen or she might have laughed. Stephen had recently lost his chastity to 'a charming and gracious lady who had taken pity on, or become irritated by, my virginity, and then, after a few months, gently dismissed me'. He felt deeply sunk in vice. Years afterwards he wrote of this affair:

'There had been difficulties. A talented lady had taken me in hand, but even her natural tenderness and subtle physical knowledge could not reform my uncouthness. Sexually I was a hobbledehoy, a country bumpkin.'

Betty Meinertzhagen had three sisters, all mad as happy children are mad. In their thirties they were still children: looking back on them from middle age Stephen attributed their 'pixilated' (a post-1939 word) quality to an excessively happy childhood at Mottisfont, their country house near Stockbridge in Hampshire, where each daughter had her own private garden.

Laurencina, the maddest, was Mrs Herbert Warre-Cornish. Marjorie (Margie) was married to George Booth, descendant of Lord Macaulay, who had been Director-General of Munitions in the War and was, among many directorships, a director of the Bank of England. Beatrice ('Bobo') was Mrs Robin Mayor. With Bobo Stephen discussed endlessly the question of whether he was happy or not. It would happen suddenly in the middle of another conversation: 'Are you happy?' Stephen didn't know. 'You hesitate,' said Bobo, 'which means that you *are*, probably wildly happy, because not to know whether you are is the only way of knowing that you are.'

The Meinertzhagens (their name, Stephen knew from philology, meant 'my heart's shelter') liked him because, to them, he too was mad. Bobo lived in a small house in Campden Hill Gardens. Her flower-filled drawing-room had furniture of fashionable, un-varnished, 'scrubbed' wood from Heal's. Vlamincks and Van Goghs (originals?) hung on the walls and there were sculptures by Gaudier-Brzeska, whoever he was. No more Huxley! Bobo was *Bloomsbury*. Virginia Woolf sometimes came to tea. Bobo also knew Ouspensky, author of a vast book called *A New Model of the Universe*, a mystic who held 'meetings' rather than classes. What exactly was mysticism? It was all rather vague, un-Shaw, un-Joad. But Bobo would not explain; nor would she take Stephen to Ouspensky's meetings.

Meanwhile, one had to earn money. Well, perhaps it had better be teaching after all – it would do to tide him over until his first masterpiece. This meant applying for jobs through either Truman & Knightley or Gabbitas & Thring, scholastic agencies. He chose Gabbitas & Thring who required 'four copies of at least three testimonials'. The best Gabbitas & Thring could do was

Windyridge Preparatory School at Bicksworth, Norfolk – salary according to qualifications but not to exceed £200 a year. He would have to teach practically everything, including geography and Latin . . . but Norfolk! Too far from London where everything happened. Ah, here was something better: 'F.S.McNalty Esq, 67 St George's Square, Pimlico, SW'.

'Mac's' was not exactly a crammer's, nor yet a school for backward boys, but something in between: a school for boys who, through illness or temperamental inadequacy, had difficulty with exams, including Army exams for getting into Sandhurst. 'Seeing myself as Nicholas Nickleby approaching the establishment of Wackford Squeers,' Stephen afterwards wrote, 'I was in for a shock.' 'Mac' didn't believe in corporal, or any other, punishment. He had the fashionable 'scholar's stoop' which had been so popular at Oxford. He taught by treating all pupils (and their age-range was thirteen to eighteen) as equals; by teasing and laughing, as Stephen himself learned to teach. 'Mac' teaching arithmetic, for example: 'My darling old nonsense, the square root of sixteen is *what* squared? *Two*, that's it!'

The McNaltys, Frank and Mary, lived at no. 67 St George's Square, and the school's boarders lived at no. 56. Both were tall pillared houses, most of whose rooms were used as classrooms, the McNaltys living in the top of the house. Mary McNalty had once been married to the legendary Harry Quilter, a painter of the Camden Town school, an enemy of Whistler, who had bought Whistler's studio in Tite Street where he died in 1907. Harry was the cousin of Roger Quilter the composer, and his daughter, Gwendolen, also a painter, had married the *Punch* writer A.P.Herbert.

Stephen found himself housemaster in charge of no. 56, which meant deserting 36 Old Park Avenue and actually living there. Billiards, ping-pong (until he was beaten by a thirteen-year-old), and golf at the Royal Wimbledon took up his leisure – and there was a Steinway piano with calf-bound volumes of Beethoven. The McNaltys also set about Stephen's own education. Girls, for example – he was still very awkward with them. Mary McNalty, petite and energetic, taught him to dance. The twenties dancing and nightclub craze was now well under way – slow fox-trotting to *Poor Butterfly*, waltzing to *Three O'Clock in the Morning*, quick-stepping to *I'm Just Wild About Harry*. All these tunes one could hear (sometimes direct from America before publication in Britain) at the Riviera, a new nightclub on the Thames embankment opposite St George's Square. The McNaltys, discreetly taking charge of Stephen's poverty, took him out dining and dancing, providing him with partners of baffling beauty with whom he found it difficult to make conversation when he took them out without the McNaltys. Sometimes the McNaltys would be at a neighbouring table, watching. Hence Stephen's first lesson on Winemanship: 'My dear old idiotic splendid, why give such a nice girl one of the heaviest and most stupefying Burgundies on any known wine list? You'll just send her to sleep!'

The McNaltys also introduced him to Well-Known People, including Artists. They took him along to Alan Herbert's Boat Race Party at 12 Hammersmith Terrace. Here, almost the only guest in a conventional three-piece suit ('my *good* suit'), he observed that actors dressed like actors in check suits, and painters like painters in polo-necked sweaters and corduroys. How did writers dress? Surely not like sailors as A.P.H. did. He must find out. One of the corduroyed painters was a girl with very clear grey eyes who seemed to be known by her surname, Attenborough, or Att for short. Why? Because she had been at the Slade where surnames were the fashion. She was only twenty-three but had already exhibited in London and the provinces. 'Her skin,' he noted at the time, 'glows with unquenchable health.' Most of her friends seemed to have been at the Slade too. Stephen pondered on this. Perhaps Oxford wasn't so wonderful after all. The Slade people seemed much more grown up. . . .

As for the Boat Race, the crews flashed past and one heard the result a few minutes later because the Herberts had a wireless crystal set, the wonder of the age, whose future Stephen had treated so disrespectfully by turning down that well-paid job in Birmingham.

He might not have noticed Att so keenly – after the McNaltys' soigné nightclub girls, Att's un-made-up face and corduroys worried him a little – had she not done her party piece. With another ex-Slade student, Roger Furse the stage designer, she sang to her own accompaniment on that symbol of the twenties, the ukelele. The two of them specialized in songs from American folk-lore. Att's was not a beautiful voice but it somehow brought out the satirical or sociological humour or pathos of what she sang. Everyone knew

'Frankie and Johnny', but others were entirely new to London's Bohemia. This one was sung to a slow blues rhythm:

My Monday girl, she buys me coats and shoes,
My Tuesday girl, she plays the weary blues,
My Wednesday girl, she buys me cocaine beans,
My Thursday girl, she says don't leave me please,
My Friday girl, she lives on Front and Main,
My Saturday girl, she anything but plain,
My Sunday girl, she lives on Main and Broad –
She's hair like Venus, she walks just like the Lord:
O Lordy Lord, the Good Book tells you now –
O Lordy Lord, I got religion now!

Recitals often ended with this tribute to the Statue of Liberty, sung fast with a punching rhythm:

There's the Argentines, and the Portuguese, the Armenians and the
    Greeks;
They don't know the language,
They don't know the law,
But they vote in the country of the free –
And a funny thing,
When we start to sing
'My Country 'tis of thee' –
None of us know the words but the Argentines,
And the Portuguese and the Greeks

.   .   .   .

But who is the gent
That collects the rent,
At the end of each four weeks?
Ah! that is all done by the Argentines
And the Portuguese and the Greeks.

When this was sung at Slade parties the applause was often led by Ralph Vaughan Williams.

Twelve Hammersmith Terrace, W6, has been called 'the Holland House of the 1920s'. It was (and is) one of a row of narrow Georgian houses, backing on to the river, which are said to have been built for the mistresses of George II. At the bottom of the garden was a low brick wall with steps down to the water for getting into boats: at this time Alan Herbert had a barge called *The Ark*. He had taken a long lease on no. 12 at the miraculously low rent of £55 a year. As their family increased, the Herberts bought no. 13 next door and knocked the two houses into one. Nearby was a famous Victorian pub, the Black Lion, with its beer garden and skittle alleys.

In the Herberts' seething L-shaped drawing-room on Boat Race day, drinking mulled claret, you met everybody. Literature was represented by Sir John Squire, the cricketing poet and editor; Gerald Barry and his wife; the Aldous Huxleys; Robert and Sylvia Lynd; St John Ervine, dramatic critic of the *Observer*; H.G.Wells; Arnold Bennett and Dorothy Cheston; Sir Owen Seaman, editor of *Punch*; and Rose Macaulay. From the theatre, Charles Laughton – not yet famous, not yet in Hollywood, not yet married to Elsa Lanchester who was also there with Harold Scott the actor and the beautiful Baddeley sisters, Angela and Hermione. Among painters there were Mark Gertler, Edward Wadsworth, Richard Nevinson, Julian Trevelyan, Eric Kennington, and a small Russian named Vladimir Polunin who did décors for Diaghilev's Russian ballet.

Young Stephen Potter was overwhelmed by all this. He did not easily adjust to new environments, tending to blame the limitations of 'no. 36' for his own conservatism. Back at St George's Square he began to wonder about teaching as a career. Knowing his own immaturity it seemed to him that for men a parental instinct was necessary (women were born with it). He was twenty-four – only six years older than his oldest pupils. Teaching one boy history he found his pupil disbelieving most of what he was told about the Hundred Years' War. Why? Because the boy was a Roman Catholic and had been taught to see English history from Rome.

As housemaster he had to deal with personal problems. One boy came to him because he wanted to confess that he masturbated three times a day. 'Promise you won't tell Mac?' the boy said anxiously. Stephen, fearing for the boy's health, broke his promise. The boy never forgave him. Another boy – Stephen's favourite, the boy who had beaten him at ping-pong – was caught 'talking after lights out'. Choosing the wrong moment to assert his authority and 'make an example', Stephen caned him. The boy refused to speak to him for the rest of the term. Stephen had lost his self-confidence: he resigned.

Back to Gabbitas & Thring who now came up with a tutorship. Sir L.M. had a son who had missed two halves at Eton through illness. Would Stephen coach the boy, who was eighteen, in Latin? Sir L.M. had hired a house at St Leonards-on-Sea so that the distractions of London would not interfere with the boy's studies.

'But, sir, classics is not my subject.'

Sir L.M., impressed by Westminster, the Guards and Oxford, said: 'Nonsense. I'm sure you're good enough.'

Banishment to the Sussex coast was as undesirable for Stephen as it was for the boy. The house was full of assegais, tribal masks and other relics of Africa. It was bookless and pianoless. He and the boy dined every evening in dinner jackets and silence. Frantically Stephen mugged up English translations of Latin prose from cribs. The boy calmly helped him over the more difficult passages.

Stephen, by his agreement with Sir L.M., had every other weekend off. He spent this time trying to repair his awkwardness with girls. How did one pick them up? How did one cope with the fear of getting too deeply involved? There was the 'haven't we met before?' method which could be given a touch of originality by adding: 'Was it at Alan Herbert's by the river, or perhaps in Studio "B" at Elstree?' Sometimes it meant taxis; and too many evenings ended with the mistake of *asking* for a kiss instead of just taking it. There were tea dances he could almost afford, and dinner dances he certainly could not afford, at the Criterion, the Trocadero, even the Savoy, where you could dine and dance for only five shillings if you ate nothing but hors d'oeuvres. His favourite partner was Christine Lindsay, sister of the great Kenneth Lindsay, who had been President of the Oxford Union. To her he could say, in the rough laughing way that seemed to work with nice girls, 'My God, you've got to come out with Potter!' With Christine, too, he had the essential 1920s experience of being in a nightclub when it was raided – something you could boast about for months afterwards. Christine, exquisitely pretty, kind and unselfconscious, gave him dancing lessons and self-confidence. Her surviving contemporaries describe her as 'the perfect flapper . . . everyone was in love with her.' Stephen confided to his diary: 'She was gentle.'

On one weekend off, he went to a party given by Neil and Nora Mackintosh at the Berkeley. Neil had been at school with him; and with Nora he had carried on a flirtation by letter – his letters to her were usually decorated with caricatures. Their father was a doctor in Hampstead and one of his patients was the dramatist Henry Arthur Jones. Jones had for years been carrying on a one-sided feud with Stephen's hero, Bernard Shaw – one-sided because Shaw had always spoken well of Jones. Their disagreement had not been about drama but about the War, patriotism and the Irish question.

Jones could not forgive Shaw for having advised all soldiers in France to 'shoot your officers and go home'.

On his next weekend off Stephen contrived to meet him. Henry Arthur, now seventy-three, was feeling his age: he was struggling against a series of nervous breakdowns, thought himself a back number, and sought reassurance from the intelligent younger generation. He took at once to Stephen who was careful not to mention that he had first heard of him through Shaw's *Saturday Review* essays. Henry Arthur said he hoped they would meet again and seemed to mean it.

It was over three months since Stephen's banishment to St Leonards-on-Sea. He now saw a golden opportunity to end it. He wrote Henry Arthur Jones a letter saying he was surprised that he had no secretary. If he wanted one, Stephen would be delighted to fill the position at £5 a week. He had no shorthand but Henry Arthur would find him (in a fine, delicate phrase) 'not without knowledge of the typewriter'. To his delighted surprise, Henry Arthur said yes. Stephen gave Sir L.M. a month's notice, bought a typewriter and a copy of Pitman's Guide, and taught himself to type at a speed of about two words a minute.

With £5 a week in his pocket he took the plunge and left 36 Old Park Avenue, SW, for a boarding house in Frognal, NW. He found himself the only male among a crowd of elderly spinsters. Somehow this was not quite what he had meant by 'breaking away from the family'.

Henry Arthur lived in Kidderpore Avenue, Hampstead. He had been writing plays since 1869: some of them had been thought shocking in their day. He had been part of the 'Renascence of English Drama', and had written a book with this title. His plays – *Mrs Dane's Defence, The Lions* and many others – were 'powerful'. He was eloquent on the need for a National Drama and a Theatre of Ideas. Certain critics were irritated by his tendency to tell them what to think. He loved visiting America where he lectured on contemporary theatre at Harvard. He had lately been lecturing and writing about popular education on which he held unfashionable views: the masses, he thought (and Dean Inge of St Paul's Cathedral agreed with him), were predestined to manual labour and should not be educated too highly.

He was the son of a Buckinghamshire farmer and, like Wells, had once been apprenticed to a draper. He still had a rustic look about him with his white hair, fresh pink complexion, very clear blue eyes and thrusting little beard. Having a secretary seemed to fill him with energy. He dashed upstairs two at a time, he strode about the room (in Stephen's own manner); at a rehearsal of one of his plays some years before, his exasperation had been so great that he took a running leap from the stage over the orchestra pit and into the stalls.

His wife had recently died. He himself had had cancer and prostate operations, suffered from recurrent angina and chronic catarrh, insomnia and periods of depression. He had not had a new play produced for several years and had unwisely sold some plays outright to film producers. His *The Lie* had been revived in 1923 by Lewis Casson and Sybil Thorndike: for him, it was an ovation, a comeback, but it had been withdrawn after 187 performances to make room for Shaw's *St Joan*. His health was not improved by his habit of drinking sherry by the tumblerful.

What Henry Arthur Jones really needed was not a secretary but a companion. Perhaps 'social secretary' was the right expression. His daughter, Doris, was his nurse; Stephen was the personification of youth, and youth brought out the best in Henry Arthur. He showed Stephen reviews of his early plays and critiques which all seemed to say: 'He forces you to think.' Nobody could remember a name like Jones; but Henry Arthur Jones – that was different, wasn't it? He gave Stephen an important piece of advice: 'I notice you sign yourself S.M.Potter. Don't do that. *Stephen Potter* – much better.'

There was not a great deal of correspondence: Stephen's typing speed had now risen to two letters an hour. Indeed, there was not a great deal of work at all and most of his mornings were free. Stephen could not cure Henry Arthur's main spiritual wounds – Shaw's imaginary persecution of him and the fact that no knighthood had come his way (was it because of his attacks on censorship that he did not share the honour which had gone so naturally to Pinero, Barrie and even W.S.Gilbert?) – but he could surround himself with intelligent young men. Lionel Millard was one of them. He was briefed beforehand by Stephen: 'Henry Arthur will ask you: "And what kind of plays do the younger generation like today, I wonder?" You are to answer with words to this effect: "I think they would put you very high on the list, sir – possibly at the top." '

Henry Arthur expanded Stephen's social horizon by taking him to the first famous club he had ever visited – the Reform. They dined with Max Beerbohm. Stephen wanted to make him talk about

Shaw, whom he had known for more than thirty years, but Max wanted to talk about D.H.Lawrence, whose novels he detested. So, at this stage, did Stephen, having tried and failed to read *Kangaroo*. Max's unqualified praise was reserved for a romantic best-seller called *The Constant Nymph* which was about to be made into a play starring Noël Coward, who was understudied by an unknown young man named John Gielgud.

The job of being Henry Arthur's part-time secretary and companion obviously could not last. To Jack Collis Stephen wrote from his Frognal bed-sitter: 'To be unemployed is doubtless torture, but to be in work, yet not used to full capacity – that is worse.' Jack was recovering from an operation in Kings College Hospital. 'I am going to make very definite efforts to get rid of H.A.J. tomorrow afternoon . . . and get to see you.'

Could Henry Arthur be combined with the new job which was now on the horizon? It would be his first steady job: junior assistant lecturer in English at Birkbeck College at £200 a year. Four lectures a week, usually in the evenings. Added to his £250 a year from Henry Arthur it would make the heady almost unimaginable wealth of £450 a year. On £450 one would be able to afford *all* the courses at a Savoy Hotel dinner-dance. Henry Arthur in the afternoons, Birkbeck in the evenings . . . preparing lectures and playing golf in the mornings. But, for once, some kind of long-term prudence, or more probably the inevitability of parting from Henry Arthur, intervened. He gave in his notice.

At no. 36 there was rejoicing. Uncle Willie (Josh) said: 'Now you're beginning to talk, Step,' and gave him a fiver for luck. He was carrying on the academic tradition started by Muriel. From Birkbeck he would surely go on to a proper university, London or even Oxford or Cambridge. The prodigal son had stopped being prodigal.

Chapter 7
Taking big steps

Birkbeck College, one of the many institutions that make up London University, began in Glasgow 180 years ago. Dr George Birkbeck, a medical graduate, had started a science class for working craftsmen at Anderson's Institution. Coming to London in 1823 he founded the London Mechanics' Institution at the Crown & Anchor tavern in the Strand. This was three years before University College, London, began. There were no examinations or homework: the course was simply to help pupils become better mechanics. Birkbeck was always progressive. In 1830 women were admitted to lectures (but not to classes). Six years later Benjamin Robert Haydon, friend and debtor of Keats and Leigh Hunt, introduced revolutionary art classes involving the 'naked figure'. By 1866, twenty-five years after Birkbeck's death, it was known as the 'Birkbeck Literary and Scientific Institution', and in 1885 it moved to a new building in Fetter Lane. It was now firmly academic, balancing science and the humanities.

It has been said that up to 1898 its pupils were 'mostly self-improving clerks'. Yet its students had included Mrs Annie Besant, Sir Arthur Pinero, Sidney Webb, Ramsay MacDonald and Albert Richardson, later President of the Royal Academy. In 1920 Birkbeck College was admitted as a school of London University.

With his conscientiously held left-wing principles, Stephen should have welcomed this 'workers' education' atmosphere, this honest endeavour by spare-time self-improvers, many of whom had passionately wanted to go to a university but had not been able to afford it. Hardly the same as High Table at Merton and vintage port after dinner; but one could approach it with enthusiasm, a chance to open young eyes to the wonders of Eng. Lit. They were not in fact very young eyes; about two thirds of his students were older than Stephen himself. No need to make them work: for them, Birkbeck was not a social institution like the senior universities. Birkbeck was growing fast. It had an excellent library. Stephen's pupils started their academic day at 6 pm, having done a full day's work first. They were hungry for knowledge, hungrier still for degrees. Birkbeck today has more spacious premises in Bloomsbury; but in 1926 the lecture rooms were (as elderly graduates now remember) in 'the dungeons of Breams Buildings'.

Dr Lobban, head of the English Department, a small amused Scot, lived in Downshire Hill, Hampstead, just round the corner from Keats Grove. This seemed to Stephen an eminently suitable address for a young Eng. Lit. lecturer, even on £4 a week, so he moved there too. With his usual luck he found a room – almost a summer house – at the bottom of Dorothy Edwards's garden. She afterwards became Lady Archibald. Here he found a piano and a collection of original Van Goghs, for Dorothy's first husband had translated the letters between Vincent and his brother Theo. Stephen began a period of Van Gogh-Was-The-Greatest-Modern-Genius.

To prepare his lectures he had to re-read large chunks of English literature which he had not touched since Oxford four years ago. He discovered a new enthusiasm for Chaucer who had seemed medieval and dead at Oxford. Milton, too – Milton had been brought alive for him by Henry Arthur Jones reading *Comus* aloud to him. A typical Potter lecture on Milton would go something like this: read Comus's first speech aloud – then take two particular words and talk about them – 'the *nice* morn on the Indian steep', 'our concealed *solemnity*' – five minutes on each. Then about seven minutes on Milton's spelling. Further time could be taken up by making students read aloud, especially from Shakespeare, often in flat arhythmic Cockney voices, until he could bear it no more. These fill-ups were necessary for Matriculation English because the classes were two hours, which is seventy-five minutes longer than any class's capacity for concentration.

Two things he learnt about teaching, after a short while at Birkbeck, were: 'Things I really liked were the only things I could really teach;' and 'You never learn something till you've taught it.'

Stephen was discovering a talent for 'waffling' his way through. Even if he had prepared the wrong lecture – and this sometimes happened ('But, sir, you were going to talk about Animal Imagery in the Metaphysical Poets!') – he could somehow keep it going with or without facts. This afterwards became a 'party turn' – the nonsense lecture on a random subject such as 'the influence of Swift on Walt Whitman', a lecture which always began: 'Now I don't want you to take out your notebooks yet,' and went on to such brilliant generalizations as 'the outward form of a writer is the worst guide to inner content'.

His students, some of whom are now in their late seventies and early eighties, remember him as 'young Apollo, golden-haired . . . delighting us with his (as it seemed to us) quite original views on English literature – so very much in contrast with those of our two other lecturers, Professor Lobban and Miss Marjorie Daunt, who were much older than this young spark'. Occasionally, to relieve the tedium of that long two-hour period, he would tell them stories of school and university – 'I well remember with what gusto he described his own claim to fame as having obtained the largest piece of pancake when it was tossed among the boys at his public school.'

Some of Stephen's classes were part of 'three-year tutorials' for the Workers' Education Asociation. These students responded gratefully: 'Drama, Poetry and the Novel were dealt with,' writes one of them (who was seventeen at the time), 'and this was my true education. My reading was random and undirected before, but now a whole new world was opened up and books were available from the University of London library at South Kensington.' This student was a junior civil servant in the Ministry of Health and mixed in with much older and more advanced students. 'I sat shy and astounded at what they knew already. I could contribute nothing to the discussions and with great difficulty produced the required written work. . . . I have always been grateful for being led into literature by such an excellent guide.'

Another older pupil remembers him as 'tall, broad, fair, with a loud, rather rasping voice; wearing Oxford bags in the fashion of the time, tweed jackets and brogues. He gave the impression of having just strolled in from a country walk.' If any student's essay showed unusual promise, 'he advised us to go on writing. . . . He had a freshness and terseness of phrase which was arresting.' Sometimes he shocked students by using words like 'gutsy' to describe, say, the heroic couplets of Dryden's *Absalom & Achitophel*: it was a trick he had probably learnt from Sir Walter Raleigh.

'Stevie always dressed in a most interesting and exciting way,' reports another ex-pupil. 'I always carefully observed his ties which were gay, wide and colourful. He was like somebody I had never met before, coming from a suburban grammar school as I did.' This lady has preserved a list of 'twenty books an educated person should have read' which Stephen used to distribute to Matriculation classes. They reflect Stephen's own reading to date, with one or two improbabilities:

Chekhov – *The Cherry Orchard*; Sinclair Lewis – *Dodsworth*; Dostoevsky – *Crime and Punishment*; Arnold Bennett – *Riceyman Steps*; Virginia Woolf – *To the Lighthouse, Mrs Dalloway*; D.H.Lawrence – *The Boy in the Bush, Women in Love, Kangaroo, The Woman Who Rode Away*; Tolstoy – *War and Peace*; Whitman – *Leaves of Grass*; H.G.Wells – *Outline of History*; Hardy – *Jude the Obscure*; E.M.Forster – *A Passage to India*; Shaw – *Major Barbara, The Doctor's Dilemma*; Samuel Butler – *The Way of All Flesh*; and James Joyce – *Portrait of the Artist as a Young Man*, and *Ulysses*.

How his Birkbeck pupils were to get hold of *Ulysses* was a mystery: they would presumably have to buy it in Paris and smuggle it into Britain in their luggage. What, no Proust? And only two Americans? No matter: 'He gave us a feeling for English, and he was very keen on punctuation – "Now don't sprinkle commas about like pepper".'

For the Intermediate Arts examination, needing a year's preparation, there were three 'set books' which always cramped Stephen's style. 'For two and a half terms Steve took us laboriously through ... a Shakespeare play and Milton's *Comus*,' reports another woman student. The third set book was Burke's *French Revolution* which Stephen had never read. 'As the exams in June began to loom large on the horizon and there was still no sign of Edmund Burke we became more and more restive. At last up spoke one of our number (later to become Professor of Geography at Raffles University, Singapore): "Sir, *can* you tell us something about Burke's *French Revolution*?" Steve was evidently caught on the hop, and paused a moment before replying: "Well – er – I gather he was against it." '

'Stevie' seems to have been popular with his colleagues, with the possible exception of Arthur Jones, MA, Reader in History. In an age when one could buy an old car for as little as £1 10s, do it up and sell it for £3 (Jack Collis actually did this with an old Morris-

Cowley) Stephen went in for decrepit sports cars, usually with open tops. Arthur Jones, who regarded the Intermediate Arts course as rather beneath him, had one of those thin, r-less voices that are associated with the nineties. 'When his polished discourse was suddenly interrupted by a fiendish clatter from Fetter Lane outside,' an ex-student remembers, 'there was no doubt whose car it was. Arthur paused until the noise was lost in the far distance, then continued: "And now, ladies and gentlemen, that my young fwiend, Pottah, has departed in his dung-wagon, we may wesume our studies." '

From Stephen's viewpoint, one of the most unsettling things about Birkbeck was that he was never quite sure whom he was talking to. He would sometimes find himself lecturing on Dryden's *Essay on Satire* to 'three printers' apprentices, five junior clerks from Cripplegate and four nuns. . . . Nuns, as every lecturer knows, are the best audience in the world.'

Because he had not, after all, kept on the Henry Arthur Jones job in parallel with the Birkbeck lectureship, Stephen's scale of entertainment remained much the same. If we are to believe his own nostalgic broadcast, looking back on these years from 1948, his direct approach to dating a girl went something like this: 'My income is £256 per annum, as you know. We will have food at Lyons Corner House [it should be explained to the young that in the twenties the three Corner Houses in London had different orchestras on each floor and a large variety of apparently sophisticated cuisines]. We will then go to the Savoy Grill and eat the cheapest single course, which will entitle us to dance in the ballroom to the music of the Savoy Orpheans. Total cost fourteen shillings for two. This I can exactly do. If you can contribute, so much the better. Right?' While dancing, his conversation still tended to be instructional, showing little interest in what the girl thought about anything: 'You *must* read *Man and Superman*. And then see it, with Esmé Percy, in its entirety. Five hours. Wonderful.'

He was always trying to convert other people to his own enthusiasms. But then, other people were always converting him to theirs. G.B. Edwards, for instance: was he not getting a little tired of G.B.? An astonishing thought crossed his mind: all his life so far he had been seeking extraordinary people and now he knew that the reason he was not perfectly at ease with G.B. was that *G.B. isn't ordinary enough.* Ordinary meant public school-games-university. He, Stephen, must sort himself out: after all he was a university lecturer, moulding the minds of others. But he had still published nothing. Everything he was doing was an excuse for not writing. There must be another self-discovery walk, a liberation from G.B. Liberation, too, from a girl called, in Stephen's diaries, 'D.'. D. was married to 'Tom'. Tom and D. belonged to Stephen's fringe-of-Bloomsbury period. He had met them first at the Cave of Harmony, Elsa Lanchester's day-nightclub where she and Harold Scott sang Victorian music-hall songs in a speakeasy atmosphere, and John Armstrong, the painter, served drinks through a window. The image of D. stayed with Stephen all his life: in middle age he would see girls who reminded him of her, and this would plunge him into ecstasies of nostalgia.

Tom and D. came from the Slade School set – Att's milieu; they were, Stephen told his diaries, 'flat-in-Chalk-Farm-top-floor-of-Mecklenburg-Square people'. Tom was a commercial artist, working chiefly for advertising agencies and specializing in the (then) new technique of scraperboard. D. had been one of the great beauties of the Slade. 'Her face was pale, her profile pure, her hair done in the new Eton-crop manner. . . . Her slow, reasonable voice made her seem wonderfully poised.' Yet, in a second, her face could be transformed 'with feeling, quickness of response; she flushed easily, laughed with marvellous abandon'.

Music was the real life of Tom and D. They belonged to the new movement, led by Arnold Dolmetsch, to revive old music and instruments. He played the guitar and had *met* Segovia. She played that most difficult of stringed instruments, the lute. He sang songs by Byrd and Gibbon to her accompaniment. They introduced Stephen to Elizabethan music which he found monotonous. They offended him by not liking Wagner ('but he's *funny, Sturm und Drang*, he's for adolescents!'). They thought nothing of his great god Shaw, preferred Aldous Huxley, were unfashionably right-wing in politics. Most important of all, they introduced Stephen to the Russian Ballet, to Stravinsky, to the French moderns such as Auric and Poulenc; and to Falla's *Three-Cornered Hat*.

Stephen writes of D. in romantic, very young terms (it was, after all, the decade of Michael Arlen and *The Green Hat*): 'Farewell, D. I shed a tear, but . . . The sense of freedom was immense. The pleasure of falling out of love, if it's mutual, can be delicious. . . .'

Out of his system? Not quite yet. The Long Walk was the only answer.

This time he would deliberately exhaust himself and do forty miles a day. He did actually achieve this distance once or twice, but his average was twenty-three miles a day. It was early spring. He took a train to Warwick: of course he would begin in the Shakespeare country. He had no clear idea where he was going: he would end up, 522 miles later, in St Ives, Cornwall. In his knapsack were three books – *Leaves of Grass,* a G.B. recommendation, Raleigh's book on Wordsworth and Garrod's selection from Coleridge. After Stratford he found himself walking through the Cotswolds towards Bath along Fosse Way. Should he strike southeast and visit Jane Austen country? That would require a decision. For the moment what mattered was just walking: 'I had augmented my usual state of complete health into that beyond mere health. . . . The last shred of misplaced mucus or irrelevant lymph is kneaded out of the farthest corner of limb or brain. To exist is the only pleasure.' Soon he was in Coleridge country, the poet's cottage and the stream nearby, the lane by which the 'person from Porlock' had come to interrupt *Kubla Khan.* In the Quantocks he met a hunted stag, followed by red-faced sweating huntsmen.

Coleridge, Wordsworth and Whitman were all 'nature' poets in their ways. 'There's a flower that shall be mine, 'Tis the little celandine.' But he didn't even know what a celandine looked like. And what did Whitman mean by, 'If you want me again look for me under your boot-soles'? What *was* under his boot-soles? Plants. He realized he knew nothing about botany and bought a book on it. Another lifelong study had begun.

From Nether Stowey to Lynmouth, then across Exmoor to Dartmoor and Hay Tor where he had booked a hotel room. To his consternation, G.B. was waiting for him, full of welcome: G.B., to shake off whose influence he was taking this enormous walk! He had found out where Stephen was by telephoning his father. They spent the evening together and to Stephen's relief G.B. went on his way to visit friends at Dartington. From Moretonhampstead Stephen posted a letter to Jack Collis:

. . . the heaven of 3rd class roads on 1-inch Ordnance maps. . . . For Cotswolds my successful route was Warwick – Stratford – Chipping Camden – Stow (White Horse Inn) – Burford – Lechlade – Cirencester – Bristol. Another route taking in Tewkesbury I have done with pleasure.

Don't stick to route! . . . Wash feet in cold water, no tea. Surgical spirit for blisters. If you can, go to Quantocks and Porlock (Ship Inn).

Back in London, the original purpose of the Long Walk was forgotten in the discovery of botany. This was going to be helped by the great revolution in the Potter family. Father had bought a new house in Reigate. It wasn't so different from no. 36 Old Park Avenue but it was in the country. And the country was full of botany. Wood spurge, horned poppy, goat's beard – one day these names would seem funny and he would invent bogus ones in the cod-lectures which were his party piece. That summer at Swanage the family holiday was transformed by wild carrot, ploughman's spikenard, cow parsnip, and their splendid Latin names. Even golf was illuminated by the knowledge that a lost ball could be lost in ladies' tresses or fruiting bog asphodel.

In September there was an invitation to join the Meinertzhagens in Normandy: they were paying guests at a house at Omanville, near Cherbourg, which would be full of family and children. The franc was 175 to the pound, and France in the summer seethed with English families living luxuriously on the equivalent of about 15p a day per person and doing exactly the same things they would have done on holiday in England. Stephen was suspicious of Abroad and spoke no French. Was it worth abandoning Egdon Heath, Hardy country, for this? Bobo Meinertzhagen, foreseeing this negative reaction, had provided him with a courier, a girl, who was to be one of the guests. She would translate for him, see him through the customs, prevent him from falling overboard. They were to sail from Southampton on the *Carpathia*, a transatlantic liner which, after Cherbourg, would go to New York.

The girl-guide turned out to be Att, Mary Attenborough, the painter he had met at the Herberts', the girl who sang songs to her ukelele and wore those off-putting corduroys and that 'arty' hat. She talked in a very British way, lips half closed, like a general explaining the battle plan. Any open space tempted her to run which she would suddenly do without any warning. Stephen watched her running round the *Carpathia*'s broad deck: the idea that an artist could also be an athlete was new to him. She had, it seemed, been invited to play lacrosse for the Southern Ladies. At Cherbourg Bobo's organization went wrong: there was no one to meet them and they had to find their own way.

At Omanville there was tennis, in cool, overcast weather. Att was a powerful tennis player too. She played 'like a tiger'. 'Tiger!' she would shout through her teeth as she smashed at a forehand drive; or 'Nobody *concentrates* enough!' Stephen had never before met a girl who played to win. He was a word-man with little knowledge of painting beyond what sister Muriel had taught him during a brief holiday in Florence. Att was a colour-girl who could not describe things in words. A conversation with her Slade friend Ivy McCusick, discussing a post-Impressionist painting, would produce fumblings like, 'It's got this marvellous chip-chip roughstuff on the right, all sliding-gliding into the warm-swarm. Gorgeous!' When the two girls went water-colouring together nobody could speak to them. Stephen watched the unbelievable contortions of Att's face, screwing up her eyes to catch some elusive effect on paper or canvas. To Stephen a shadow was 'dingy dark'. To Att it had 'lots of purple – and specks of umber'.

How did he feel about Att? He observed and envied her rollicking success with the various broods of Meinertzhagen children. (He was afterwards to become extremely Good with Children himself.) Att came from his own sort of background – Beckenham, Kent, almost SE London, was not so different from Clapham Common, SW. 'We had the same sort of homes, the same sort of uncles and aunts,' Stephen remembered many years later. 'We had both "broken away from the family".' Most of the people Att knew were richer than his friends and some of them came over to Omanville to see her. People like John Howard the painter, Att's friend from the Slade; Philip Nichols, who was going to be a diplomat, and his sculptor-sister Anne, married to Henry George Strauss who was certain to be a KC and probably an MP too. (He afterwards became Lord Conesford.) Was he jealous? Oh, but Att – or Attipops, as Ivy called her – was too 'Slade' for him. (His ideal of sophisticated feminine beauty at this time was Benita Hume, an actress of twenty who dressed in black and carried an ebony cane. He had unwisely taken her to the 1917 Club once or twice. She would one day go to Hollywood and eventually marry Ronald Colman.)

Att, a scholar of the Slade, had been taught drawing by the great Professor Henry Tonks, Principal, who believed in the hard pencil and not much rubbing out. He was brutal to his favourite girl pupils, often making them cry; 'Can you knit, Miss X? You'd be better employed knitting than trying to paint.' Her professor of painting was Wilson Steer whose mumbled praise seldom exceeded, 'Carry on, carry on'. Many Slade students entered the school as young as sixteen. Boys and girls so thrown together tended to have very early love affairs and were sometimes married at seventeen. They went about in gangs, to each other's houses, abroad, anywhere, but always together.

They were used to the nude body at life classes and had little reticence. Every morning Stephen and Att ran down to the beach to swim, peeling off their clothes as they ran, till they were naked; something one wouldn't dare do at Swanage or anywhere else in England, and therefore, especially in the 1920s, a gesture of defiance and deliciously Bohemian.

With Att he felt easy: no 'pillow-bites'. Philip Nichols lectured him about his bad manners but Att didn't seem to mind. 'It was never implied', Stephen wrote afterwards, 'that there should be spells of courtly admiration; nor was there the slightest atmosphere of tick-off if she had to light her own cigarette or carry her own suitcase.'

Att remembers things differently: 'He was terribly gauche, no manners at all. I used to force him to carry my bag for me, and put big stones in it to make sure it was heavy.'

Stephen to his diary: 'Attenborough is going to be my friend.' No more than that? 'I was going around in the Slade gang and being pursued by rich and rather grand men,' Att remembers. 'Only Stephen was shy and undemanding.'

It was not what you would call a whirlwind courtship. Tennis twice a week in Battersea Park, just across the river from Cheyne Row, followed by tea at a tea-shop, 'going Dutch'. Att was used to being taken dancing as often as four nights a week. Stephen could manage a nightclub only occasionally and he took her to the Fifty-Fifty (this was the club which had been raided when he took Christine Lindsay there). When the Fifty-Fifty was closed down part of its clientèle became the nucleus of the Gargoyle in Dean Street. The Gargoyle was started by a BBC announcer, the Hon. David Tennant (who was married to Hermione Baddeley the actress), his father Lord Glenconner, Lord Henry Cavendish-Bentinck and A.P.Herbert. All these, and H.G.Wells and Arnold Bennett too, were to be seen at the Gargoyle, as were Francis Meynell and his wife Vera, already met at the 1917 Club and one day to become close friends. Francis, with his high, gentle voice, was an all-round designer and typographer, founder of the

Nonesuch Press and editor of the best-selling *Week-End Book*, conscientious objector, great gamesman, wit and good cook, and the object of Stephen's lifelong admiration; a man of Elizabethan versatility, scion of a literary family, a Roman Catholic who was to abjure his faith, a careful dresser who had silk shirts made to measure. He was the great gentleman that Stephen had so often wished to be.

Bertie Farjeon was another object of Stephen's admiration. Thirteen years older, he was the son of Benjamin Leopold Farjeon, a prolific but forgotten novelist. His maternal grandfather was the American actor Joseph Jefferson about whom there was a legend that he had spent the best part of a lifetime touring in *Rip Van Winkle*. At the age of seventeen Bertie himself had acted one-night stands all over America. He was now an author and dramatic critic who had written for everything from the *Sunday Pictorial* to *Vogue* and, with Osbert Sitwell and Siegfried Sassoon, had been one of the original band of writers on the Socialist *Daily Herald*. His brothers Harry and J. Jefferson were respectively a composer and a writer of detective stories, and his sister Eleanor wrote children's books. Bertie also wrote song lyrics of which the most famous was, 'I've danced with a man who's danced with a girl who's danced with the Prince of Wales,' first sung by Elsa Lanchester.

Stephen often met the Meynells at the Farjeons' small Georgian house, the Round Cottage, in unfashionable Forest Hill, SE. Bertie Farjeon was editing the Nonesuch Shakespeare which Francis would design and publish. One of the bonds between Bertie and Francis was cricket: at Lords or the Oval they would place bets on the numbers of runs, catches, lbw's. Above all there was tennis, fierce, playing-to-win tennis. Stephen fell into the habit of taking Att there once a week. When they were not at Round Cottage they were often weekending at the Booths' (Marjorie Booth was a Meinertzhagen) who had a country house, the kind Stephen longed for, at Funtington, near Chichester, Sussex.

The Potter parents, their children having flown, lived at Wychwood, their newly built villa in Reigate. Reigate was then still a rural market town, amid glorious country. Stephen was quick to sponsor and magnify a legend that it took its name from Milton-under-Wychwood in the Cotswolds, where a sixteenth-century Potter had poached on the estate of the poet's grandfather. It was to Wychwood that Stephen brought Att to meet his parents. 'They were terribly relieved,' she remembers, 'because I wasn't an actress, wasn't too pretty and used no make-up.' Stephen was duly presented to the Attenborough parents at Beckenham, making an immediate impression when his weekend attaché case burst open all over the floor. All his life Stephen favoured very old luggage held together by straps which were always too long so that they tripped people up and caught in revolving doors.

But they were now engaged – in a state of declared love. Love, in Stendhal terminology, had 'crystallized' on a weekend walking tour in Berkshire, doing fifteen to twenty miles a day: Att, her friend Ivy McCusick, John Howard the painter and Stephen. A downhill slope, like the decks of the *Carpathia*, was irresistible to Att: she must run. She was wearing an unbuttoned yellow cardigan which streamed behind her as she ran. Stephen said suddenly: 'Doesn't she look marvellous, running like that?' John Howard stared at him oddly. *Something had gone wrong*, Stephen thought. *The very thing that most attracted me – the impossibility of falling in love with her – had that gone wrong?* That this should happen after a platonic friendship of nearly two years. . . .

He had been silent all that evening and two days later wrote her a letter: they must stop seeing each other, it would be painful for him. . . . We do not know what else went on in his mind for his diary at this point becomes maddeningly reticent: all it says is 'Four months later, on 7 July, at the Beckenham Baptist Church, we were married.'

To Jack Collis ('c/o Middleton Murry' at Chesil Beach) a postcard written in the 1917 Club: 'Att and I are getting married on 7 July. . . . Marks must be on a new and terrific scale (for taking big steps) – best man? Don't think we will have one. My parents so nervous they can't speak, only smile.' This was followed by an elaborately printed wedding invitation in beautifully embossed silver script: 'Elm Road Church, Beckenham, on Thursday 7 July at 2.30 pm, and afterwards at 60, Scott's Lane, Shortlands.' Stephen scrawled across it: 'Please keep this. Surely marks on or off, on some scale never before used, for having name in silver writing.'

The Attenboroughs were all correctly dressed. Stephen's usher, from the 1917 Club, wore a jacket and stained flannel bags. Att wore a red silk dress. Stephen, prevailed upon to find the best man, had chosen Bertie Farjeon, although he was not a bachelor. A lapsed Jew, he had only been in a church once before and knelt in what

Stephen called 'a Moslem attitude' and Att described as 'Court curtsey sitting position'. Stephen wore a new double-breasted suit with a cigarette burn by one lapel. At a splendid reception, complete with marquee, he made a pillow-bitingly unsuitable speech; and then Att's brother drove the couple to the desolation of Chesil Beach where Jack Collis had lent them the ground floor of the coastguard's cottage which he rented from Middleton Murry.

The surroundings, for a honeymoon, could not have been more gloomy. Jack Collis, eating out of tins, was pining for a girl who had gone back to her home in America. Middleton Murry, living next door, had just discovered that his second wife, like his first, Katharine Mansfield, had TB, for which there was no cure. Nearby lived H.M.Tomlinson, author of *Galleons Reach* and other nautical stories, who had just seen his son drowned in the sea off Chesil Beach five weeks before.

But young love is tough. 'To the sound of the waves and the gulls and the swans flying towards Abbotsbury,' Stephen wrote, 'we walked off, blissfully happy when the sun came out, sometimes making love on the shingle on our bed of pebbles which seemed as soft as down.'

Chapter 8
Riverside days

Two Riverside, Chiswick Mall, was, and is, a tiny three-storey house beside the Thames opposite Chiswick Eyot with a small garden behind and a little river-bank garden in front. Built of dung-coloured brick and stone it may be late Georgian or earlier: Stephen claimed it was Queen Anne. Three doors away is Walpole House, reputed to be the original of Miss Pinkerton's Academy in *Vanity Fair*; and Hogarth's House was in the immediate neighbourhood. Railings and flowers, distracting views and artists living all round made it an eminently suitable setting for the nurture of a young writer. Not, of course, that he had actually written anything yet.

This was the home to which the newlywed Potters returned after their honeymoon. Everything about 2 Riverside was small. Kitchen and dining-room were in the basement. The ground floor had a bathroom as big as the dining-room, and another room which would eventually be used as a nursery. On the first floor was a room best referred to as a studio: here Att painted her pictures and Stephen wrote. It was also their bedroom: a double bed folded back into a white cupboard during daytime. There was a spare room but it was unusable because it was full of boxes and trunks belonging to a certain Major B.L.Montgomery who would one day command the Eighth Army at El Alamein. On the top floor was Deaky, Miss Deacon, Alan Herbert's retired Nanny; it was his house, rented to the young Potters at 19s a week plus £12 a year rates.

Stephen, when working, always paced up and down. There really wasn't enough room for this; moreover, when Att was in her 'fish still-life' phase, the fish model began to stink after a few days and conditions, in a room used for living, working and sleeping, became intolerable. The pacing, to Att, was the worst, and she eventually banished Stephen to a wood-and-glass hut in the garden. Here he had a truckle bed so that he could work at night if good golfing weather made it undesirable to work during the day; moreover there was the garden to pace up and down in. He had achieved the dignity of a study.

Two hundred a year: in 1928 a young couple could just about survive on it. Yet within a few years Stephen was also renting a country cottage at Heyshott, near Midhurst in Sussex, at five shillings a week. It is impossible not to think that both the Attenborough and Potter parents were, directly or indirectly, subsidizing such projects: after all, Stephen was going to write a great book and great books presumably earned money. The most convenient way of getting to a country cottage was to have a car. It would, Stephen told his father, be 'so useful for holidays and taking you and Mother out for drives'. So Father paid most of the £65 needed to buy a second-hand car.

Who was knowledgeable about cars? Why, good old Mason, Edgar de Bois Maison, the Conners' chauffeur in Eastbourne. Mason found him a 1921 six-seater Studebaker open tourer. The way Stephen sat at the wheel convinced Mason that he had never driven before which was true except for two lessons with a cousin. 'Here's how you do it, sir – that's it – off you go.' Stephen drove the Studebaker back to London, narrowly avoiding a crash when he risked overtaking on a narrow curve.

He was now at last seriously at work on a novel, *The Young Man*. To make time for it he decided to write fewer letters to people. 'When we write letters,' he wrote on a postcard to Jack Collis, 'so much creation is taken out of us. Perhaps we owe it to the Future to stick to postcards.' Yet soon he was sympathizing with Jack about his broken love affair, offering advice on writing: 'You cannot, I believe, say "A quarter of a year has passed and still I have not got over it: therefore I will *never* get over it!" ' This letter ends with a tiny confession: 'Faint worry over debts and honesty.' About the manuscript of a book: 'I think you should rewrite completely much of the first four pages, which are written in a style utterly unlike your own.' Jack was still in correspondence with Bernard Shaw who had sent him £50 when he was hard up and a Christmas card: 'Courage, friend! We all hate Christmas but it is soon over.'

The role of Potter the Married Man was soon swollen into Potter the Father. The birth of his son Andrew in March 1928 was an anxious time, in the cramped discomfort of Riverside with Stephen administering the chloroform. 'Att getting better,' Stephen wrote to Jack Collis, 'the baby is well, but of course his crying tendencies are increased by the operation business. I write in the sound of roaring tears.' The operation was for pyloric stenosis, a thickening of the pyloric muscle which prevented food from leaving the stomach, causing vomiting after every meal. Stephen was critical of the doctor for being slow to diagnose it; but it had the effect of stimulating his lifelong interest in medicine, an interest complicated by a squeamish revulsion from hospitals which he had to force himself to overcome.

The Young Man was a curious 'self-conscious' novel which, twenty years later, Stephen described to me as a 'put-it-all-in' book. There were stream-of-consciousness passages, some in the historic present, showing the influence of Virginia Woolf. Everything is described and deliberately 'felt'. If the hero eats biscuits, he 'snaps their shapes with his teeth'. Self-expression must be divorced from any idea of entertaining the reader. Most of his friends were in the book which was a résumé of his life to date, the Long Walk and everything, Bobo Meinertzhagen, G.B., Collis, Father, Uncle Willie – yet the portraits are never clear: we never know what they are like because we are only told the narrator's self-obsessed reactions to them.

Stephen was a twopenny notebook keeper at this time and the rather solemn observations he jotted in them are all in the novel. The book opens: 'A young man, David Voce, lately an undergraduate at Oxford, now a lecturer in London, who had a few minutes before got out at a station of the Metropolitan Railway on the outskirts of London, was beginning to take his Sunday morning exercise. . . .' He sees a Wesleyan chapel: 'How long are we to have the corpses of a dying religion rotting on our countryside?' He thinks about Oxford: 'The cemetery of young men . . . the institution's institute.' Why was he not writing? 'There was only some tenuous thing preventing him.' Is he the same person as his undergraduate self, who had felt he was 'a sort of Steerforth, good at everything'? Words must be used to convey the abstract as well as the concrete. But this does not always work. At one point words fail to describe music so he reproduces eight bars of a Beethoven score in the middle of a page.

He drops in to see J. (Collis) at his country cottage: they play the 'life scoring' game – 'take 70 complimentary marks for this unexpected visit – take 100 situation marks for the place your cottage is in.' The words 'meat' and 'meaty' had special meanings in Stephen's vocabulary – 'would you like some good father meat?' meant 'interesting news about my father'. The code-talk reminds one of Isherwood and 'Chalmers' with their Cambridge-begotten Mortmere saga.

Should Voce take a manual job – down a mine, say – to find out how workers live? Why does he keep thinking about 'my genius friend' Gessler (G.B. in real life) – is J. right in his opinion that the attraction of Gessler for Voce is physical? Voce eventually goes for a long country walk with a girl and two painters, Felix and Lydia. He has an agony of jealousy because he thinks Felix and Lydia are having an affair, suddenly has a row with Lydia and leaves the party. The difference between painters and Oxford graduates is that painters 'accept the body'. He realizes he is in love with Lydia. . . .

The situation of jealousy stimulating love would have been comic in the hands of Jane Austen. But there is not one hint, in this book, of the future humorist and satirist. Potter had several stages to go through first.

The book was sent to Chatto & Windus, who politely declined it, and Martin Secker who did the same. Stephen tried Jonathan Cape who invited Stephen to his weekly directors' luncheon in Charlotte Street. ('Down, down, thou bounding bosom!' Stephen said to his diary.) Cape was collecting promising young men at this time; it was always said in the trade that he 'hated authors', but Stephen saw no signs of it. Cape said he would print 1,250 copies. Stephen took Att to the Gargoyle to celebrate.

When the book came out late in 1929 he could not help noticing that the whole of the back of the jacket was devoted to an advertisement for *Poet's Pub*, a light funny novel by Eric Linklater whom he had never met but who would one day be one of his greatest Savile Club friends; and that the jacket of *Poet's Pub* bore no such corresponding advertisement for Potter's *The Young Man*.

The critics were on the whole kind: there was an unwritten agreement among them that first novels were to be let down lightly. Vita Sackville-West praised the book on the radio. L.P.Hartley was favourable; Edward Shanks in the *New Statesman* noted that the hero's name was Voce but 'had no connection with the Nottinghamshire bowler, who at any rate was effective'. Gerald

Gould, friend and tennis partner, wrote a long piece about the book in the *Observer*. Forrest Reid thought it full of 'subtlety, irony and humour. . . . a distinguished contribution to intellectual fiction'. The anonymous reviewer in *The Times Literary Supplement* congratulated Mr Potter on 'the exceptional keenness of his observation and his gift for phrase', but deplored his hero's 'muddled and rather second-rate thoughts', and concluded that 'Mr Potter has many of the gifts of the analytical novelist'.

There was a curious by-product of all this. Stephen had long been aware of a kind of secret homosexual freemasonry in the artistic establishment; had even wondered whether it was militating against him. At the Cave of Harmony four years before he had met an immensely fat, white-skinned actor, producer and designer of scenery and costumes. This man asked the unwary Stephen back to his flat for a drink and to show him his priceless collection of porcelain vases. On the piano were erotic figurines. 'I don't know about you,' he said, 'but I'm bi-sexual,' and he suddenly kissed Stephen wetly on the mouth.

Wriggling desperately out of the embrace, Stephen stepped back and knocked over one of the huge four-foot vases which shattered and lay in a thousand pieces on the floor. Shouting apologies, he ran out of the flat and never saw him again.

The experience came back to his mind when, soon after the publication of *The Young Man*, he received encouraging letters from E.M.Forster, J.R.Ackerley and Forrest Reid. All three invited him to lunch. The hint of homosexuality in the novel had touched them. With E.M.Forster he dropped a brick, a reference to a mutual friend who had probably missed a university appointment 'because he was a bit of a homosexual'. Forster, it seems, never forgot this. For Stephen, it was a recurring 'pillow bite' for the rest of his life.

The Young Man sold 1200 copies and earned £40 over a period of eight years. But already he was at work on another book, a critical study of D.H.Lawrence to whom he had been converted by G.B.Edwards. Cape saw him as a new young critic, liberated from classical tradition. At work? There were so many distractions in Chiswick Mall. 'The light on the water, the big tides, swans swimming nearly up to the front door . . . that wild and mad island Chiswick Eyot,' the discovery of a new plant called hemlock water dropwort; and, in the winter of 1929, the Thames in flood, so that it was possible in the basement kitchen to see water spurting through the keyhole.

It was a 'dropping in' neighbourhood of informal parties and every temptation not to work. At Said House, with its huge bow window, lived Sir Nigel Playfair, proprietor of the Lyric Theatre, Hammersmith, with his family; along Chiswick Mall were the A.P.Herberts with their enormous circle of friends. Next door lived Vladimir Polunin, Diaghilev's scene designer; his parties always ended with the Volga Boat Song. People lived in their front gardens and on the pavement as much as in their houses.

Perhaps writers shouldn't have friends: they can be so distracting, especially if you play golf and tennis with them several times a week. One can, of course, make the excuse that one is storing up characters and impressions for future masterpieces. The keeping of a diary can be the greatest excuse of all for not getting on with the writing of a book. Stephen tried the experiment of tying his leg to his chair with Att's old skipping rope so that he could not keep getting up to look out of the window or even answer the telephone which was halfway up the stairs. It didn't really work.

Parties and weekend invitations abounded for this was the silver age of the country-house weekend party. The popular young Potters were invited to three or four cocktail parties a week. The Meynells at their Gordon Square town house and Bradfields, their country house in Essex, had the principles of *The Week-End Book* down to an art. Everyone had to play games invented by Francis Meynell – the Roof Game (throwing a ball so that it touched the roof and had to be caught and thrown again) and Tishy Toshy, a kind of slow table tennis played with a tennis, not a celluloid, ball. In their games-rivalry, physical and verbal, Meynell wrote in his autobiography, Stephen was 'better at tennis, equal at ping-pong, worse at cricket, supreme at tricks of the tongue'. The Meynells had as their country neighbours Sir Leslie Plummer of the *Daily Express*, and Raymond Postgate, Marxist writer and food and wine expert: all this was part of what Stephen called 'the Left Wing-Liberal colonization of Essex'; and it was somehow essential to left-wingery that in summer everyone should bathe naked. Less leftish, but more luxurious, were weekends with Philip Nichols, the rising diplomat and his wife Phyllis at Lawford Hall, their beautiful Elizabethan mansion at Manningtree.

There was, too, cricket, organized by Francis Meynell in the literary tradition of Sir John Squire the cricketing poet and his 'Invalids'. Meynell's team, the 'Long Primers', was named after a type-size familiar to book designers, and in it Stephen found himself playing, on perfect village greens such as Aston Clinton near Aylesbury, in company with Miles Malleson the actor, John Strachey the ex-communist theoretician, Alec Waugh, Clifford Bax and Bertie Farjeon. The 'Long Primers' sometimes used Gamesmanlike methods of overcoming their adversaries: playing against a village team at Great Yeldham, Essex, they all wore caps with very long peaks to intimidate the enemy.

But there were other games, word games. With Elsa Lanchester, whom he had met at the Herberts', he played the Occupational Disease Game. Most of its highest scores were for unpublishable inventions based on the idea of 'housemaid's knee'. Elsa Lanchester's favourite was, 'I once knew a musician who suffered from cellist's crutch.'

The decision to write a book on D.H.Lawrence had two main reasons. *The Young Man*, Stephen realized, had shown that he either could not write fiction or was not yet ready to do so. He therefore chose a medium which he had long suspected was his true forte and which went naturally with his lecturing job: 'philosophical criticism'. The second reason was chivalrous: he resented the recent runaway success of the, to him, destructive and negative Aldous Huxley, and the fact that – especially after the notoriety of *Lady Chatterley's Lover* – Lawrence now seemed both neglected and persecuted by reviewers who used phrases such as 'sewers of French pornography'. Bloomsbury did not like him. Max Beerbohm dismissed him as 'pages and pages of stuff'. Edith Sitwell mocked him as 'the Jaeger poet'. Meynell had had a row with him. Nobody else on this side of the Atlantic had written a full-length book on Lawrence. He, Stephen, would be the first.

It was now 1930. The first half of the book, *D.H.Lawrence: A First Study*, went well and fast: he now hardly ever needed to tie his leg to his chair. He showed it to Cape, who wanted it. Stephen had no literary agent so he consulted Arnold Bennett whom he had met at the Herberts': was his contract all right? Bennett, always kind to young authors, had been slightly put off Stephen because Stephen had made the mistake of calling him 'Enoch', a first name used only by close friends, which was too familiar from a younger man to an older. Bennett also knew Lawrence and knew how ill he was; he had been instrumental in sending a young TB specialist, Andrew Morland, to the Villa Beau Soleil at Bandol to try to save his life. Stephen wrote to Lawrence asking if he might come and show him the manuscript; if Lawrence disliked it, he would withdraw it. He received this reply:

9 Jan 1930

Dear Mr Potter,

I believe my books are published pretty well in the order in which they were written: I don't think there are any serious divergencies. Only *Women in Love* was finished by the end of 1916 and didn't get published till some years later – was it 1922? – I haven't got any unprinted works and I don't think any exist.

We are here till the end of March, and I shall be pleased to see you if you really want to come down – though I hate reading about myself and my 'works'. The Hotel Beau Rivage here is quite pleasant, costs about 45–50 francs a day – and is ten minutes distant from here.

About a photograph – perhaps my sister would lend you one that was taken for my 21st birthday, clean-shaven, bright young prig in a high collar like a curate – guaranteed to counteract all the dark and sinister effect of all the newspaper photographs.

I don't know the name of your novel, or I would order it. Please tell me.

All good wishes,

D.H.Lawrence

Almost immediately afterwards came a telephone call from Arnold Bennett: 'D-d-don't go out to see Lawrence. He will be d-dead by the time you get there.' Lawrence was at Vence, nearly a hundred miles from Bandol. Stephen was shocked yet relieved at not having to meet him. In March Lawrence died.

The book was already in proof, and it was published in the spring list. It reads today like notes for a series of lectures – by a lecturer who assumes that you have read the whole of Lawrence first. In this short book (barely 35,000 words) Stephen finds that most of Lawrence's readers are 'youngish, normally educated, somewhat conventional men . . . attracted by hearsay knowledge of Lawrence as a breaker-down of established things'. Lawrence had 'stepped into Bernard Shaw's shoes as a "fearless" . . . and bannable young writer'. If you read him for sex, he is already *vieux jeu*. His 'philosophy' is the least important part of his work.

Stephen goes on to discuss the Lawrence Hero – the opposite of Hamlet, not introspective, by no means incapable of action – and the Lawrence Heroine, who must be fulfilled by sexual experience.

The Lawrence Man hates ideas, which are 'like nails stuck into the bark of a growing tree'. The Failure of Love, the Failure of Friendship, the Failure of Leadership (in *Kangaroo*), the search for some ultimate solution to the human condition in the North American continent – these themes are explored in turn. In a sudden flash of humour, Lawrence's dialogue is compared with Jane Austen's: can one imagine a Lawrence heroine repulsing a suitor as Elizabeth Bennett repulses Darcy by asking quickly, 'Are you pleased with Kent?' Stephen notes that Lawrence never describes faces, only bodies and gestures; and, unsmiling, invents a terrible word, Lawrentiomorphism, to cope with the description of Lincoln Cathedral in *The Rainbow*: 'The far-off clinching and mating of arches, the leap and thrust of the stone. . . .'

The book ends with affirmations: 'It seems as if an appreciation of Lawrence must always be made in a half-antagonistic way;' and – 'To me and to many thousands he is the greatest living writer of this generation.'

Reviews were mixed. One noticed an unfortunate misprint in a chapter heading: 'Sex and Sardinia' for 'Sea and Sardinia', which, as the tale passed from mouth to mouth, soon became 'Sex and Sardines'. One or two writers, thinking the book had been rushed out to capture the topicality of Lawrence's death, used the words 'indecent haste'. Arnold Bennett, then reviewing for the *Evening Standard* at the enormous fee of £70 an article, was kind. *The Sunday Times* sneered, but the impression was counteracted by Desmond MacCarthy the following week in a few defensive paragraphs. *The Times Literary Supplement* was sniffy:

> It is true that [Lawrence's] disciples were not altogether helpful. Mr Potter's book brings home this unhelpfulness. He . . . is not content that Lawrence could do something supremely well; the hero of his worship must be a great philosopher and a great leader too. . . . Talk of Lawrence's 'otherness' is meaningless, and it is almost ascribing divine attributes to say that a writer is seeking for a new element in life. . . . It should be said, however, that [Mr Potter's] study is well written, will be pondered by 'Lawrence men', and is ingenious in its construction of a biography from Lawrence's own writings.

The worst review, in the *Adelphi*, was by his 'genius friend' G.B.Edwards, to whom he had unwisely shown the book in proof. It looked like the end of this friendship which was already being worn thin by G.B.'s endless requests to lend him ten shillings.

The book remains a 'first study' which all other writers on Lawrence have had to take into account; it established Stephen as an 'authority on Lawrence', and justifies Stephen's claim in after years that it had 'made quite a splash'.

It pleased some of Lawrence's friends, notably S.S.Koteliansky, translator of Chekhov and other Russian authors, who offered Stephen a large quantity of Lawrence's letters to edit. Stephen refused them, a decision he regretted for years afterwards. It even pleased Frieda Lawrence who came sailing round to Riverside in an outrageous hat. From the Potters' Dorset holiday in August that year, Stephen wrote to Jack Collis:

8, The Parade, Swanage – How much off for address? Interesting day with Mrs. D.H.L. last week. She is *not* a formidable German Frau, very much the wife-of-a-dead-genius. I hear there are 5 more Lawrence books to come. She is having an awful time with her co-executor – Lawrence's brother George who comes up to town, she says, in an enormous collar and puts his foot down about the publication of *The Man Who Died*.

The young Potters were now expecting their second child. Nineteen thirty-one was the year of Epstein's *Genesis*, which, like most of the sculptor's larger works, had caused a scandal. Lionel Millard remembers a party at Riverside with Att, very pregnant, posing as Genesis. The Potters now had a new party piece. Stephen had always been a little jealous of Att's songs to the ukelele and they now developed a double-act called 'The Village Choir', in which the hymn – or it might have been 'Nymphs and Shepherds' – got flatter and flatter in each successive verse. Stephen also had his 'cod-lecture' act, which he sometimes improvised with John Howard as pupil; sometimes this took the form of a burlesque of Tonks of the Slade whom Howard could imitate wonderfully; and sometimes a lecture on a given subject, such as sponges, wrapped up in invented, meaningless, pseudo-scientific jargon.

Howard's niece, the novelist Elizabeth Jane, then a very small child, remembers the two of them fooling about to entertain children at her family's house in Sussex – bounding about in drawing-room or garden being gorillas and sea-lions: 'Stephen had body-humour.'

Nineteen thirty-one, we know, was the year of Joad's Gambit: it was also the year in which, some time in March, Stephen wrote to Francis Meynell discussing a forthcoming tennis match against two difficult opponents (who they were is uncertain, but it seems probable that they lived at or near Great Yeldham, Essex) and using, for the first time, the word Gamesmanship. The letter unfortunately has not survived.

Julian, Stephen and Att's second son, was born in March 1931. Like his brother, he began by being 'poorly', but in a very different way: double pneumonia and whooping cough, so that he did not go to school until he was six. But he had the great advantage of being taught at home (in the garden hut) by Stephen, so that he eventually arrived at school in a state of some precocity. At McNalty's Stephen had learnt how to stimulate a pupil's interest by using coloured inks for diagrams and marking. Apart from some elementary arithmetic, he ignored all educational theory by drawing on his own reading. Thus young Julian learnt snippets of evolution culled from *The Science of Life*, by H.G.Wells, his son G.P.Wells and Julian Huxley; and some astronomy taken from a massive volume called *The Story of the Heavens*. All this, and writing, Stephen combined with lecturing four nights a week at Birkbeck.

Among his students about this time was Jack Hargreaves, one day to create a popular country programme on Southern Television after a varied career in veterinary surgery, radio, advertising, fishing and journalism. 'I had had rather too much Latin and Greek at Mill Hill,' he says today.

I wanted to expand and humanize my education. So I took Stephen's English literature course at Birkbeck. He always walked into the lecture room with a rucksack full of books from which he sometimes read aloud. I thought his lectures brilliant but disorganized. He never looked at his audience, sort of spoke sideways while looking out of the window; and he sometimes mumbled. His voice would have been fine for broadcasting, but he couldn't project it to the back of the room.

Hargreaves was, years later, to meet him again at the Savile Club and other unexpected places.

In May of the following year Att, somehow coping with two infants, housekeeping and her own painting, had her first one-man exhibition at the Bloomsbury Gallery. John Armstrong, in the *Spectator*, singled out 'Still Life No. 5' for special mention: 'She places her fish and plaster cast and other objects against the glittering background of the river with all the delicacy and grace which is traditional in the feminine arrangement of flowers.' No doubt he remembered the view from Riverside, and perhaps the smell of the fish. 'The pale colours . . . she commonly uses,' said another critic, 'are saved from insipidity by the variety of roughened textures she gives to her paint.' And in the *New Statesman* T.W.Earp thought that 'Mrs. Potter is quiet and forceful and particularly happy in still life.' The exhibition was visited by Duncan Grant who was overheard saying: 'I wish I could put paint on like that.'

D.H.Lawrence, selling between three and four thousand copies, had been enough of a success to encourage Stephen to think of himself primarily as a critic. What should he write about next? He yearned to edit a volume for Meynell's Nonesuch series. Not for the money – Meynell was reputed to pay his editors as little as £5. The author Meynell wanted was Coleridge whose work and life Stephen knew well. There was a firm prospect of its being simultaneously published by Random House in New York.

Why Coleridge? He was not the best of the Romantic poets but, to Stephen, he was the most likeable. 'He had a kind of unscrupulous innocence, which is very appealing,' a modern critic, Alan Gibson, has written; 'he was the child of his father's old age, what is sometimes called a spoilt child,' victim of his own 'aberrations from prudence'. Books about him were often more interesting than what he wrote; and he had exasperated men like Hazlitt by his failure to make full use of his talents. Did Stephen see, in Coleridge, something of himself? His next three years, and two more books, were to be devoted to Coleridge.

Coleridge: Selected Poetry and Prose (1933) had consistently good reviews. The warmest came from Robert Lynd in the *Star*:

> Mr Potter seems to me to have done his work extremely well. . . . Most readers will find the genius of Coleridge far more impressively and inescapably here than in a collected edition of his works. . . . The selection of letters and 'table-talk' helps to bring Coleridge the man as well as Coleridge the thinker before us, and discovers him to us in his loftiest as well as in his most Micawberish moments.

Was it Meynell's or Stephen's own idea to follow it up with a book on Mrs Coleridge? No matter – *Minnow Among Tritons* (the title was a misquotation from *Coriolanus*) was a true literary discovery: forty-two letters from Sara Coleridge to Thomas Poole of Nether Stowey, 1799–1834, edited from original manuscripts in the British Museum Library. In his introduction Stephen acknowledges the help of Edward J.O'Brien, for telling him of the letters' existence, and the strange fact that they had never been published before; and J.I.M.Stewart of Christ Church, Oxford ('Michael Innes' the detective-story writer), for his knowledge of other Coleridge manuscripts.

The letters tell the story of Coleridge's unhappy marriage to Sara Fricker, most stupid of several sisters, two of whom were married to his friends Southey and Lovell. Coleridge and Sara never remotely understood each other: it was all part of Coleridge's dream that they should all emigrate to Susquehanna, Pennsylvania, and there establish a Pantisocracy or community of equality. Poor Sara! In 1816 she writes: 'Oh! When will he ever give his friends anything but pain? He has been so unwise as to publish his fragments of *Christabel* and *Koula-Khan* [*sic*]. . . . We were all sadly vexed when we read the advertisement of these things.' Dorothy Wordsworth called her 'a sad fiddle-faddle'; but the reader is made to sympathize with a wife left at home without money while husband Coleridge tours Germany with the Wordsworths and absents himself abroad for long periods – 'If he does not shortly *recollect* that he has a *wife and three children* in the *North* of England, who can *now less than ever* do without his pecuniary aid, I believe they must all travel South and join him. . . .'

Of several favourable reviews, Harold Nicolson's was probably the best: 'These letters, which are prefaced by a wise and sympathetic introduction by Mr. Stephen Potter, force one to take Coleridge's side.' The letters, says that introduction, are important for those who 'only know him as a man made up of inexplicably disconnected components, fascinating by his poetry, alternately stupefying and animating by his prose, and at the same time exemplifying, by famous weaknesses, a failure in the art of life. . . . Coleridge's life begins to seem more important than the isolated perfections of his published work.' For Harold Nicolson, Coleridge was 'the greatest potential genius since Shakespeare. . . . Nothing that I have read about Coleridge has made me like him so much.'

The Potter holidays, in these years, ventured abroad more often. Dorset was still the favourite, *en famille* with the Potter parents, and largely at their expense; but there were exciting invitations to France from the Meynells who held holiday parties at the Hôtel de l'Abbaye, Talloires, on the Lac d'Annecy in Haute-Savoie. There would be camp-fire cooking and perhaps a little Bloomsburyish nude bathing; but if Att wanted to look at Chartres on the way she would be allowed only ten minutes. To be worthy of a Meynell holiday you had to be a good tennis player for this was how much of the holiday would be spent.

As Andrew and Julian got over their childhood illnesses Stephen's home-education system was replaced by schools. It was assumed that, backed by Stephen's parents, Uncle Willie and sister Muriel, the boys would eventually go to Westminster, Stephen's old school; despite his theories about education, Stephen never risked anything like Dartington Hall or Bedales. Muriel, since 1927, had been Headmistress of a Girls' Public Day School Trust school in South Hampstead; for some years she was the youngest public school headmistress in the country. She was turning South Hampstead High School into one of the most brilliant and advanced girls' schools in the country.

The boys were eventually sent to Burgess Hill in Hampstead. Dick Mitchison, Labour MP and socialist theoretician, and his wife Naomi, prolific authoress, were neighbours in Chiswick Mall and their son Avrion went to the same school. The Potter boys were therefore driven to school and collected in the afternoon in the Mitchisons' huge chauffeur-driven Packard. This happened every day, except Friday, when Stephen himself would sometimes drive them, telling them stories on the way about a multilingual and on the whole antisocial parrot named Squawky who nearly thirty years later would be the subject of a book for children.

Stephen as a father was alternately strict and lax. Lax about tidiness – his own example was never conducive to it. The cramped muddle of the Riverside living-room was often complicated by the boys' model railway on the floor. It was a real *steam* engine, heated by methylated spirits, inherited from Stephen's own boyhood. Strict about manners, such as shaking hands with people you are introduced to. On one occasion this went wrong. Invited for the weekend to a fairly stately home with many servants, young Andrew greeted two footmen with outstretched hand: 'How do you do?' The footmen, not accustomed to being spoken to by guests, and eyeing Stephen's old two-seater with dickey suspiciously, retreated nervously. On the homeward journey Andrew commented: 'They had some awfully shy butlers, didn't they?'

Just as he never could bear not to know things, Stephen pounced upon ignorance in his sons. Reading a newspaper over his father's

shoulder on top of a bus, Andrew asked: 'Who is Lindbergh?'
Stephen looked over his shoulder, hoping that nobody had
overheard. As Andrew had been minus one year old at the time of
the first solo flight across the Atlantic he could hardly have been
expected to know. He was now told in no uncertain terms and has
never forgotten it.

Stephen taught his sons that 'in the country, nothing matters'.
There was a spot near this same stately home where Kent, Surrey
and Sussex meet, and this was the family's favourite place for
relieving themselves before arrival. 'It's wonderful!' Stephen
explained. 'Here you can pee into three counties at once!' There are
worse ways of teaching geography.

The Nonesuch *Coleridge* and *Minnow* had established Stephen
firmly as an authority on Coleridge. Jonathan Cape, who had
published both *A Young Man* and *D.H.Lawrence,* was now
bringing out his Life and Letters series and asked Stephen to
contribute a short critical life of Coleridge. The result was *Coleridge
and S.T.C.* (1935). The idea that there were *two* Coleridges was not
new but it suited Stephen's desire to break through the conventional Eng. Lit. view of Coleridge based on only partial reading: we
must read *all* of him, realizing the Jekyll and Hyde in all of us. Do
not, he says, accept his contemporaries' view of him, especially
Hazlitt's, and blame everything on drug-taking. Like Stephen
himself, Coleridge was a diarist, an autobiographer, a 'notebook
man'. To avoid the Teutonic vagueness of terms like 'inner self', the
man is divided into 'Coleridge' (a developing Personality) and
'S.T.C.' (the better known Fixed Character). Coleridge, hating his
Christian name Samuel, preferred to be called S.T.C. Character
and Personality, Ego and Self, are not the same: we relapse
periodically into our fixed characters.

Coleridge, as at one time Stephen had threatened to be, was for
years at a time a writer who did not write. His health was poor, his
teeth, in an age of primitive dentistry, were bad – certain
biographers believe that some of them were agonizingly impacted.
Hence the laudanum? Not necessarily – the character may have
caused the excessive drug-taking, not vice versa. Coleridge as
'S.T.C.' even invented a word – 'estecean' – to describe his own
faults: indolence, for example; an annuity from the Wedgwood
family nearly paralysed his creativity, yet a quarrel with
Wordsworth could spur him to action.

Stephen tries to analyse Coleridge's style, 'at its best when at its worst': disregarding usual standards, we can be excited by his *non-style* – parentheses, looseness, italics – 'this, if good writing is successful self-revelation, is the perfection of authorship'.

Yet, in efforts at precision, Coleridge (like Stephen himself) invents funny 'bad-style words' – 'a tall old Hag, whose soul-gelding ugliness would chill to eternal chastity a cantharidised Satyr'. Coleridge as critic, Coleridge as poet, Coleridge's view of friendship (that it has a natural end, that 'dependence is fatal to it'), the neglected importance of his political writings, the belief (found also in Lawrence) that 'deep thinking is attainable only by a man of deep *feeling*', his spiritual journey from adolescent atheism to Anglicanism – all these are covered in what Stephen calls 'essays' rather than chapters.

By a last-minute piece of bad luck, not unlike the bad luck of D.H.Lawrence's death just before Stephen's Lawrence book came out, I.A.Richards published *Coleridge on the Imagination* just before *Coleridge and S.T.C.* appeared. Richards, very *avant-garde* and fashionable, dispensed with 'S.T.C.' altogether and tried to 'settle' the merits of Coleridge by scientific literary analysis.

'Mr Potter stops short of the credible psychological and intellectual biography which is necessary if this thesis of the two Coleridges is to be really convincing,' said *The Times Literary Supplement* in its vinegary anonymity. 'What Mr Potter has given us is notes for such a narrative. . . . Mr Potter has posited the problem more thoroughly than it has been posited before. That is a great deal.'

At Birkbeck, Stephen was getting restive. Dr Lobban was retiring and he was to be succeeded by Professor James R.Sutherland who was exactly the same age as Stephen. He had held lectureships at Saskatchewan, Merton (Stephen's old college), Southampton, Glasgow and University College, London. He had a string of degrees and publications to his name. Stephen could scarcely have hoped for Lobban's job, but there was obviously not much hope of anything substantially better than an assistant lectureship. Four pounds a week on which to keep a wife and two children was a situation which could not last much longer.

It was about this time that Stephen began to write freelance scripts for the BBC. Like so many aspirants he was tried out in the Schools Programmes. There are a number of claimants for the honour of having 'discovered' him but the award must probably go to John Pudney. Pudney, an off-beat personality for the BBC in that, although public school, he had not been to university, was a poet who had started on the staff of the *Listener* and eventually joined what was then called the Empire Programme. Before the *Listener,* he had been a Soho rent collector. He claimed to be the only member of Broadcasting House who was 'self-educated'. Colleagues used to ask him carefully: 'I forget which college you were at. . . . Perhaps it wasn't Oxford but the other place?' Pudney had been married for two years to Alan Herbert's daughter Crystal when Stephen first met him.

For the Schools Programmes between September 1936 and November 1937, Stephen wrote sixteen scripts in a Senior English series, most of them produced by Pudney and some featuring Stephen himself as narrator. (He was seldom if ever allowed to speak poetry, a thing he dearly wished to do; he was given a voice test by another producer, Mary Hope Allen, who cut him short: 'Stephen, it's hopeless! You sound just like Donald Duck!') His favourite reader was 'Hobbo', Carleton Hobbs, a pillar of the BBC Repertory Company. 'Spheres of Action: a Programme about Games' took younger listeners into familiar Potter territory. 'Dr Johnson: a Dramatic Biography'; 'Famous Writers' – William Morris, Daniel Defoe, Lewis Carroll; 'Enjoying Life', a poetry programme – to all these, Stephen gave an inventive freshness that was new to radio. Soon he graduated to main feature programmes beginning with one on tobacco, produced by Leslie Stokes.

The impulse to work really hard had several causes, above all the need for money, but also the need for change. He had always been a polite borrower and an overspender; and there had been, as we have seen, an endearing tendency to invest large quantities of time and energy in games, of which golf was paramount. His chief golfing crony for some years had been Edgar Lansbury who was about his own age. They had met at the 1917 Club usually among the crowd who gathered round the long table known semi-seriously as the 'communists' table'. Edgar was one of several candidates for the role of 'best friend', like Jack Collis, like Ronnie Simpson, like Lionel Millard: men whose affection never changed, who tolerated all his weaknesses. Edgar was the son of old George Lansbury, whom A.J.P. Taylor calls 'the most lovable figure in modern politics', leader of the Labour Party in the early 1930s and former editor of the *Daily Herald*, a figure of the 'emotional Left' who appealed to the vague political idealism in Stephen. George Lansbury, from the East End of London, very popular with the Royal Family (his friendship with George V extended to their showing each other their operation scars), was famous for 'Lansbury's Lido', a mixed-bathing establishment beside the Serpentine in Hyde Park which reflected his fatherly desire to make people happy, and which, together with his Christian socialism and his out-and-out pacifism, has perpetuated his name to posterity.

Stephen was godfather and unofficial uncle to Edgar's daughter Angela, a pupil of Muriel Potter at South Hampstead High who would one day go to America and become an actress of international renown. Edgar, still with a trace of Cockney in his speech, was an extraordinarily handsome man, unintellectual but highly intelligent. He ran a timber business in Bow with success because everyone liked and trusted him. Married to an actress of luscious beauty named Moyna Macgill, he was a man of flamboyant generosity who enjoyed the good things of capitalist life – 'thinking Left but living Right' – and loved to take his friends to dinner and dancing at expensive restaurants and hotels; there he was the despair of head waiters because he had never lost his old East End habit of pouring vinegar over everything.

What was the bond between Edgar and Stephen that went so far beyond ordinary friendship? They were certainly united by golf which Edgar played extremely well. Two rounds before lunch was nothing to him. Edgar was also a good Lifeman: once, watched by an admiring cluster of spectators, he and Stephen drove off from the first tee and both landed on the green in one. It was the purest fluke that two good golfers should have achieved two such magnificent shots on the same occasion. The spectators applauded. Edgar and Stephen exchanged a silent glance but no more. They picked up their bags and strolled nonchalantly down the fairway, not a muscle of their faces moving to betray the fact that they did not play to championship standards every day of their lives.

Edgar, so different from Stephen, was good for him, cheering him up when he was tense, lending him money, and when necessary puncturing his occasional pompous utterances with a 'Come *orf* it, Steve!'

For a few years the Potters and the Lansburys shared a weekend holiday cottage at Berrick Salome, near Wallingford in

Oxfordshire. It was mainly Jacobean with an enormous hall which could be used as a living room; and here, at weekends, old George Lansbury sometimes joined his son and daughter-in-law and grandchildren with the Potters and their small sons. Like the holiday at the Collis house in Ireland more than a decade before, this was a period of friendship that Stephen never forgot, and memories of it came back to him repeatedly for the rest of his life.

It was as if Edgar's appetite for life and wild generosity hid a premonition that he was to die young. For the last year or two of his life he knew he had cancer. An operation at the London Hospital in Mile End Road failed. At his funeral in 1936, which was attended by the Meynells and other members of the 1917 Club, Stephen broke down and wept helplessly.

This was Stephen's first experience of early death, his Lycidas, the first realization that life is short, that he must get on with his own career. His diaries refer only obliquely to Edgar as if the whole friendship was too personal and its end too painful.

With a new release of energy Stephen was now working his head off. There were embarrassing occasions when he forgot to go to his own Birkbeck lectures and Att had to telephone explanations about sudden indispositions. By now he was beginning to write, for Cape, something he had been meditating on since Oxford – an irreverent criticism of the whole Eng. Lit. establishment to be called *The Muse in Chains*.

One chapter of this was delivered as a lecture to the Saintsbury Club, formed in 1935, of which Stephen was an original member. It met twice a year to commemorate, with wine and food, the great literary critic and historian George Saintsbury who had died aged seventy-eight in 1933. Saintsbury, who had taught English Literature at Edinburgh University from 1895 to 1915, was the author of many books on English and European literature, and of lives of Dryden, Scott and Matthew Arnold. He was also a connoisseur of wine and his *Notes on a Cellar Book* (1920) was to have been the seed of a huge all-embracing book on wine which was the real aim of all his ambitions and which, of course, he never completed.

The Saintsbury Club was restricted to fifty members of the utmost distinction. They have included, over the years, Vyvyan Holland, the son of Oscar Wilde; the Duke of Devonshire, André Simon, Sir Ralph Richardson, Sacheverell Sitwell, Reginald

Maudling, and Sir Francis Meynell. On the night of Stephen's lecture, 6 April 1936, the horseshoe table, chaired by Sir Stephen Gaselee, classical scholar of King's College, Cambridge, was adorned by the Marquess of Hartington; E.F.Benson, the novelist; Ralph Straus, the literary journalist; H.Warner Allen, wine-writer; André Simon (Hon. Cellarer and wine merchant); A.J.A.Symons (Hon. Sec.), author of *The Quest for Corvo*, collector of musical boxes, inventor of games and historian of the Nonesuch Press; the Hon. David Tennant; Martin Armstrong, novelist; Percy Fender, England cricketer; and Charles B.Cochran, theatrical producer. The lecture, like the menu, was 'printed at the Fanfare Press for Francis Meynell' – on handwoven paper, of course. Only twelve years before Stephen had confided to his diary that he wanted to know 'notable people'; well, here he was, among them and one of them. This was Clubmanship at its most brilliant.

Saintsbury, admired by Stephen partly because he had managed to rise above the stigma of 'only getting a Second' (in Greats), had embraced *all* literatures; he had been an anti-pedant, not writing for degree hunters; and, unlike any other critic (except Housman, who could not understand why certain phrases of the Authorized Version moved him to tears by the words alone, not by what they meant), he confessed that he could not define poetry: 'I do not believe that anyone knows . . . why certain words in a certain order stir one like the face of the sea, or like the face of a girl.'

The Muse in Chains, while it was being written, brought Stephen in touch with Rupert Hart-Davis who was to become one of his heroes, the kind of Englishman he longed to be. His mother Sybil had been a prominent Edwardian hostess at whose house Francis Meynell, as a young man, had met Lady Tree, Lady Diana Manners, and Alfred Duff Cooper who was Rupert's uncle. How wonderful to be as well-connected as Rupert! Rupert had not exactly defied Oxford; he had found it irrelevant to his life-design. After only two terms at Balliol he had asked to see the Master, A.D.(Sandy)Lindsay, and said to him:

'Master, I want to go down.'

'Oh, Mr Hart-Davis? Why?'

'Well, Sir, it seems to me that there are only two possible things to do at Oxford: either work like hell and get a first, or do no work at all and enjoy oneself. I don't want to do either.'

'What *do* you want to do, Mr Hart-Davis?'

'I want to go on the stage.'

The Master looked extremely grave. 'I'm afraid you won't find many Balliol men *there*.'

Rupert accordingly joined the Old Vic School and afterwards played at the Lyric, Hammersmith, then managed by Sir Nigel Playfair; it was the Potters' local theatre for which Alan Herbert had written musical shows such as *Tantivy Towers* and *Derby Day*. Then, on tour, he found himself playing opposite Peggy Ashcroft; they were married and, four years later, divorced. Meanwhile he had changed his profession to publishing, becoming at twenty-six the youngest director of Jonathan Cape.

I read *The Muse in Chains* when it first came out. I had read the Hons. School of Eng. Lang. and Lit. and taken my degree just eighteen months before and, for me, the book said all that we had felt about it. The dons had been so afraid lest we should enjoy our studies and so they forced us to do Anglo-Saxon and Middle English in which only a few eccentrics like W.H.Auden had found pleasure. 'English Literature', my Anglo-Saxon tutor told each new intake of undergraduates, '*died* with the Canterbury Tales.' The book is subtitled 'A Study in Education' and dedicated brashly to 'Students of Eng. Lit., the best of all subjects for education'. (This dedication was borrowed from Swinburne's friend, John Churston Collins.) Eng. Lit. is not English literature: it is what remains (like History in *1066 and All That*) after the scholars have been at it. 'Eng. Lit. is an example of the interpretation of the greater by the lesser: of great English writers by anecdotalists, antiquarians, hero-worshippers, pedants and collectors.' It leaves the mind littered with clichés like 'willing suspension of disbelief . . . killed in a tavern brawl' – all the phrases Stephen and Lionel Millard had giggled over at Merton. There was a fixed Order of Merit, dividing writers into Geniuses and Non-Geniuses, ranking or seeding them like tennis stars – 1. Shakespeare; 2. Milton and Wordsworth; 4. Chaucer; 5. Keats; etc.

Stephen had fun with histories of English literature and their chapter headings – 'Heyday of the Picaresque Novel', 'Death of the Sonnet', 'Dryden and the Age of Criticism'. There are the critics who chop up literature into 'romantic-classical-romantic' sandwiches. There are 'note-men', like Mr A.W.Verity, MA, whose editions of Shakespeare we had all used at school; Stephen invents one called T.E.Copp. He then has a go at *The Times Lit. Supp.* and reviewers generally: 'A good novel will get a paragraph. . . . But a new edition of Mason's letters to Thomas Gray's old nurse will get the top reviewers, and a good 1,200 words of well-spaced large pica.' Eng. Lit. (or Inglit) is about *externals*: critics do not seem to understand the motives of creative writers. Poets are arranged by 'schools', 'sources' and 'borrowings'.

This, Stephen says – and it is a very angry-young-man thing to say at the age of thirty-seven – is due to the conservatism of all education, the search for precedents. Thus the professor of Eng. Lit. at Edinburgh University (Saintsbury!) was not so called, but had to be given the title 'Professor of Rhetoric and Belles-Lettres'. Oxford had tagged along behind provincial universities by not starting an Honours School of English until 1893, when there were only three students.

Oxford, Stephen says, gives 'only super Sixth form teaching'. Oxford 'hates any branch of education which is directly useful. . . . To get English taken seriously it must be made to look like a *dead* language.' He jeers at the scholars who saw Middle English as 'acres of unedited text' which they turned to with 'salivating relish'. English literature was only really appreciated in continental universities which were 'centres of discovery'.

How, then, to account for the wonder of Walter Raleigh at Merton, appointed Professor of English in 1904? Both Saintsbury and Churton Collins had badly wanted the job and been turned down. Raleigh had got only a second in History at Cambridge. He had been Professor of English at a Mohammedan Anglo-Oriental College at Aligarh, India – 'corresponding, in the church, to a bishopric of Eastern Uganda – the kind of post from which no traveller returns'. He had then taught at Owen's College, Manchester; then succeeded A.C.Bradley (of *Shakespearean Tragedy* fame) at Liverpool. Raleigh, loved by senior and junior common rooms alike, was a rebel, unacademic, using words like 'gutsy' to describe poetry; he even wondered whether literature *could* be taught. . . .

The jacket design was a montage of Eng. Lit. clichés, largely contributed by Lionel Millard – 'Killed in a tavern brawl – *saeva indignatio* – Ph.D, D.Phil, LL.D, B.Litt – lisped in numbers – cf.cp. – Uncle of the Sex Lyric . . .'.

There was no hope of finding appreciation in *The Times Lit. Supp.* which analysed the blurb on the jacket: 'This is a casebook and a diagnosis, pungent, well-informed and entertaining, serious in its intention and implications. . . . Mr. Potter makes a bold attack on the spirit and methods which envelop the teaching of English Literature in schools and colleges today. . . .' The *T.L.S.* quite failed to find the attack: 'Mr. Potter nowhere professes to expound the true standards of taste, still less of enjoyment . . . tedious at times – his style is very often jocular. . . .' The review ended in a nasty jab with a suggestion that the author has 'a grudge against his examiners at Oxford'.

The *New Statesman* was better: 'Mr. Potter has written a good, angry history of Eng. Lit. . . . Lit. is the pompous discussion of unimportant aspects of unimportant books by people who can't write.' And in the *London Mercury* Reginald Scott-James praised 'Mr. Potter's elaborate joke. . . . With his scholarly competence and nice satire Mr. Potter has effectively shown up the difference between the work of literature and the usual but more menial services of its professional acolytes.'

Professor Sutherland, Stephen's head of department at Birkbeck, thinks the book 'a just and deserved exposure of the pedagogic editing of English texts for use in schools and colleges. . . . It also anticipated a good deal of what the New Critics in America were beefing about some years later.'

Nineteen thirty-seven in general was an outstanding year for Stephen. In March he was elected to the Savile Club of which Francis Meynell was already a member. He was proposed by W. Elliot Reynolds (that splendid Uncle Willie or Josh who 'knew people on the stage') and his sponsors included Moray McLaren of the BBC, writer on things Scottish, Raymond Postgate, G. P. Wells (H. G.'s zoologist son), and V. C. Clinton-Baddeley. There is no London club quite like the Savile, which takes its name from Savile Row where it began in 1882, though the Garrick (mainly actors and lawyers) and the Savage (stage, literature, law, science and medicine) have elements in common. The Savage and the Savile each claims a remark made about one or other of them by a member of the Guards Club with which one or other of them once shared premises: 'Those fellows look as if they made their own trousers.' Oscar Wilde, after visiting the Savile, called it 'a real republic of letters – not a sovereign among them'. All three clubs are tolerant of eccentricity, even look for it in their members. The Savile has always had a reputation for good talk; at the time of Stephen's joining the talk was usually led by Compton Mackenzie and later by Gilbert Harding. Until only a few years ago it enjoyed, like other clubs, the kind of ancient club servant who would say things like Frank the wine-steward's 'You dropped this £5 note in the Card Room, Mr Kipling – it's a good thing, sir, that it wasn't a member who found it;' and, after Kipling's death, 'he was a very irascible gentleman for such a small member'.

Social life at the Savile tends to centre on the billiard room where a special game called Savile Snooker is played – a version of Volunteer snooker (leaving out yellow and green) designed for players who wish to complete the game in their lunch-hour. Nobody knows who invented it but its secrets were handed down by Uncle Willie to Stephen who officially codified the rules in the 1960s. The only other place on earth where it is played is Fiji because a Savile member was once resident there. The Savile, even more than most West End clubs, is masculine and has no Ladies' Annexe; there is a story that many years ago it held a Ladies' Night of which the Oldest Member said, 'It has been such a success that we *must* do it again – say in about twenty-five years' time.'

Election to the Savile was the first big step towards Potter, the well-known Clubman. He would eventually belong to five clubs at once; not a record, for that is believed to have been held by E.V.Lucas of *Punch* (Harold Scott's father-in-law) who was a member of fifteen, including the Athenaeum, National Sporting, Beefsteak, Garrick, Buck's and the MCC; with Harold Macmillan as a possible runner-up (Athenaeum, Carlton, Turf, Pratt's, Beefsteak and Buck's).

Nineteen thirty-seven was also a landmark in the improvement of Stephen's golf. From Swanage, a postcard to Jack Collis: 'I have had great SPORT positive curves. 2 silver cups and name in the *Bournemouth Echo* – my handicap has been reduced from 8 to 5. Marks?'

He had now been offered a permanent job as writer-producer in the BBC. Together with Rayner Heppenstall, Denis Johnston, Cecil MacGivern, Jonquil Anthony, Wynford Vaughan-Thomas and Jack Hargreaves (whom he had last seen as one of the Birkbeck students a few years before), he was one of a band of new talents who had recently come out of the BBC Training School. He worked at first with John Pudney and Leslie Stokes. Of Birkbeck he retained one souvenir: a microscope which he had borrowed, failed to return and kept all his life. 'It was my only theft,' he told his sons. 'But they never asked to have it back.'

From Schools Programmes, through the Empire Service, Stephen progressed to independent features. His work immediately attracted serious critical attention. 'Victorian Negative', produced by Mary Hope Allen in January 1938, was daringly different from most BBC features both in writing and microphone technique. It was a portrait of his old god Samuel Butler, played by Charles Lefeaux, who, in a great deal of soliloquy, was required to utter such un-BBC thoughts as 'Morality turns on whether the pleasure precedes or follows the pain. If the headache came first, it would be moral to get drunk.' Gladys Young played Christina, Carleton Hobbs Theobald, and Norman Shelley Festing-Jones. The dialogue was spare and fast and transitions were quick, even sudden – the device known in films as 'jump-cutting'. Squeamish incidents, such as Butler's servant Alfred wanting to have his master's ashes in a jar on his mantelpiece after cremation, were handled ruthlessly.

To his sister Muriel Stephen wrote about the experience of interviewing the real Alfred in his old age: '. . . talking to him for a quarter of an hour in a studio and *recording* without his knowledge – he heard the record after and was delighted . . . his naturalness and mixed loving admiration overlaying laughter at details of the cremation were perfect.'

In July 1938 Stephen's 'Guide to the Thames' was broadcast. It made history in more ways than one. 'Mr. Potter followed the Thames from its source to its mouth in anything but a guide-book style,' wrote one anonymous critic, 'with little snatches of conversation, phrases and tunes which made an exact picture of each place he was describing.' He made felicitous use of a radio device known as 'cross-fading' – 'the criss-crossing of gramophones on the river awoke one's memory of days in punts. . . . There is about Mr. Potter's writing a hint of mockery which is delightful, but which does not obtrude when the picture should be serious.'

The *Observer* radio critic, at £10 a week, was a girl of twenty-eight named Joyce Grenfell. She praised 'Guide to the Thames' because it made the listener feel as if he were eavesdropping, instead of being addressed like a public meeting which had been the besetting fault of old-style radio. The dialogue sounded almost improvised. The whole had 'pace, humour and style'. Mrs Grenfell knew the Philip Nicholses who knew Stephen through the

Meinertzhagens. Could she meet and interview Stephen? A dinner party was arranged during which Joyce found herself describing a talk at her local Women's Institute at Cliveden, the Astor estate, in Buckinghamshire, where she and her husband Reggie had their country cottage. The subject of the talk was how to make Useful and Acceptable Gifts. . . . The Potters laughed unrestrainedly. There were to be unexpected results from this.

But first came the Munich crisis in September which jolted the Potters enough for them to send Andrew and Julian, ten and seven respectively, for safety to the Mitchisons' 'castle' in Scotland. It looked as if such peaceful subjects as the Thames might soon be out of order. Several of Stephen's programmes during the next few months took on a nostalgic quality as if he were looking back at a world soon to be destroyed.

In February 1939 Stephen's father died. Dressed for the office, after a hearty breakfast of bacon and eggs, he suddenly said to Minnie, 'I've got a terrible headache –' It was a heart attack. He had never completely retired from Bird & Potter, toiling up to London several times a week from Reigate. To Lionel Millard Stephen wrote a postcard: 'I want you to write to my Mother and say your happiest times were spent with us, and you admired my father more than any other man alive. The above because he has just died.' Lionel obeyed and made a bereaved lady extremely happy. To Lionel Stephen rarely showed emotion; but to Jack Collis he scribbled (on the back of an invitation to an exhibition of Att's paintings at the Tooth Gallery), 'I don't know whether you remember Father well – he died suddenly yesterday of a stroke. Salt, salt tears – eye-stinging. Do send one of your letters to Mother. . . .'

There had meanwhile been a further meeting between Grenfells and Potters – a 'Friday the 13th' party at Riverside – a mixture of BBC, stage, painters, Meynells and Farjeons. Stephen suddenly clapped his hands for silence and ordered Joyce to give her WI lecture which was mostly about how to turn an old biscuit tin (obtained by 'making love to your grocer') into a wastepaper basket. Farjeon asked her to write it down for his new revue, *Little Revue*, which was soon to succeed his successful *Nine Sharp* at the Little Theatre. It turned out that Farjeon not only wanted the sketch: he wanted Joyce to be in the revue and do it herself.

This was the beginning of Joyce Grenfell's career on stage, radio, film and television. So important was that Potter party that she recorded, in her autobiography, a precise description of the Riverside drawing-room-studio which had obviously been ruthlessly tidied for the occasion. Supper was for twelve people: 'Long French loaves of bread, a board covered with cheeses, a big block of butter on a dish and plates of Austrian *apfelstrudel* were laid on top of the piano, among other places, and most of us ate sitting on the floor.' Att's decoration was mostly in white – 'white walls, white sofa, white-covered divan and one scarlet-patterned armchair; Mary's [Att's] pictures framed in light wood hanging on the walls. . . .'

'Mr. Potter is striding up the ladder,' Joyce wrote in the *Observer*, saluting his 'The Last Crusade', researched by Ivan Vinogradoff, which told the story of the Spanish Armada from both sides in a way that no English history book had ever done.

Soon after Frank Potter's death Stephen and Att moved into a much larger house, Thames Bank, a little further along Chiswick Mall, early Victorian with a bigger garden. Here Stephen could indulge his fondness for gardening ('digging up the chives I'd planted' is Att's version of this), or at least his passion for botany. They had the end of a short lease – but the future seemed so uncertain that they could not look very far ahead.

Ever since Munich the country had been organizing something called Air Raid Precautions, against remarkable public apathy. In March 1939 Hitler marched into Czechoslovakia, bringing war one step nearer. Stephen was asked to devise a programme which, while providing dramatic entertainment, would explain to the great mass of people who had not seen the Spanish Civil War exactly what could be expected in an air raid even if the disaster never came.

'Air Raid' was built up beforehand by a careful press campaign: there must be no national panic, as there had been in American radio eight months before when Orson Welles had launched his 'War of the Worlds'. 'Listeners will hear a modern air raid,' the London *Evening Standard* told its readers on 17 June, 'complete with explosions of bombs, shrieking of sirens and shouted instructions to gunners and searchlight crews. Air raid wardens will reassure people and decontamination squads report on gas conditions.' The narrator would continually 'convince listeners it is only a play. . . . Any towns or villages mentioned are fictitious.' The programme would be produced with 'the co-operation of five Whitehall departments', including the Air Ministry, Home Office, Scotland Yard, Ministry of Health, War Office, anti-aircraft and searchlight detachments, the Women's Voluntary Service and a Surbiton ARP post.

'Air Raid' presented two families, one sceptical – 'It's just a noise' – the other alert, fully prepared. Mr Leversuch, head of the sceptical family, fiddling with his radio, finds a ministerial speech on 'being prepared' and crossly switches off. Mr Cudworth, the local air-raid warden, calls to test their gas-masks; we hear the absurd muffled speech of people trying to converse in respirators and Philip, the precocious son, remarks: 'It is appalling that the noble countenance of man should be reduced to this sheepish uniformity – even Father is made meek!' Mr Leversuch is persuaded to visit an ARP operations room and listeners are treated to a montage of shouted reports – 'H.E. bomb exploded. . . . Electricity main broken. . . . No casualties . . .,' and the special jargon of the Auxiliary Fire Service – 'Third floor *well* alight . . . this is a chair knot, used for lowering insensible persons. . . .'

Mr and Mrs Leversuch's reasons for not lending a hand *yet* are totally middle-class suburban: 'But there's the bridge committee, the charity dance, and who would walk the dog?' Mr Leversuch switches on the radio again; music is interrupted by war news: '. . . sudden deterioration in the international situation . . . reserves mobilized, leave cancelled . . .' Mr Leversuch: 'Of course, *our* fellows are better prepared.' A further montage of actual intercom messages, air to ground staff, drill commands on AA guns and realistic snatches of air-raid shelter conversation finally convinces the Leversuch family that they must *do* something.

In the last few weeks of peace Stephen, like anyone who had enjoyed life intensely and was not a member of the 'submerged third' of the population who were statistically 'below the poverty line', looked back on his life with aching nostalgia. To Jack Collis he wrote, on 22 July:

I had one moment of intense and painful Killiney pleasure when I got your letter. I shall never, never forget Killiney, the exact position of the tennis court, the effect of the roller, the withered billiard table, the current dog, the road down to the station, one beautiful girl . . . you are now more than ever indissolubly connected with me because of your connection with my starved and unsatisfied Ireland-pleasures.

What had happened at Killiney? The beautiful girl? Something too private even for his diaries? We do not know.

Stephen's last notable programme before war came was sheer nostalgia. 'Undergraduate Summer', broadcast just three weeks before the first real air-raid siren sounded, was recorded at Oxford during the summer term. It begins with morning bells, scouts waking people up, a Latin grace before meals; we hear the awkward conversation of an undergraduate entertaining his family to lunch in his rooms, the splash of punts on the Cherwell, bits of a Union debate, a rehearsal of Leslie French's production of *The Tempest* at the OUDS. The Union debate has Father Ronald Knox and Evelyn Waugh making uncomfortable jokes about 'Germans pouring into Poland' (which they did, less than a month later). The fictitious undergraduate hero, Philip Trotwood, is of course writing an Oxford novel. His sister asks embarrassing questions like, 'Do you often wreck people's rooms?' As a final triumph Stephen enlisted the Senior Common Room of Merton College with Deane Jones holding a tutorial on Cromwell's foreign policy; Garrod and Geoffrey Mure contributed their specialities; Professor Wyld talked on eighteenth-century pronunciation and Nichol Smith lectured on Pope. Nothing, it seemed, had changed in twenty years; and all to a background of cross-faded gramophones mixing Duke Ellington with Bach.

When it came, the outbreak of war found the Potter family on holiday, as usual, in Dorset, this time in a cottage at Langton Matravers. Like fifty million others they heard Chamberlain's ragged voice saying, 'We are now at war with Germany.' Att started to cry. 'Don't *cry*,' Stephen said angrily. 'Whatever happens to us now we've had a very happy life.'

Chapter 9
Potter at war

For a year there was little war action on what was known as the Home Front: only the fall of all Europe leading to the expectation of invasion. The 'phoney war' had its own kind of action at home: the apparent need to move almost everyone to somewhere else. The BBC Drama Department (which in 1939 included Features) found themselves in the fruit-rich Vale of Evesham, Worcestershire, at Wood Norton Hall, once the home of the exiled Duke of Orleans. Wood Norton was at once re-christened 'Hogsnorton' after the imaginary milieu of Stephen's namesake, the comedian Gillie Potter. Wood Norton was for some time deeply suspicious: it had never before seen so many men with beards on bicycles, all looking like spies.

The BBC had laid its war plans well, as long ago as spring 1938. Because radio transmission could guide German bombers, broadcasting had to shrink to one Home Service. In an air raid a local transmitter would go off the air for the duration of the raid but the listener would hear only a drop in volume because another transmitter would be working in a raid-free area. The Germans had not thought of this. By contrast, for propaganda purposes, overseas broadcasting became enormously important: all through the War the BBC, with four overseas networks, was broadcasting for ten hours a day in forty-six languages.

But by mid-October Wood Norton was already too full and it had been decided that most of Drama should be based in Manchester. Lawrence Gilliam, head of Features, had gone on ahead to stay temporarily with D.G.Bridson, one of his writer-producers, who lived in Manchester. To most BBC people, being Southern sophisticates, Manchester was regional and therefore limbo.

Stephen to sister Muriel: 'There is gloom among us all, from Val Gielgud downwards, at having to go North.' It was to mean living out of suitcases (or, for Stephen, rucksacks and cricket bags) for months on end as they were shifted around to new billets when the old ones became too full.

Stephen set off from Wood Norton by car, taking with him Mary Hope Allen, then (with Barbara Burnham) one of the two first women radio producers. She had hidden her sex for some years under the initials M.H., and had produced some of Stephen's own scripts. Her great talent, other than some brilliant productions of what were then thought to be 'highbrow' subjects, was puncturing his occasional boastfulness. Except for certain rejuvenation exercises, Stephen affected to despise clothes – 'A chap who buys a new suit is trying to prove something.' Mary Allen noted that to go north he had a smart new blue hopsack suit. She wondered how long it would take for its wearer, a notoriously careless chain-smoker, to drop his first smouldering stub on it and ruin it. 'Carpets and chair-covers in the houses of his friends were scarred with little black holes where his ash had burned,' Joyce Grenfell says. 'You could push an ashtray toward him but he never saw it until too late.' The Savile Club is full of Potter-burns. He once set an entire sofa on fire. It was wise, if Stephen were a regular visitor, to have a special Potter Ignition clause in your insurance policy. Knowing this, and knowing that no preventive action could be taken, Mary Allen waited for it to happen. She had only half an hour to wait: a round black hole in the new hopsack trousers made it just like all other Potter suits.

There were several billets in and around Manchester. A postcard to Jack Collis in November 1939 bears the splendid address 'c/o Mrs. Allen [not Mary Allen], 1001 Watling Street, Sandiway, Cheshire ...'. Soon, however, Stephen, complete with family (during school holidays at least), found himself in the extraordinary commune of 66 Platts Lane, Rusholme. This was a spacious Georgian brick house with an imposing flight of steps up to the front door. Until the War began it had been the newly and beautifully furnished home of a just-married young doctor and his wife. The gorgeous towels in the gleaming bathroom were such as nobody had ever seen before. Here a very large number of people, both permanent staff and visiting firemen, lived in such crowded conditions as would be condemned by most local government bodies if only for not having enough cubic feet of air per person. If the old criticism of Broadcasting House and its outposts had been that staff and grades were too remote from each other, communicating too often only by memoranda, there could be no such complaint now.

Flung together in Platts Lane the inmates alternated between hilarity and tension. Drink being hard to come by there were black looks if someone was known to have a bottle of whisky in his room but did not share it; or if so-and-so smelt of expensive scent yet was behindhand with her rent and prone to borrow money.

There were Lawrence Gilliam and his assistant (afterwards his wife) Marianne Helweg, specialist in adapting plays and novels for radio; Maurice Brown, Music Adviser to the Features and Drama Department, and his wife Thea. Brown had just written a book, *We Sailed in Convoy*, describing life in a merchant ship crossing the Atlantic, and would soon leave Platts Lane to join the Navy as a rating. Val Gielgud and Lance Sieveking, veterans of radio drama, put in occasional appearances. There were also at various times Moray McLaren and his wife Aline, who called each other Miaow; actors Robert Eddison and Valentine Dyall, soon to be nationally famous as the Man in Black, introducing horror stories; Jo Plummer, Stephen's assistant, afterwards a producer of Children's Programmes; and, after the fall of France, an irrepressible Frenchman named Maurice Thierry. All these were occasionally joined by J.B.Priestley, then recording, in a rich Yorkshire voice, the controversial 'Postscripts' which were heard in every home in the land, but also writing regularly for radio. His 'Return of Mr Oakroyd' and a series, 'Listen to My Notebook', grandly announced to a theme from Elgar's Second Symphony, were both produced by Mary Hope Allen.

The splendid Yorkshire broadcasting voice, carried over into private life, sometimes became too much of a good thing so that the irreverent inmates of no. 66 cried out: 'Come off it, Jack, you can stop being Huddersfield now.' The Potter boys remember Priestley as a sort of funny uncle who gave them a Masonic-type handshake, thumb bent inward, saying solemnly, 'Excuse my wart.'

At 66 Platts Lane the 'wives and concubines' took it in turn to queue for rations and cook; and, when the bombs finally came, everybody was allotted tasks in air-raid precautions and fire-watching, with Stephen as chief fire-watcher. He was also a sergeant in the Home Guard, armed with a truncheon. The unit had only one rifle with one round of ammunition and this was in the care of the actor Norman Claridge. Henry Hallatt, the actor-manager, who enjoyed the rank of corporal, had no weapon at all.

Att somehow went on painting, if necessary in her bedroom, doing portraits of everybody in the house. She had never liked cooking much – even at Riverside she had managed to afford a daily cook – but now she learnt from Marianne Helweg and Thea Brown.

Mary Hope Allen had started as a student at the Slade where she had known Att. Tonks had never succeeded in making Mary Allen cry; 'I knew I was no good – I just laughed at him.' For three years she was secretary to Naomi Royde-Smith, then literary editor of the old *Weekly Westminster Gazette*. Mary soon found herself being relief dramatic critic, the only woman in the stalls with James Agate, St John Ervine, and Herbert Farjeon, who ribbed her unmercifully ('Got a pencil, dear?'). She was also a regular visitor of the Herberts at Hammersmith Terrace whom she knew through Thorpe (nobody ever knew his first name), dramatic critic of *Punch*, white-haired and always in a black cloak; he had taken to journalism after being rejected as a Jesuit. She was a genuine pioneer of broadcasting, having joined the BBC at the old Savoy Hill studios in 1927.

Stephen admired her as a producer: 'She's so quick at seeing what's wrong with a line – it's like talking to the eardrum itself;' or, in a less unmixed metaphor, 'like talking to a naked optic nerve'.

Getting an education in wartime was not easy. Burgess Hill school was evacuated to Cranleigh School in Surrey; then for a time Andrew attended a prep school at Seaford, while Julian lived at Reigate and went to a local school there. For a brief fortnight they both went to a school at Kirkby Lonsdale, Cumbria. The sheer difficulty and slowness of civilian transport in war made every journey an ordeal. The family, however, were all together at Platts Lane on a critical day in June 1940. Lionel Millard, who had been teaching for most of the 1930s at St Jean de Luz in France and was now a gunner, came over from Liverpool where he was stationed. He remembers Stephen 'saying the salving thing' about the fall of France, the general assumption that Britain would be invaded, and the unspoken assumption that the War would be lost. 'We're finished. But it may not be as black as it seems now,' Stephen said – meaning that a compromise way of life would be found under German occupation? We cannot tell. Andrew remembers being recalled from the nearby park, where he was playing, by Att who told him France had fallen. It was 4 June 1940. Together she and the boys and other members of the Platts Lane household listened to the famous Churchill speech: '. . . we shall fight on the beaches, we shall fight in the fields and in the streets. . . . We shall never surrender.' Mary Allen, coming back from the studios, was met by Andrew, bounding out of the house, his twelve-year-old face shining: 'It's all right!' he shouted. 'Churchill says we're terrifically *safe!*'

We now know (what none of his Drama Department colleagues seemed to know at the time) that this broadcast version of Churchill's speech was spoken by Norman Shelley of the BBC Repertory Company, imitating the great man's voice.

Stephen's mood goes up and down in his diaries:

A delightful day recording – the only thoroughly nice thing about this job . . . [Att] reproves me about my unnecessary overwork. . . . So many day-dreams about a car – it's awful not having one. . . . I have just read a good novel, *The Power and the Glory* by Graham Greene – makes me want to write again – must leave avenue of escape from BBC. . . . At the moment the Germans are marching through a dead Paris – the feeling is not unlike what I have sometimes tried to imagine, being under sentence of death from cancer. One wants to run round and have a last look at things.

J.B.Priestley's radical scripts and talks were upsetting officialdom in both Government and Broadcasting House. Stephen, who had hoped to produce some of them, resented 'the casual coldness' of certain colleagues in accepting these policies. 'Of course I feel disappointment permanently. It was to have been quite a big thing for me – I would have worked *with* Jack, at his house, and learnt a lot about writing and dramatic techniques in the process.' (There were Priestley programmes after all, but they were generally produced by Mary Hope Allen.) Stephen always wanted to get closer to Priestley and lists four reasons why he liked him: '1 He speaks confidently to me and seems to like me. . . . 2 His imitations, the fact that he can tell, or rather act, a story better than anyone. 3 His firmly derogatory assessments of a friend's character (but God, what does he say about *me*?) 4 His knowledge of events and affairs.'

The lack of a car, it seems, was not permanent: Stephen was skilful at getting round BBC and wartime regulations. Maurice Brown, a fellow producer, remembers 'an old two-seater with a dickey' (a fairly typical form of Potter transport) which frequently required unorthodox starting methods. One day it stalled in front of a Manchester Corporation tram in the centre of the city. The tram driver gesticulated impatiently, telling him to get out of the way. Stephen unhurriedly got out to survey the problem, realized at once that the tram driver was completely in his power, and said cheerfully: 'I think they just about fit, bumper to bumper,' got leisurely back into the two-seater and shouted to the tram driver: 'Give us a shove, will you?' It worked.

Maurice Brown was one of the few people who could thrash Stephen at ping-pong. Stephen brooded over this for days; then, in the BBC Club, stood Maurice a great many beers. Maurice, knowing that Stephen was not normally a lavish drink-stander, should have suspected something, especially since Stephen was drinking frugally himself. At length, Stephen said casually: 'How about a game of tennis?' They repaired to the local courts where Stephen had his revenge.

Two Manchester defeats are on record: Stephen, in the BBC Squash Championships, took on an opponent without first finding out who he was: he just happened to have played for England. And, because he did not know the north, Stephen had yet to discover how seriously the north takes snooker. Any member of the Hallé Orchestra could beat him, and many did.

The dictates of war meant that Stephen had to produce a proportion of documentary, not to say propaganda, programmes. Many of these were done at high speed with few rehearsals: gone were the days of over-rehearsal, of multi-studio productions in the Sieveking manner. All productions were 'live' and, if there was sometimes an air of improvisation, this was now felt to give (a new word) 'immediacy'. *The Eagle Under the Sea* (February 1940) dramatized the escape of the Polish submarine *Orzel*, 'reconstructed with the help of the crew and the Admiralty'. The story, beginning in Tallinn, Estonia – 'one of the neutral capitals of the Baltic' – showed the crew trying to escape to England, pursued by a German destroyer's depth charges. . . . As he often did, Stephen quickly mastered the technical jargon and used shouted orders with great effect. He used this knowledge again in *Patrol of the Salmon*, another reconstruction, this time of a North Sea patrol whose mission was to relieve a Polish submarine. We hear the alert in a British port, police stations rounding up the crew who are on furlough, messages read from stages in cinemas, the taking aboard of stores, potatoes, corned beef and biscuits. Again tension is built up by routine commands (you could invent them, only submariners would know if they weren't genuine) – 'Port main motor speed, sir' – 'Starboard main motor speed . . . Half speed ahead together. . . .' The *Salmon* sights the German *Bremen,* sinks a U-boat and two other German warships; but, after the rescue is effected, we are assured that everybody behaved DOH ('according to the dictates of humanity') and that 'as the *Bremen* was unarmed it should not be torpedoed'.

Stephen, who genuinely itched for a more active role in the War, tended to be rather full of himself when researching this kind of programme. Mary Allen thought it was her daily duty to deflate him:

Stephen: 'I was in a submarine yesterday.'
Mary: 'Oh. Did it go down?'
Stephen (furious): 'You're spoiling my story!'

The Battle of Britain and the winter air raids that followed put an appalling strain on the little band of broadcasters in Manchester. Stephen was producing, and sometimes writing, two shows a week, and the overworked actors were playing up to three parts a week. A postcard to Jack Collis who, awaiting his call-up, was working on a Sussex farm for £1 a month, his wife and daughters having been evacuated to America: 'Shall we have a personal championship of bomb-avoiding? Suggested scale of marks – 10 off for your own life and so on, down to 5 for injury to closest friend's bathroom.'

The Platts Lane commune had a floating population and, after some months, there was a movement out of Manchester to seek escape from bombing and the chance of a few hours' sleep at night: it was led by Ronald Simpson and his wife Lila, who rented a charming little old house in Mobberley. The Potters moved out to rooms in Hale, about nine miles from Manchester. Here, despite a difficult landlady, they could be happy, for Ronald Simpson, who had acted in so many of Stephen's productions, was nearby.

So too were the Moray McLarens, at the Bird in Hand, a pub in Mobberley. Maurice Thierry was a frequent visitor and it was in this period that Stephen added croquet to his compendium of games. Moray McLaren eventually provided him with another club, the Edinburgh Croquet. Mobberley also started another lifelong enthusiasm for Stephen, allied to his love of philology and word-history: the study of English place-names. Mobberley, he discovered, meant 'a *leah* or glade with an assembly mound'.

At another billet, the Red Arch at Hale, near Altrincham, about four miles from Mobberley, he met Betty Johnstone. Betty was married to the BBC's Head of Music for Northern Region and her husband had just left her. She needed a job. Stephen, whose regular secretary had recently died, was eventually able to give her one. She became not only Stephen's secretary but the organizing genius of all his productions and managing friend of the family. She knew a lot of music he didn't know, especially Dohnanyi and Borodin, and was often able to suggest the absolutely right background music. And when Att, deep in her painting, forgot to buy anything for Christmas dinner, it was Betty who knew a local farmer who could let them have an unrationed goose – and cooked it too.

Lifemanship had not yet been defined but 'life-scoring' was a standing joke between Stephen and Mary Allen. She once threw him completely by announcing one morning, as she opened her mail, 'Oh, the Sitwells have asked me to Renishaw for Christmas –' Stephen grinned in disbelief. She had not said it for effect. In her *Weekly Westminster Gazette* days she had helped Naomi Royde-Smith with her literary parties. She was shy and used to being ignored by the guests except when their glasses were empty. She was just the secretary and nobody talked to her except the three Sitwells, Osbert, Sacheverell and Edith. They not only talked to her – they *listened*. Since then she had adapted some of Osbert's stories for radio.

Stephen and Att had also been entertained by Osbert and Edith Sitwell at Renishaw, in the freezing cold of a wartime winter. They were met at the station by a chauffeur-driven car, and shown round the stately home, marvelling at a wing known as the 'visiting servants' quarters'. Stephen enjoyed Osbert's stream of anecdotes about very rich people but in general seemed ill at ease. There had been much talk of painting which delighted Att but bored Stephen because he knew little about it. In these grand surroundings she was completely at home and talked animatedly. Stephen sat uncomfortably, his nerves assaulted by Osbert's instructions to his butler Robins. The repetition of the name oppressed him: 'A little more wine for Mr Potter, Robins – thank you, Robins – Robins, would you mind just – thank you – Robins. . . .'

This was the devoted Frederick Robins, successor to Henry Moat: he had been with the Sitwells for more than thirty years. To Edith, Osbert and Sacheverell, servants were friends, even if first names were never used. Robins had been Osbert's batman in the First World War; had been taken prisoner and survived to jeer at his captors; had been in charge of the palace at Montegufoni; had been taunted and bullied by the Sitwells' eccentric father Sir George.

Mary Allen tossed the invitation over to Stephen. 'You are rather far from home,' it said, 'and we are not far away from Manchester. Would you care to come for Christmas?'

Mary played her trump card. 'Oh, I shan't accept,' she said. 'I'm going home to my family. Besides, what on earth does one give Sitwells for a Christmas present? A Modigliani?'

March 1941 saw the first performance of Stephen's *Married to a Genius*, based on *Minnow among Tritons*. It was revived several times in the next few years. Out of the unpublished letters to Thomas Poole, the cultured tanner of Nether Stowey, found in the British Museum, he fashioned a funny-sad dramatization of Coleridge debating whether to marry poor Sara. ('So commanding are the requests of her relations . . .') She is obviously in love with him; but he misses his old friends William and Dorothy Wordsworth and wants them all to live together. Sara cannot keep up with the conversation of poets and seeks refuge in her 'little days' among her children. The story is linked together by Mr Poole as he reads extracts from Sara's letters to him.

Most of the BBC Repertory Company were in Manchester, the majority on a flat rate of £12 a week, which meant casting Robert Eddison as Coleridge, Arthur Young as Southey and Gladys Young as Mrs Southey. For Sara, Stephen picked Betty Hardy: he had heard her as Mrs Micawber in a production of *David Copperfield* and knew she was 'good at doing hysteria'. It was the first time she had played for Stephen and she did it so well that he cast her, whenever he could get her, for many other productions. There were only six actresses in Manchester at the time and Betty found herself in up to seven productions a week.

'I loved working with him,' Betty Hardy says. 'It was so rewarding – his face lit up when actors gave him what he wanted. His warm, undiluted response to good performances made him unusual and thrilling to work with.' Occasionally he would say: 'Gladys Young and Betty Hardy are the two best actresses in radio –

and neither can read poetry!' Who *could* read poetry? Stephen was slow to praise any who tried. It remained an obsession with him, so much so that he wrote unkindly to a girl student at the Royal College of Music who was doing 'Piano, Singing and Drama', and who had written to him asking for an audition. 'My dear Miss Foster,' he replied, 'only one voice in a thousand can read verse. Go on with your course and stop writing silly letters to producers.'

Addressing the Association of Teachers of Speech and Drama he committed himself to the unpopular opinion that 'men's voices are better on radio'. He had, he said, auditioned 350 people in fifteen months and (in the true spirit of Professor Wyld and *Pygmalion*) claimed that he could localize four main types of Cockney – west of Paddington, east of Paddington, north-east London and south London. How much of this was a leg-pull can only be guessed.

Betty Hardy's praise of Stephen as a producer with an unusual capacity for enthusing his cast is echoed by Dr Robert Gittings, poet, biographer of Keats, and playwright, who worked with Stephen on scripts about this time. Supervisor in history at Jesus College, Cambridge, he had been a conscientious objector on the outbreak of war but was allowed to do 'educational work of national importance' and was now moving into radio as a writer-producer. Stephen found him by chance in someone else's office at Broadcasting House, casually picked up a script Gittings had put on the other producer's desk, and said: 'This looks like the sort of thing I'd like to produce.' It was one of a series called Famous Meetings – actual, not imaginary – and dealt with the curious encounter between Garibaldi and Tennyson in the Isle of Wight. The originality of this lay partly in Stephen's insistence that Tennyson should speak not in a grand Poet Laureate's voice but with a Lincolnshire accent, copied from the BBC Archives' famous phonograph cylinder of Tennyson reciting *The Charge of the Light Brigade*.

This was followed by 'Beethoven and Goethe', 'Wellington and Nelson', 'Stanley and Livingstone', 'Hans Andersen and Charles Dickens', and 'Mendelssohn and Queen Victoria', a hilarious affair in which composer and Queen sing songs together at Buckingham Palace, the Queen singing flatter and flatter so that Mendelssohn has to keep transposing the piano accompaniment a semitone lower. It was like Stephen and Att's party piece, years before, 'The Village Choir'.

'I was an historian, so I felt no exaggerated respect for Eng. Lit.,' Robert Gittings recalls. 'Stephen and I felt the same way about literature, laughed at the same things.' For example, the black humour of *Too Much of Water*, a dramatization of Millais painting Lizzie Siddal as Ophelia drowning: the poor consumptive girl was required to immerse herself in a bath which grew colder and colder so that, teeth chattering, she could only answer 'yes' and 'no' to Millais's haranguing. One snag in this production was that the actress who played Gertrude, in an excerpt from *Hamlet* to set the scene with, 'There is a willow grows aslant a brook . . .', could not get the speech right at rehearsals. 'You know, this girl can't act,' Gittings murmured to Stephen. 'What can we do?' Stephen's solution was an order to the sound engineers: 'Turn the music up as high as you can.'

The few mistakes Stephen made in casting were always due to some lapse from logic. Of another actress who plainly lacked experience, if not talent, he said, in answer to Gittings' complaint that she could not act, 'Such a pity – she's the daughter of X.Y. the rackets player.'

The exhausting variety of Features in these years, Stephen wrote long afterwards, meant 'stuffing the air every week with endless documentary programmes on the War Effort, alternating with Poetry and the Lives of Authors (Escape Programmes, angled on English Heritage). I would return on Sunday from spending a week in the Tanks area of Dorset to dig straight into a delicate Life of Jane Austen for sensitive production next Saturday.' All this 'caused me to drink, particularly on air-raid nights, more, or at any rate less scientifically, than ever before or ever since'.

Gerald Moore, the great accompanist, tells in his autobiography *Am I Too Loud?* of a concert given by the Irish tenor, Count John McCormack, in Manchester, which was followed by a supper party at the Midland Hotel. McCormack's parties, for which he spent enormous sums on champagne, tended to develop into all-night affairs. 'We were joined in John's room by Fay Compton [Stephen was doing a programme on her life] and Stephen Potter. After an hour or so, Stephen quietly slid out of the room and telephoned me from the hall porter's desk below to say it was so terribly late and he had a broadcast the next day; would I make his excuses to John.'

Stephen had with him 'the fine, big, bound producer's copy of the script which I liked to carry around for effect.' Having finished his telephone call from reception he picked up a fine, big volume and went muzzily back to the BBC where he could get a bed in the firewatchers' post in the basement. Next morning, opening his script to study it before the broadcast, he found himself reading things like 'No. 185. Mrs Gathorne 8.15. Coffee', and 'No. 188. Admiral and Mrs. Halsey. Full breakfast'. He had picked up last night, instead of his script, the Call Book of the Midland Hotel. 'Five hundred and forty of the 600 rooms were occupied . . . 50 wrong pairs of cleaned shoes were delivered, 500 incorrect kinds of breakfast served, and 450 people called at wrong or disastrous times.'

Stephen enjoyed his War Effort programmes. The Tank Corps feature had needed War Office cooperation. The only man he knew who was both a trooper and had experience of broadcasting was Jack Hargreaves, then a cadet at OCTU. He demanded, and got, Jack and no one else, and the commanding officer of the officer training unit allowed Jack to wear civvies so that he could enter the officers' mess without difficulties of rank. There were to be several other Potter-Hargreaves collaborations before the end of the War. It was the nearest Stephen could get to some kind of action. Others who had joined the BBC at about the same time as himself – Wynford Vaughan-Thomas, Richard Dimbleby, his old friend Howard Marshall – were now war correspondents. Stephen went so far as to have a uniform made (was he not a second lieutenant in the Coldstream Guards?) but Lawrence Gilliam would not hear of it.

The floating population at Platts Lane floated a little more and the Potters moved back to London towards the end of 1942. The lease at Thames Bank was running out and they had to find somewhere to live quickly. They sought refuge among the moneyed Essex socialist colony: Dick Plummer had Berwick Hall, an empty and dilapidated house at Toppesfield, near Great Yeldham, which he let them have for £3 a week. It was huge, cold and uncomfortable. Splendidly placed at the end of an avenue of limes it had eight bedrooms, one lavatory, grand staircases, oil lamps, and a charlady called Mrs Letch. In winter it was possible for a hot-water bottle to freeze. All water had to be pumped from a well which also froze in winter. The whole family wore a garment known in the Army as drawers, woollen, long. There was a ha-ha and a croquet lawn, however. Stephen now stayed at the Savile Club several nights a week and spent weekends at Toppesfield, covering the three miles from the nearest railway station, Great Yeldham, on an old green bicycle, carrying a battered suitcase or haversack on the handlebars; for at this stage of the War nobody without a special allowance of petrol could run a car. That green bicycle was also used to get Stephen about London in the general wartime shortage of transport. German raids were now very bad and a bicycle could get you through the rubble very much more quickly than anything on four wheels. At weekends the bicycle was put into the guard's van between Liverpool Street and Marks Tey where Stephen changed for the branch line to Great Yeldham. Often he forgot to get the bicycle out of the guard's van so that it was carried on to Cambridge or Ipswich. His secretary spent a great deal of time organizing its return.

His secretary was Betty Johnstone who, with her baby daughter, was a frequent guest on working weekends at Toppesfield. Stephen, never renowned for the elegance of his clothes, now had a threadbare look. 'You could see pink knees showing through his trousers,' Betty remembers. This was at least partly due to clothes rationing and the strain of keeping and clothing two growing boys at boarding school. Betty was now indispensable, looking after the whole organization of Stephen's productions – choosing sound engineers, booking studios, hiring the cast, informing the *Radio Times* six weeks ahead of transmission – everything except writing the scripts.

As Stephen never kept an engagement diary of his own, and always took on too many activities, the job of being his secretary took on heroic proportions. Betty was rewarded with illegal days off, breaking BBC rules. Stephen wanted to make her an assistant producer but only administrative grade people could promote a secretary that far. Betty was one of the few women – indeed perhaps the only woman – to be admitted to a bedroom at the Savile Club, for the purpose of recording in shorthand a meeting at which Moray McLaren, Compton Mackenzie and Stephen planned a programme on the life of Fay Compton. Often her problem was to find Stephen; she would telephone the Savile Club only to be told: 'He's just left, Madam – he only stayed long enough to start a small fire.' Another badly-aimed cigarette butt! Betty, in London, was being bombed all the time; Stephen would telephone instructions from

Toppesfield, adding cheerfully: 'No point in my coming to London just to be bombed!'

He usually spent much of the week in London, however, sleeping at the Club – well, not sleeping very much, by his own account: 'Wartime memories of the billiard room are rather confused. . . . There was often an influx about midnight. People were keen. I remember that if I came in after 1 a.m. and found the Club in darkness I would hunt out the bedroom numbers of players like Howard Marshall – a master – or the less classical but more fiery Eric Linklater. It was taken for granted that, being wakened, they should dress, come down, and play.'

In 1942 the Features Department had recruited Douglas Cleverdon who was destined to do great things in broadcasting, among them devising, with Howard Thomas, the famous 'Brains Trust' programme, and forcing Dylan Thomas to finish *Under Milk Wood*. Douglas, who had started a bookselling and publishing business while still at Oxford, had written freelance scripts for West Region, and had then risen, via 'Children's Hour', to features producer. His bookshop in Bristol, specializing in first editions, had been bombed out, so he came to London. He and Stephen saw eye to eye on many things; with Edward Sackville-West they constituted a 'literary group' within Features, liaising with the Literary Committee, chaired by Stephen and calling on the advice of outside authorities such as Desmond MacCarthy and Geoffrey Grigson. Together Douglas and Stephen devised a programme called 'How'. It began as a serious feature explaining how things worked. Then, after they had made a programme 'How to Argue', starring the irrepressible Professor Joad, laughter began to break in.

Since the Farjeon revues Joyce Grenfell had been entertaining the Forces all over the world but had found time to broadcast seven sketches produced by Stephen. Stephen now saw 'How' as an all-satire feature in which how-not-to was one of the most fruitful sources of laughter; also as a full collaboration with Joyce writing as well as acting. It is strange that two such different temperaments could work together so well: Joyce, always early for trains, non-smoking, teetotaller; Stephen, a last-minute man if ever there was one, chain-smoking and setting everything alight. 'How' was improvised, not 'written' in the normal way; Stephen and Joyce threw out ideas and lines of dialogue which might or might not work, everything being taken down in shorthand by Betty

Johnstone since there were no tape-recorders in those days. Sometimes they worked in Stephen's office in Rothwell House; sometimes in Kew Gardens (not a good idea, because Stephen kept being distracted by botanical specimens); but most often in the kitchen of Joyce's flat in King's Road, Chelsea. 'I don't think any of the "How" scripts were completed until the day before transmission,' Joyce says in her autobiography, 'and quite often Betty arrived at the studio just before rehearsals began, with extra scenes for the cast typed out on flimsy sheets of paper to be clipped into our scripts.'

There were to be twenty-nine 'Hows' during the next twenty years, containing many of the seeds of Joyce's future sketches and of Stephen's Games/Lifemanship books. They covered how to broadcast, blow your own trumpet, talk to children ('Who's got beautiful new blue shoes on then!'), give a party, woo, cope with Christmas and be good at games. The formula never failed. A section of the BBC Repertory Company became the 'How' Repertory Company, with guest stars such as Robert Donat and Celia Johnson. The programme was introduced by an announcement punctuated by loud chords from the orchestra – 'A How! (chord) *How!* (chord) HOW!'. The whole series would nowadays be considered middle-class, but it was middle-class mocking itself and middle-class (and above) loved it. At Sissinghurst Castle, on 2 August 1943, Harold Nicolson, having spent the afternoon at the local village fête, throwing darts at large cartoons of Hitler and Mussolini, and cheered by the nine o'clock news announcement of the Allied invasion of Sicily, settled down to an evening with the wireless and wrote in his diary: 'A really brilliant feature by Stephen Potter about how to talk to children.'

Many of the 'Hows' are dated but not 'How to Woo' (September 1944) which began with various 'Lovers' Voices', from *Henry V* ('Kiss me, Kate!') to an approach which sounds very like Stephen himself: 'Do you know that you're the only woman I've ever met who has the rare gift of being able to *listen*?' Elizabeth Bennet of *Pride and Prejudice* is there with her 'Are you pleased with Kent?' and there is a parody of D.H. Lawrence: 'Clarissa . . . knew that the cold blood was mounting through her veins in an agony of restive repulsion.' There is Jack Tanner, in *Man and Superman*, shouting 'Ann, I won't, I won't, won't marry you!' merging into serious Shakespeare, spoken by Celia Johnson, and the awkward 1920s 'I'm

afraid I'm terribly fond of you.' There is advice on 'how to bring out
the mother in her', 'how to be the friend of your friend's wife', 'how
not to woo' (e.g. 'I'm not worthy of you – I'm too poor.'). It will
nearly all appear, more than twenty years later, in a book, *Anti-
Woo*.

Roy Plomley, one day to be nationally famous for 'Desert Island
Discs', was then a versatile member of the BBC Repertory
Company, playing as many as nine different characters in one
'How'. One thing he had in common with Stephen was a love of
collecting catchphrases. Whenever Roy was approached with an
offer of a part or a script-writing assignment, he would say: 'I'll do
anything for money, lady,' which was certain to produce explosions
of laughter from Stephen. In war the nation lived on catchphrases
from radio shows, especially Tommy Handley's 'ITMA'(It's That
Man Again). Stephen knew a publican who used them as
conversational stopgaps: 'Mind my bike,' 'Time I gave it the old
one-two,' 'Don't forget the diver.' People used them, he thought, to
establish some common ground, say in air-raid shelters, with total
strangers who had no natural material for conversation. Stephen at
rehearsal, Roy says,

was a casual dresser and, in the studio, discarded his tweed jacket at the first
opportunity, pulling the knot of his blue woollen tie halfway down his chest
so that he could open his shirt. There are some men whose hips are such
that they need neither belt nor braces, but this was not the case with
Stephen; and by the end of the day in the studio his trousers would have
slipped down to the lowest possible limit of safety.

'How no. 14', he would begin, crisp as a military command. The
read-through would involve much cutting and addition so that
everybody's typescript was covered with scribble. Stephen always
wrote one scene for himself: 'He was a good actor, because his sense
of timing was superb, but a limited one because his voice was flat
and rather nasal,' (what Stephen himself called a *plonking* voice). As
a producer he 'gave out confidence', welcomed suggestions, and
loved trying out funny accents (but the Professor Higgins in him
insisted that they be genuine). Little BBC affectations, encouraged
by the Spoken English committee, such as an excessively aspirated
*H*olland *H*ouse, aroused a devil in him. 'Cut this, add that –':
Stephen rubbing the back of his head at a point which would soon
become his bald patch was always a sign of another impending
script alteration. You had to have your wits about you.

Some transmissions went out from the old Grafton Theatre in Tottenham Court Road. The stage, deep in the bowels of the earth, was the microphone area. One day a heavily made-up woman came into the theatre and sat beside Stephen. The cast took no notice: Stephen often brought friends into the control room to watch the show. Everyone was waiting for the red light – 'on the air'. Suddenly the woman took out a cigarette and in a slurred voice asked loudly: 'Anyone got a bloody light?' Stephen hustled her out just in time before they were on the air: she was an elderly tart, very drunk, who had wandered in off the street to rest her feet: he hadn't even noticed her until she spoke. One minute later she would have been heard all over the country.

Despite his failure to become a war correspondent Stephen was having a good deal to do with the Army. Jack Hargreaves, a rapid riser in any environment, was now a major at the War Office and gave him facilities for a programme on infantry training. For Stephen it was not enough to watch, he must *do*. Despite all his chain-smoking, Jack says, 'Stephen's physical fitness was incredible. He was over forty yet he did the whole of that fearful assault course at Barnard Castle with the Durham Light Infantry without training at all; and at Ringway, Manchester, he did a test parachute jump from the tower – he wanted to do a real jump from an aircraft, but they wouldn't let him.'

By the autumn of 1944 it was clear that the invasion of Europe was going well and victory was in sight. Anglo-American relations had not always been easy and the authorities felt that some appreciation of the United States' war effort should be demonstrated. A spectacular show called *To You, America!*, sponsored by the *Daily Telegraph* in aid of King George's Fund for Sailors, was planned for the Royal Albert Hall on Thanksgiving Day, 23 November, after a Thanksgiving service at Westminster Abbey. Stephen was to write the linking script. John Barbirolli was to conduct the Hallé Orchestra, Henry Ainley was to recite, Malcolm MacEachern (the bass half of Flotsam and Jetsam the singing comedy duo) was to sing, there were to be massed bands and choirs, and the whole was to be produced by Ralph Reader, producer of innumerable Boy Scout Gang Shows.

More to Stephen's taste was a little dramatized documentary, written in collaboration with James Fisher, the ornithologist, on the extinction of the Great Auk, and also produced in 1944; but his showmanship was required for bigger things as the war came to an end. Again he sought Jack Hargreaves's help in planning a Victory in Europe Programme for 1945. 'When you suggested ideas to Stephen,' Jack says, 'he received them with little grunts – you couldn't tell whether he was really interested. Then, when you saw the script, you'd find he'd used the lot!' It was Jack who thought of the title, 'The Road to the Reich'. It was to be a quick history of the whole War leading up to the King's speech to the nation and the Commonwealth. Jack had a speaking part in it and contributed many of the ideas – notably the idea that the feature should break with all BBC precedent by having an actual soldier to do much of the narration. Jack found a Lancashire sergeant on leave before going to South-East Asia (thus emphasizing that victory over Japan was still to come). The sergeant was rewarded by Lawrence Gilliam with £100 to enjoy himself in London. The programme was introduced by veteran announcer Frank Phillips ('You'd like my *big* voice, I expect?').

When Hiroshima and Nagasaki brought the shock of peace the Potters, like most families, were exhausted. There had been one family holiday in Anglesey during the Manchester period, and a brief excursion to Scotland using a BBC car, with James Fisher, whose war work had consisted largely of a study of the feeding habits of rooks: this had been a joyous interlude of freedom from wartime rationing for in Scottish farmsteads there were plenty of eggs and butter. Otherwise it was holidays at home in Toppesfield, swimming and tennis with Meynells and Plummers, and bicycling picnics carrying tin hats and gas-masks.

Stephen also had money worries, as he did all his life. He was a big spender with a tendency to entertain people at Claridges and the Savoy on a scale far in excess of what was considered reasonable by the BBC. Both Andrew and Julian were now at Westminster School which, after being evacuated to Buckenhill House, Bromyard, Worcestershire, was returning to London. Stephen's salary had begun at £750 a year in 1938 and was now just under £1000. Sister Muriel often came to the rescue: in a letter to her about this time Stephen wrote: 'Your £30 has made a most terrific difference to keeping the boys going – I am often hoping to be able to say to you NO MORE. Mr. Gentle has just rung up . . . to remind me I am not out of the wood yet.'

George Gentle was the manager of the Bond Street branch of the

Royal Bank of Scotland – Uncle Willie's bank; but Uncle Willie had died during the War. Stephen could not always clear his overdraft but he could bring Mr Gentle more customers: soon all his Savile Club friends had accounts at the Royal Bank of Scotland and later, when there was some risk of George Gentle being transferred elsewhere, Stephen organized an appeal to the Bank to let him stay because he understood his Savile Club customers so well.

Muriel, the unmarried and comparatively well-off headmistress, with no direct dependants; Muriel, the eternally generous aunt of all the family, was now aware that, as both Andrew and Julian were destined for Oxford, there would be more expense. She knew that Stephen could never discipline himself about money. And there were his occasional outbursts of generosity – sometimes with other people's money. The Potters had had only two wartime holidays but Betty Johnstone had had none. Stephen's method of rectifying this was to organize a whip-round of fivers from his friends until he was able to present Betty with £40. 'Don't use it to pay bills,' he ordered. 'Have a good holiday.' With £40 in 1946 you could have three weeks in Norway, which Betty did.

When Stephen began a letter to Muriel, 'My dear old Sis', she knew he was in money trouble and, as his middle age crept on, she who had been big sister and second mother became a kind of aunt as well, sending him fivers on his birthday as good aunts do.

He was now augmenting his salary by reviewing books for the *News Chronicle* and plays for the *New Statesman*: the former was edited by Gerald Barry, the latter by Kingsley Martin – both old friends and Savile Club members. Stephen admitted candidly that the Savile was the best job agency he knew. He was a good and fair book critic though apt to say things like 'my own favourite bedside book is a volume of the *Oxford English Dictionary*'. His theatre criticisms had a kind of elegant excellence and sound judgement based on his Eng. Lit. classical approach.

The London theatre was enjoying a boom in the immediate post-war years: Shakespeare galore – *Antony and Cleopatra*, with Godfrey Tearle and Edith Evans; Donald Wolfit at the Winter Garden, reviving *Cymbeline* among other plays; young Peter Brook's *Love's Labour's Lost* at Stratford ('very young and intelligent', but he had 'produced the play to pieces'); Jack Hawkins in *Othello* at the Piccadilly with Anthony Quayle as Iago; Alec Guinness in *Richard II* with Ralph Richardson as John of Gaunt.

Among a feast of new plays there were O'Casey's *Red Roses for Me*; Priestley's *Jenny Villiers*; Freda Jackson in *No Room at the Inn*, a play about the pathos of evacuee children in war; and Cocteau's *Eagle with Two Heads*. Small, barely furnished theatres in unfashionable districts such as the Mercury and the New Lindsey, both at Notting Hill Gate, flourished as did the Granville at Walham Green. There was a return to the stage of tumescent, extravagant verse in Christopher Fry's *A Phoenix Too Frequent* and other plays. It was the silver age of revue. Bertie Farjeon had died untimely, in an accident five days before the German surrender, but revue was now in the speedier and more ruthless hands of Alan Melville, in *Sweet and Low, Sweeter and Lower* and *Sweetest and Lowest*. 'Issimus is the best of the three,' Stephen wrote, noting that 'the homosexual joke, once limited to the music-hall, is now accepted in the best revue circles'. Sad to have to castigate his admired Noël Coward for *Pacific 1860* ('flat lyrics, predictable plot – there should be a new word, counterpart of "amateurish" – "professional-ish!" '), but cheering to be able to hail a revival of *Present Laughter* at the Haymarket as 'the perfection of high comedy', noting with glee that Robert Eddison as the angry young man 'has a copy of the *New Statesman* bulging out of his pocket'.

The outstanding review he contributed to the *New Statesman* was a total demolition of the actor-manager Donald Wolfit, not yet knighted. For those days it was very strong stuff, all done by mercilessly accurate descriptions of what Wolfit actually did on stage. The in-joke of the day in theatre circles was 'Donald's *Lear* is not a *tour de force,* it's just forced to tour.' The kind way to describe him was as 'an actor-manager of the old school'.

'In Mr. Wolfit's productions', Stephen wrote, 'the play is subordinated less to a principal theme than to a principal actor.... It is said, maliciously, that Mr. Wolfit under-produces and undercasts the rest of his company in order to stand out by contrast: that he builds up a part as he builds up an entrance, by the hundred better-known devices of lighting and stage position....' (Only the word *maliciously* removes this from the brink of libel.) Are these charges true, Stephen asks? No – with reservations.... But they *are* true, as anyone who ever saw Wolfit will remember. 'He greets the polite applause demanded by such entrances with an almost but not quite invisible bow, fittingly contrasted with his appearance at the end of the play, when he clutches the curtain for support, just as exhausted . . . whether he has been laying himself out with King Lear or trotting through thirty minutes of Touchstone.' As for the rest of the 'remarkably bad' cast, 'too many of the "difficult" speeches are shot off at rapid fire by an actor, who, the moment he has delivered them, is electrified into making his exit with a brisk, clockwork kind of walk, as if he were a defaulter being marched off after company orders.'

There was yet more of this, including a reference to 'the basic sing-song' of Wolfit's voice – 'You can't sing-song a line like "That old lord, look you mock him not".' A furious exchange of letters with the actor-manager followed: Wolfit never forgot this criticism and, some years later, when Stephen added the Garrick to his list of clubs, he found that he had nearly been blackballed by Wolfit. The two men made their peace at the bar a few years afterwards; but it was a fragile peace.

The Potters, who had had six temporary homes during the war, now moved back to London and took a flat in Harley Street, the top three floors of no. 135 where they were to stay for five years. Andrew, now doing his national service in the Royal Artillery, had had a mild form of polio and it was good to have plenty of doctors handy. They were also near Doyne Bell, paediatrician at Charing Cross Hospital and one of his great non-gamesmanship friends; Stephen had done a radio feature on him in a series called 'Professional Portraits'. But the literary association which gave Stephen the deepest satisfaction was that their landlord at no. 135 was Andrew Morland, the lung specialist who had tried to save D. H. Lawrence in those last years at Bandol and Vence.

Chapter 10
Famous man

The island of Skomer, 700 acres of igneous rock, is about $1\frac{1}{4}$ miles off the mainland of Pembrokeshire. A hunger for botany, which had been neglected during the War, and a growing friendship with James Fisher the zoologist and bird specialist, whom he knew through the Savile Club, led to Stephen's joining an expedition in May 1946 mainly to study bird life on the island. The party included Dr Julian Huxley, ex-Secretary of the London Zoo and Director-General of Unesco, Keith Piercy, chairman of Bedfordshire Natural History Society, and a Lincolnshire postman named Reg who had remained a bachelor because he feared that marriage might interfere with his birdwatching.

Before crossing to the island in a dinghy they visited the nests of red kites of which only ten known pairs remained in Wales, and were delighted to hear a farmer refer to the local postman as 'Evans the post'. Waiting for the boat at Martinshaven they all leaned against a wall in whose crevices Stephen discovered pennywort.

Landing at North Haven they climbed a rough track to an abandoned eighteenth-century granite farmhouse where they were to live for five days – or longer if the weather turned too rough for dinghies. They were welcomed by Ronald Lockley, the Chief Warden, who was setting up a bird observatory on Skomer. He had lived on nearby Skokholm before the War, had written several books about it, and was an authority on Manx shearwaters.

The farmhouse was grim and almost unfurnished: Fisher, Piercy and Stephen shared a room, sleeping on iron bedsteads. The only touch of colour, Piercy noted, was two pink scarves, for both Fisher and Potter were members of Leander, having rowed for their colleges at Oxford – 'Leanderthal Man', Julian Huxley called them.

By day they watched puffins, razorbills, guillemots, kittiwakes and (James Fisher's speciality) fulmars, and saw large colonies of herring and lesser black-backed gulls. There were a number of great black-backed gulls too; as this is a predator of other seabirds it was permissible to take its eggs which were a bonus (hens' eggs were still rationed in the shops) and could be made into omelettes or custard. One of the weirdest sounds was the screaming return of the male Manx shearwaters from the sea to their nests in rabbit burrows: this happens at midnight for if they came by daylight the gulls would slaughter them. Lockley lectured the party on this bird which, by ringing, is known to forage as far afield as Bilbao in Spain and to be able to fly to Brazil, some 5700 miles, in fifteen days. As for flora, Ronald Lockley and John Buxton's book on Skomer records that 'specimens of the very large variety of the bucks-horn plantain (*Plantago Coronopus*) attracted the attention of . . . Mr Stephen Potter and Dr Julian Huxley'.

In the evenings there was talk round the oil lamps and washing-up. Stephen invented two styles of washing-up, Oxford and Cambridge – the one kept its mop in the water longer than the other. 'I got a half-Blue for wiping, you know. . . . I always get my mops specially made at Lillywhites. . . .'

The BBC was now reorganizing itself into three main programmes, to be known as Home, Light and Third. A great question mark hung over the Third which was to carry out the BBC's mission to bring culture to the cultured, if not to the masses. Its first head was George Barnes who would today be accused of 'elitism'. Introducing the Third Programme in the *Listener* on 26 September 1946 he wrote: 'We shall make no effort to appeal to everyone all the time, nor shall we try to be all things to all men.' Listeners would not be treated like Promenade Concert audiences who wanted 'programme notes' – 'there will be few "hearing aids" for listeners to the Third Programme'. It seemed that culture was to be dehumanized altogether, that it didn't matter if anyone was listening or not. In charge of presentation was a lively man named Leslie Stokes who was simply not allowed to present. One of the features of radio that made you feel you were part of the audience at a concert was the sound of applause at the end. Barnes thought this interfered with the communication between artists and listener. 'I hope, Stokes,' he said, 'we are not going to hear any of that clapping.' Invited audiences at BBC concerts were therefore asked *not* to applaud. The press called the Third 'the timeless wonder' because it had no regular time-table: you were supposed to switch on and hope for the best. And, if you had the patience, you got the best: five hours of *Hamlet*, Sartre's *Huis Clos* (which had been banned on the stage), Benjamin Britten's new opera *The Rape of Lucretia*, a new verse play by Louis MacNeice, a talk by Le Corbusier in French, the *Agamemnon* in Greek, Douglas Cleverdon's production of *Comus*. . . .

That such a man as Barnes should tolerate, let alone admire, Stephen Potter was the biggest surprise. He attended rehearsals, he seemed fascinated by this writer-producer who broke most of the rules. So it happened that the first night of the Third opened with a satire on broadcasting itself, 'How to Listen', by Stephen Potter and Joyce Grenfell. Listeners must have felt that something had gone wrong right at the start; and indeed something nearly did. Roy Plomley, as narrator – called 'explainer' – had to speak the opening words from a different studio where he could not see the rest of the cast. 'Rehearsal' and 'transmission' rings were separate and he noticed that 'transmission' was not turned on. Quickly he turned it on and began to announce. 'This was the worst moment in my broadcasting life,' he says.

No radio writer until now had allowed listeners to eavesdrop. The unseen audience was treated to a sound montage of things no listener is supposed to hear, such as the producer saying, 'rather quicker on cues, please', 'that whole line is *out*', and 'we *must* pick up ten seconds'. The explainer asks a fundamental question: 'Is anyone listening?' which is what most BBC people were wondering that evening. We are then treated to various kinds of listener, beginning with a character called Mrs Moss, who was already a well-known feature of several 'How' scripts. Remembering the post-war fuel shortage, and the fact that Average Listener was cold and hungry, you can see the point of her *non sequitur*, 'Turn the wireless up a bit, dear, it's chilly tonight.' But to bridge-players the wireless is no more than background: 'Turn the wireless down, I can't hear anyone's bids.' And to a superior person, called Felix, what is actually broadcast could not matter less: he is keen only to demonstrate his new radio built into a cocktail cabinet, arranged so that the sound comes out of a dummy lampshade.

We now meet Ideal Listener who enjoys everything: he is presumably a hermit with no friends and is never interrupted by telephone calls. He chooses his programmes well ahead, marking them in the *Radio Times*, and is sitting comfortably in his chair five minutes before transmission. What would nowadays be called a Meaningful Dialogue is held with him; all his favourite sound effects are played for him – howling gale, approaching train, that mournful sandpiper used to suggest seashores and sinister marshes (contravening Stephen's basic belief that one should 'write for the eye not for the ear') . . . but it is interrupted by an angry person from Listener Research who denies that Ideal Listener exists. Un-ideal Listener is always complaining: 'All the best programmes are when we're having dinner,' 'nothing but dance music whenever you switch on,' 'nothing but classical music and talks . . .'.

Mrs Treubel, another stock character, played by Gladys Young, makes a brief appearance: she is a recently naturalized refugee from Germany whose name was always pronounced Trooble: Stephen, who spoke no German, was not fussy about pronunciation. There being no Race Relations Board in 1946 it was OK to make fun of immigrants. Mrs Treubel enjoys almost everything: 'Ve Bridisch are full of fun and sports.' What programmes do children enjoy? Stories which begin: 'Once there was a big red bus which liked going through puddles'? Joyce Grenfell's awful child, Sidney, aged five, remains mutinously silent while she tells him, 'You like Toytown, dear, don't you?' Do people really want a cookery programme at breakfast time, or (much worse) the Radio Doctor bumbling on about 'please don't whip your bowel into a chronic frenzy'?

Stephen then inserts a bit of spoof poetic drama and a skit on one of his own literary biographies, about 'Thomas Cobbleigh, the Dartmoor poet', the cowherd who lost his kine in 1799 through reading Wordsworth while on duty. To Professor Crump, radio is simply a sociological phenomenon; to technicians, only baffleboards and something called 'woof' are important – 'too much woof, Len'. Len, in fact, was an invention of Roy Plomley's: Roy had had a solo variety act in which he impersonated a rhythm-club fanatic with a lot of invented electronic jargon. One radio critic thought the programme 'brutal', singling out for special mention a listener who said: 'I like to hear the wireless in the evening when I'm on holiday. It gives me something to look forward to all day.'

Potter weekends were now very often spent in Suffolk at Cobbolds Mill near Bildeston, the home of Francis Meynell.

Within a year Francis had been made one of the forty Royal Designers for Industry, become typographical adviser to HM Stationery Office and head of the Cement and Concrete Association, been knighted, and joined the Campaign for Nuclear Disarmament. He had also remarried: his wife was now Alix Kilroy (known as Bay) who had been his guest on so many of those holidays at Talloires. Both had spent most of the War at the Board of Trade where Francis had been Adviser on Consumer Needs and Bay had been in charge of clothes rationing. Their daily help at Cobbolds Mill was a Mrs Stowe who believed in witchcraft: 'The Black Death always comes in through *south* windows.'

Andrew Potter, then in his last year at Westminster and about to do his military service, remembers these weekends as full of 'acrimonious bridge', Francis reading poetry aloud, *boule* (which the Meynells had learnt in France), and indeed most of the games to be found in *The Week-End Book*. On a Meynell weekend you acquired merit (in the Buddhist sense) if you offered to wash up, even if your offer was not accepted. The Meynells were generous hosts and lent 'Cobbs' to the Potters for holidays when they themselves were not in residence.

Gamesmanship was practised seriously: among several members of the post-war Labour Government who were friends of the Meynells was John Strachey, then Minister of Food. John Stewart Collis has described a tennis foursome with Strachey, Joad, Stephen and himself: 'Joad was expected to cheat. John Strachey was expected never to cheat. No one was sure whether I would cheat or not. Stephen Potter leaned backwards so much against a ruling in his favour that we were bound to give him the point.'

Francis and Stephen also had a highly intellectual game which might be called 'cod philology', conducted partly by talk and partly by letter. The danger of cod philology is that it is so near real philology as to sow doubts about all philologists. 'It is not uninteresting to note,' Stephen writes to Francis,

that the expression *bowels* (i.e. boules) *of compassion*, first used in 1374, has no connection with the ancient etiquette according to which the gouttie-étranger (the gutstranger or guest player new to the boule 'carpet') is supposed to allow his host to win the 'bully up' or first rubber sequence. The term of course acquired its modern use in connection with the boule game which the Duke of Rutland played for a wager against Henry, son of Shakespeare's 'old Gaunt', time-honoured Lancaster at Hove Castle in

1381, beating him on the last throw with a half-pansy and dubbing his victim 'Bouling-broke'.

In November 1946 Stephen realized an old ambition, nurtured by Douglas Cleverdon whose idea it really was, to produce Chaucer's *Canterbury Tales*, directed by Professor Nevill Coghill from his own modern English version. This had the effect, for many people, of dragging Chaucer out of the examination room and listening to him as if for the first time. The *New Statesman* thought that 'the combination of taste in the "translation" and *brio* in the performance placed the first of this series among the very best poetry broadcasts'. Purists might think that Coghill had taken liberties with the original, showing Chaucer as a fourteenth-century Crabbe, 'with a similarly sardonic eye for the absurdities of human behaviour, a similar rather shy sense of beauty, and the same taste for making his rhymes fit with a dry click'. But at least it dispelled 'the popular illusion that poetry is always sad and difficult, and that the humour and psychological penetration of Chaucer are perceptible only by scholars'. The narrative was preceded by Coghill himself reconstructing the original pronunciation: 'It sounded like a cross between German and French read with a Scottish accent.'

For Christmas there was a special 'How' programme, a new edition of an experimental wartime script, starring Celia Johnson and Robert Donat with what was now called the How Repertory Company. On summer holidays ordinary people start saying, 'It'll soon be Christmas'; but for department stores (and Stephen invents one called Meddings & Sills) it begins much earlier: 'February has come round again, gentlemen, and the problem of next Christmas faces us once more.' The first need is to 'sell off our left-over stock as Spring Novelties'. Being 1946 this was of course an 'austerity Christmas' – if you are invited anywhere you take your rations with you. There is a discussion on awful Christmas cards: 'I'd rather have an El Greco on my mantelpiece than a Father Christmas in a silver jet-plane labelled Tons of Fun for Xmas' – and awful books for children too. Joyce Grenfell's mutinous five-year-old Sidney is making paperchains and getting glue in his hair. The carollers start arriving on 30 November. Nostalgic memories of pre-war Christmas recall bottles of brandy at 18s. Today (1946) nobody can get more than two thirds of a bottle of gin and a kind of nasty non-alcoholic Martini which Stephen calls Vermuto.

Nobody? Hear Mrs Treubel: 'Ve are spending old-fashion English Christmas with business associate friend of my husband at Golders Green, with a bridge-party for starting – bottles of whisky for men and nylon stockings for ladies.' There is here a clear implication that Jewish refugees are getting black-market goods off ration; today such a joke would be the subject of po-faced letters to the *Guardian*.

The 1947 winter was the longest and severest in living memory. We have seen that the sudden running down of the country's power resources closed down the Third Programme and gave Stephen time to write *Gamesmanship* which, within a year, would make him internationally famous and give rise to a *-manship* cult, not only in Britain and America but also in Scandinavia and Japan where, at Tokyo University, a Gamesmanship Society was formed of which Stephen was made Honorary Life President.

Had the Fuel Crisis lasted longer *Gamesmanship* might have been a longer book. Thirty thousand words, however, is quite enough for a funny book with funny-solemn pictures which people are going to give each other for Christmas. It is hardly possible that all its readers could have understood many of the private jokes; indeed there is evidence that some readers, including a number of psychologists at American universities, took at least some of them seriously. Non-games players have tended towards the view that the book is pure fantasy which never touches reality. Games players know that it touches reality all the time.

The book opens with the premise that there are 500 books on how to play games and none on how to win. There are no actual rules which say that you should not stiffen your opponent's muscles by delays and tensions on the way to the tennis courts, by wearing wrong clothes (such as Joad's yellow shirt, black socks and trousers held up by an orange scarf) – or by wearing ostentatiously *right* clothes if your opponent is wearing wrong ones. There are, too, permissible off-putting eccentricities such as Henry Cotton's left-hand glove for golf.

Is it really so unsporting to blow your nose loudly just as your opponent at billiards is taking aim, or to 'chalk your cue squeakingly' to set his nerves on edge? Should it be known that Paul Beard, leader of the BBC Symphony Orchestra, whistles a well-known phrase from Elgar *wrong* to upset his adversary? Full of false Nicechapmanship you should not spend too much time looking for

your own lost golfball but far too long looking for your opponent's.
There are despicable ways of gaining your opponent's sympathy by
talking about your 'game leg' or 'the old ticker' (we shall, in due
course, quote an example of S. Potter actually doing this).

The book goes on to cover Winner's Heartiness, dialogue attacks
or 'parlettes' and the essential conclusion that 'the Gamesman's
advantage should appear to be the result of luck'. Only in the almost
incomprehensible Appendices does the book lapse into farce,
notably at the entry on W.G.Grace who, we are invited to believe,
was really a woman with a false beard.

The time it takes for a book to appear in bookshops after the
typescript has found a publisher is hard on authors' nerves. Rupert
Hart-Davis was going to risk a printing of 25,000 copies, five times
as many as Stephen had dared hope for. He went on with 'How'
programmes and others, but gradually stopped doing *New
Statesman* theatre criticisms which were ill-paid; he wondered
whether he would spend the rest of his life in broadcasting.

In May, with only one rehearsal (never had he cut things finer),
he produced 'How to Blow Your Own Trumpet', with Joyce
Grenfell and many of the old gang, such as Betty Hardy and Ronald
Simpson. The theme of this opus was the lost art of boasting, except
in advertising: 'For royal bouquet and regal flavour, incomparably
blended with the wines of Empire, drink Vermuto. . . .' Why can we
no longer speak the bombast of Tamburlaine? Modern Britons just
show off self-deprecatingly: 'There's nothing clever about it.
Biology happens to be my subject.' 'Oh, do you *like* my nose? I
think it's silly.' Or there are more Lifewomanlike techniques such
as that of Lady Hemroid-Greeth who causes an announcement to
be printed in the paper that she 'has arrived at the Sovereign Hotel,
regrets she will be unable to accept any engagements for the next
three weeks as her doctors [plural, you notice] have ordered her to
rest'.

There follows advice on Being Popular with Artisans without
being Patronizing. Popularity Boasting includes the American lady
who says, 'I have the hardest time convincing people I'm a
grandmother'; and an ingenious technique of 'how to echo one's
own praises by praising someone else', illustrated musically by two
trumpets played in canon. While we are bound to conclude that only
children nowadays know how to boast (and they are reprimanded
for it), we may perhaps admit the lonely triumph of the elderly

graduate who, gleefully scanning the *Daily Telegraph* obituaries for the death of friends, boasts: 'I think I may say I am the only survivor of my staircase now.'

Stephen, himself an enthusiastic boaster, could, about this time, have boasted about his first meeting with Royalty. It was spoilt – indeed, turned into a 'pillow-biter' – by his frequent inability to recognize well-known faces in or out of context. The young Princesses Elizabeth and Margaret were, in these years, coming out into society and, closely surrounded by ladies-in-waiting, equerries and handpicked Guardees of good family, were often to be seen at suitable London nightspots. That, of course, was in context. For some good broadcasting reason Stephen found himself at a Girl Guides function where there was dancing. Choosing a petite girl in uniform who was some ten inches shorter than himself he asked her to dance. Making suitable semi-flirtatious conversation he asked: 'And what is a pretty girl like you doing in the Guides?' His partner murmured gravely: 'I think we do rather good work.' He realized that a silence had fallen and that all eyes were upon him but still did not know why.

At the end of the dance he asked a much bigger and older Guide: 'Who was that girl I was dancing with?' 'Princess Margaret, actually.'

In September there was another opportunity to go on a scientific expedition led by James Fisher. This time it was an aerial reconnaissance of the Outer Hebrides and beyond in a large Sunderland flying-boat, with the primary object of carrying out a census of young seals. At Calshot, Southampton Water, Stephen joined a party which included Max Nicholson, a distinguished ornithologist and secretary to the Lord President's Office; Dr Brian Roberts of the Foreign Office Research Department, a zoologist; Keith Piercy; and Eric Hosking, by general agreement 'the finest bird photographer of our time'. James Fisher would join the party at Pembroke Dock next morning. To Stephen, with his gift of the gab, fell the task of explaining to the Station Commander why they wanted a Sunderland. 'You see, pure scientific research, the pursuit of knowledge for its own sake, terribly important, you know. . . .' Had he been better briefed he could have told him that the expedition had the approval and backing of the Royal Society, the Advisory Committee on Airborne Research Facilities, and the Air Ministry. The Royal Society itself defined the objective as 'to fly over every island in Scotland and Wales to see whether grey seal colonies could be found from the air and if so, whether it would be possible to get any idea of the adult seals hauling out and the young ones born'. Among subsidiary objectives were 'oblique photography of as many islands as possible for reference purposes, and a study of all the gannet colonies of Scotland and Wales'.

First stop was Pembroke Dock where they met James Fisher, Dr Bruce Campbell, an ornithologist and broadcaster, J.L.Davies, a mammalogist from Aberystwyth University, and Ronald Lockley. After waiting a day for mist to clear they were airborne early next morning. They flew up the Welsh coast, over Lockley's farm where the family could be seen waving, past Holyhead, the Isle of Man and Ailsa Craig; then across to the east coast, over Bass Rock and so to Invergordon, landing at Alness seaplane base. Here they were joined by Dr (afterwards Sir) Frank Fraser Darling, the Scottish naturalist, like Ronald Lockley an experienced island dweller.

'Next morning,' Keith Piercy says, 'we set off early to fly north over Orkney . . . then on to Shetland, Unst and Muckle Flugga, the most northerly point in the British Isles, about 60 miles north of Cape Farewell, the southernmost tip of Greenland'. Turning south, they passed over Yell, Foula, North Rona (where Fraser Darling had once lived) and St Kilda. Eric Hosking records that the flight was enlivened from time to time by James Fisher shouting excitedly, 'Fulmars to starboard – small breeding colony, no more than about ten pairs,' and 'I say, chaps, can you see those fulmars on the port side? Must be a new colony – there's no record of them breeding here before.'

But it was seals they had come to see. They soon learned, as they flew over North Ronaldsay, to distinguish seals from seaweed-eating sheep. 'The seals breed in September,' Piercy continues, 'and during the first few weeks of their lives the calves have white coats and can be clearly seen from a low-flying aircraft. Most of the islands are bare rounded humps, and the baby seals lying on the grass "looked like maggots on a dead bird", to quote Stephen's vivid phrase.'

It was never easy to manoeuvre the huge four-engined Sunderland; you were always astonished that anything so un-streamlined could become airborne at all. In bad weather, twisting and turning to get suitable angles for photography at only 500 feet, the ride was very bumpy indeed and all the observers were airsick, except James Fisher, Stephen and Eric Hosking, who nearly fell out of the hatch responding every few minutes to shouts of 'calf on the shore to port'. Fraser Darling, sickest of all, also lost his cap which was blown off when he leaned out of the hatch.

Flying over St Kilda, whose sheer cliffs rise to over 1200 feet, the Sunderland came into an air pocket and plummeted 200 feet; even the captain admitted his anxiety lest the wings should drop off. 'After a flight lasting over $9\frac{1}{2}$ hours,' Piercy says, 'as long as it takes to fly from London to Pakistan in a modern jet, we returned to the Royal Hotel, Invergordon.' That evening was a Savile Club occasion for Eric Linklater and his wife Mary came over from Nigg, where they lived, to dinner.

On the final day they flew over the Outer Hebrides, observing seal calves on Shillay (where local people said there were none), and discovering an immense colony on the remote island of Gasker, which no naturalist had visited for fifty years; they returned, after an eight-hour flight, to Calshot.

Gamesmanship, published in October 1947, got friendly reviews but did not 'take off' quickly in the book trade. 'We must be a lot of dullards in Oxford,' Basil Blackwell wrote to Rupert Hart-Davis on 29 October. 'I have not been able to get a rise for your *Gamesmanship* – could we have a dozen copies to start with?' *The Times Literary Supplement*, always grudging, thought the word Gamesman 'has a sinister sound', like mobsman, cracksman (but not oarsman?), marvelled at the number of games S. Potter seemed to play, and concluded that 'it is impossible not to admire Mr. Potter's pertinacity in turning a joke into a book'. Tom Driberg gave the book most of his weekly piece in *Reynolds News*, and R.C.Robertson-Glasgow, that orotund prose-poet of cricket, saluted it in the *Observer*. With the hospitality of his friends on the *New Statesman*, whose paper ration allowed Cyril Joad no less than twenty column inches to review the book he himself had inspired, Stephen found his book placed immediately after a definitive work on Kierkegaard. Joad, noting that the function of most games (especially those compulsory games at school which intellectuals were supposed to be so bad at) was basically 'altering the position of balls in space', harked back to the golden age before 1914 when it was almost normal for a man both to row for his university *and* get a first in Greats. Intellectuals should be good at social games if only to prevent them from boring non-intellectuals. *Gamesmanship* was therefore 'a great book . . . destined to become a classic. . . . . It is unlikely that his work will be superseded for many years.' As for C. Joad, this was no doubt an apocryphal character.

By a skilful piece of timing, calculated to boost sales against all BBC anti-advertising rules, the next 'How' programme, 'How to be Good at Games', was broadcast at the peak listening hour of 9.15 pm on Christmas Day. Much of *Gamesmanship* was there – clothesmanship, flurrying your opponent before the game starts, two characters called Whittler and Bolderdew who illustrate how to put your croquet adversary off his game by noticing botanically interesting plants in mid-play, and the precise intonation with which, at tennis, to say 'Bad luck, partner!' Mrs Moss is there, with her 'I always let the children win!' To be topical there are Christmas games such as Pounce Patience (always played at no. 36 in Stephen's boyhood) and something which seems to have escaped the scholarship of Peter and Iona Opie and may have been invented by Stephen himself, Mumbledy-Bumbledy Mrs Mason ('Sidney dear, don't *bend* the cards.'). Two faithful pastiches of the main kinds of sportswriter of those days complete the picture – the (usually north-country) soccer man who writes things like 'Ably indeed did Walthamstow's goalie officiate between the sticks,' and Robertson-Glasgow himself ('As the last clock of bat on ball echoes over Steep Meadow, and rooks gather . . .'). And underneath all the jolly decent sportsmanship we hear a sepulchral voice like Hamlet's father's ghost intoning, 'I – play – to WIN.'

The two Potter sons, Andrew and Julian, were now respectively reading history at Merton College, Oxford, and approaching Higher School Certificate at Westminster School. By a mathematical improbability calculated at 80,000 to one against, Julian won the 'pancake greaze': there is no other record of its being won by both father and son and it is strange that the *Guinness Book of Records* ignores it. J.J.Potter's performance, which according to ancient custom appeared in a photograph in *The Times*, caused Potter Senior to be asked for a contribution to Julian's house magazine – on Greazemanship, of course: 'The expert greazer will . . . look over his shoulder to observe the angle of flight'; and, among off-putting ploys, the Spontaneous Nosebleed is recommended.

Gamesmanship had now caught on in a big way and there were many requests for -*manship* articles, still generally centred on sport. Lordsmanship, for example: 'I don't actually know Denis

Compton, but I stand near him and move my lips, which makes people out of earshot think I am talking to him.') All these would one day be used in books. Stephen was famous and he was enjoying fame. It was not the kind of fame he had wanted, but . . . He was now thoroughly accustomed to being introduced to people who invariably said, 'Not *the* Stephen Potter?' to which he invariably replied, managing a slight blush, 'I'm afraid so.'

He therefore felt rather one-down when, spending a weekend at Eric Hooper's house in Kent, he was introduced to a Mrs Heather Cox who had never heard of him. 'I had hardly listened to the radio since the War, and I hadn't read *Gamesmanship*,' she says. For some time they talked at cross-purposes – 'I thought he was *Stephen Spender*!' It was not a promising start for two people who, in seven years' time, would marry each other. Stephen, for his part, learnt that she was Heather Jenner of the Marriage Bureau, the most famous agency of its kind in Britain, founded just before the war and run on scientific but human lines: the long initial interview, the comparison of file cards (computers may do this quicker today, but not better), the sorting out of people's illusions about themselves from the truth. . . . The most likely client in those days of Empire was still the lonely tea-planter on leave from Ceylon who wanted to take a wife back with him to the plantation. . . . All this fascinated Stephen and he docketed it in his mind for future use – a radio feature, perhaps, or . . .

But how much longer would he stay with the BBC? Another possibility was on the horizon and approaching fast. A new young publishing company headed by Edward Hulton had appeared in 1938 with a revolutionary left-wing illustrated magazine called *Picture Post*. It had also acquired *Lilliput*, a satirical pocket-sized magazine, a monthly called *Housewife*, and a weekly called the *Leader*. Paper was still rationed and circulations were 'pegged'; but this would not last much longer. The *Leader* had once been a magazine entirely devoted to competitions. It was now, in 1948, a general weekly, largely built around show business, rather too similar to other weekly magazines but competitive enough to survive.

There was about Hulton Press an engaging amateurishness. The hard-faced men who ran Odhams Press could never understand it and called its staff 'lucky amateurs'; Hultons employed people with university degrees, some of whom had never done their time on provincial, preferably Yorkshire papers before coming to London. Bit airy-fairy, wasn't it? Yet it seemed to work. The management of Hulton Press was not satisfied with the *Leader* as it stood: wasn't there a more cultured public, the sort of people who used to read *John O'London's Weekly*? In the words of one director, the old *Leader* was 'no fun to publish'. But who should edit it? It must be someone out of the usual run of Fleet Street editors. Somebody of wide-ranging interests and a literary background who need not be of Fleet Street at all.

The Potters had lately been visiting Aldeburgh, that wonderfully unspoilt fishing village on the Suffolk coast, home of Benjamin Britten, the composer who was the nucleus of the fashionable Aldeburgh Festival. There was, of course, a golf-course there too. The managing director of Hulton Press, Max Raison, lived near the Old Moot Hall, and played golf. Going into the club-house one day he saw two men sitting at the bar. One of them he knew as Ronald Simpson the actor. The two men seemed to be in some kind of trouble. 'We can't pay for our drinks,' Simpson said. 'Oh? Why not?' Simpson showed Max Raison a jingling handkerchief. 'We've tied all our money up in here and we can't get the knot undone. By the way, this is Stephen Potter.'

Well, it was one way of getting a free drink. Nobody seems to have thought of cutting the knot and sacrificing the handkerchief; but then, handkerchiefs were still rationed. So began a friendship which led to a job. 'I found Stephen a most entertaining companion,' Max Raison says, 'and I thought he had ideas which could make a rather nice magazine, so I engaged him as editor. . . . I knew that he was somewhat vague at times, but I felt that Sydney Jacobson would be able to control him.' The idea was further discussed between Jacobson, a senior editor (now Lord Jacobson), Raison and Potter at an hotel in Aldeburgh: 'Stephen was in top form,' Lord Jacobson remembers, 'very gay and amusing, but at that stage there was no final commitment.' The matter was eventually clinched between Raison and Potter during a round of golf. (There is a solid British tradition of people being offered top jobs or arranging mergers either on golf-courses or in the hunting field.)

Before taking up his new job there was, in July 1948, another of James Fisher's expeditions, this time to the north-west corner of Sutherland. Fisher, Stephen, Keith Piercy and a number of botanists were joined by Tom Longstaff and his wife Charmian, who lived in Achiltibuie, a village on the promontory of Rhu Coigach. A doctor by training, Longstaff, then seventy-three, was an internationally famous mountaineer who had climbed in the Alps, the Caucasus and the Himalayas, and had explored Greenland and Spitzbergen.

The party stayed at Kinlochbervie, about ten miles south of Cape Wrath, in a fishing hotel patronized by both amateurs and local fishermen. The locals came in after each trip, their pockets stuffed with money, and got methodically drunk: sometimes the evening ended in fights with bottles. In the residents' lounge Tom Longstaff, lying on the carpet in a foetal position, gave nightly demonstrations of how to sleep on a rocky ledge high up on a mountain.

In the desolate, treeless Parphe area, with its massive bogs and outcrops of rock, Stephen found rare Arctic alpines and white Dryas with its eight-petalled flowers. A botanical journal, *Watsonia*, afterwards gave Stephen a scrap of the scientific recognition he coveted by paying tribute to 'the work of K. Piercy and S. Potter'.

The *Leader*, teeming with ideas, was an almost total expression of Stephen's personality. The main trouble was an attempt to mix old and new staff. The old staff, loyal to the old editor, never really absorbed the new character of the magazine. At the time I was on the staff of *Lilliput* and was hastily moved over as assistant features editor and general writing dogsbody for the *Leader*. Larry Solon, a brilliant American political and industrial feature writer, was hired from the *News Chronicle*, and Stephen's old acquaintance Jack Hargreaves was brought in from Colman, Prentis & Varley, the advertising agency. It was the way of Hulton Press to fling together a lot of diverse talent and then see what would happen.

The *Leader* appeared in its new form on 9 April 1949 and ran for a year. It was usual, in those days, to give a new magazine two or three years to establish itself, and the coming of commercial television was not yet regarded as a serious threat. Stephen's ideas followed the precedents of his career in radio. Each issue of the magazine usually had a 'potted classic' (beginning of course with Stephen's beloved *The Way of All Flesh*); a serious political 'problem' feature; 'One Man's (or Woman's) Week', a new form of interview with anyone from a writer to a model-girl; a medical piece; a Low cartoon; a famous crime, told in a strip cartoon; articles by Victor

Stiebel on dress, and by James Fisher on birds; a short, funny-charming piece by me (sometimes half a dozen photographs were flung on my desk on press day: 'Four hundred words in three quarters of an hour – OK?'); a 'Guide to the Arts'; sport and film features; and a new kind of puzzle called a Double-Crostic. The issue ended with two pages of 'Readers' Letters', some of which were made up in the office – Larry Solon's masterpiece was headed: 'I was a Test-Tube Baby'. The covers tended to be rather *avant-garde* and arty; the trade was suspicious of any magazine that did not have a pretty girl on the cover and circulation representatives used to come into our offices moaning: 'Another smashing Picasso this week, eh?'

Press day, for which we all drove down to Sun Printers at Watford, was sheer anarchy. The methods of Stefan Lorant, who had frequently torn up the whole of *Picture Post* the day before press day and started again, had left a tradition of how a genius-editor should behave. We were sometimes at Watford most of the night, the printers working overtime (no union would stand for it today). I once dictated a book review to a compositor as he sat at his machine.

Tom Driberg, who wrote the gossip column under the name 'Ian Paddock' in his beautiful script – never on a typewriter – put his piece together within sound of the presses and, for the last giggly paragraph, wandered frantically about asking us all for funny stories. He became known as May-I-Use-That Driberg.

Stephen was still freelancing for the BBC and also reviewing books for the *News Chronicle*: he carried his review copies around in a large green cricket bag. He made little attempt at controlling his staff but occasionally visited us in our tiny, crowded offices, peering round the door to smile: 'Everything all right? Splendid.' Nor was he happy at editorial meetings when we decided what to put in each issue. At the BBC writer-producers had an extraordinary degree of freedom and he was not used to an unruly staff full of conflicting opinions for whom a magazine was their livelihood first and anything else second. He did not much like journalists: 'They're venal,' he once told us. He set us a ruthless standard of good, cliché-free writing, however. Verbosity maddened him: 'This chap's terribly writey-writey,' he would say. 'Cut him by one third.'

I discovered that any reference to age irritated him. We were planning a 'half-century' edition for January 1950 and, at an editorial meeting, I said: 'Let's interview all sorts of well-known people who are fifty. Noël Coward, for instance – he's no longer the brilliant young man – let's get his worst enemy, Osbert Sitwell, to write him a birthday greeting.' Well, it wasn't so hot as an idea but that was not why Stephen slapped it down. 'What's wrong with being fifty?' he glared. '*I'm* fifty!'

Looking through old issues of the *Leader* one cannot fail to notice how many members of the Savile Club were contributors. Indeed, there was a rumour among us underlings that the magazine was edited from the Savile where Stephen sat in state ordering articles from anyone within sight. When the magazine eventually folded we found £7000 worth of overbought stock on file.

'He was totally untrained and inexperienced,' Lord Jacobson remembers, 'and temperamentally unsuited. He found it difficult to make decisions, and the long hours demanded by the job did not suit him. He was forever having to dash off somewhere else.' Journalists have very little social life and not much club life. Jacobson was now helping him out as managing editor. 'I used to go into his room in the evening and find him changing into a dinner jacket while his secretary, who sat in the same room, faced the wall during the trousers bit.'

They played squash together amicably, however. 'He was just about average, very keen on winning. Once we had one match each, and had a small bet on the decider. He brought his son along to watch, which rather put me off. Stephen won.'

Towards Christmas Stephen began offering his resignation almost weekly until it was accepted. Saying goodbye to Jacobson, who was to succeed him as editor, he looked beaten: 'It's the first job I've ever failed at.'

To his younger son, Julian, now doing his national service in Korea, Stephen wrote: 'It will interest you to know that I am no longer editor of the *Leader*. The poor old mag. has been losing £1000 a week. . . . In other words I've got the boot, more or less, and I am now starting a long struggle not to use up all my new and glorious freedom playing golf. They've treated me financially very well, I consider.'

The magazine folded with a circulation of 200,000 in May 1950. The official reason given was 'recent heavy increases in printing and paper charges'; but it seems more likely that Hultons needed the paper ration to swell the sales of their new and immensely successful children's papers *Eagle* and *Girl*, edited by a hitherto unknown parson named Marcus Morris from Birkdale, Lancashire.

Stephen's interview with Heather Jenner had appeared in an early issue of the new *Leader*. To write it had necessitated several meetings which, in Potter fashion, had begun by going wrong: for their first two meetings, each mistook the date. Eventually, Heather says, 'Stephen wooed me over lunches at the Apéritif on Hulton Press expenses.'

The social life, which Sydney Jacobson had seen interrupting his editorial duties, was proceeding apace. It was at about this time that Stephen began to be fascinated by peers: the way they lived, their houses, their easy assurance, their names. His New Year resolution for 1949 had been: 'Meet more lords.' He had recently got to know a man with the unbelievable name of the Hon. John Clotworthy Talbot Foster Whyte-Melville Skeffington, who would one day be thirteenth Viscount Massereene and Ferrard. ('Massereene *and* Ferrard!' Stephen would gasp with delight.) Eton, Black Watch, City company director, theatre 'angel', driver in Le Mans Grand Prix, Joint Master of Foxhounds, authority on farming, forestry, racing ... many of these were spheres of which Stephen knew nothing. As always he could not bear ignorance. The Skeffington home was Chilham Castle, Kent; the main address was Knock, on the Isle of Mull, Argyll; there was also a Clotworthy House in County Antrim.

Being invited to Mull for a weekend Stephen understood that there would be fishing. He was not the kind of man who could say to his host: 'I don't know anything about fishing – do show me how you do it.' No; he must do some quick homework with books. It so happened that Jack Hargreaves was an authority on fishing and had written books about it. Could Jack give him a crash course on fly-fishing? (The Gamesman in him should surely have sought refuge in some such remark as, 'Of course I only do deep-sea fishing, that's the real sport. . . .') His chief fear was being left out of the conversation.

Jack lent him *The Young Fly-Fisher*. 'But that's the book for boys!' 'Of course it is. You *must* begin with this. If I give you a grown-up book it will assume that you know elementary things in the beginner's book.' Stephen read it in a single evening. 'Now show me how to cast!' So Jack took him to Hampstead Ponds at dusk, when no one he knew was likely to see him, and they practised

ABOVE Christmas 1901.

LEFT Frank and Lilla,
Stephen's parents.

Young Bookman: Stephen
Meredith Potter, aged six.

Stephen's sister, Muriel.

1917: 'If the War doesn't
end soon I shall have to lay
down my blooming life for
my blinking country.'

S.M. Potter, B.A.(Hons) in 1922: 'Cockney accents cured'.

A picture letter to a 'not very serious' girl friend.

really will have to be frightfully sweet to live up to one

criterion. at 4.

I have been most gardening a lit lately.

Waking up Wagner —

with curious effects on my face

Steve.

Att, Stephen's first wife: 'very clear grey eyes . . . glows with unquenchable health'.

Att, Stephen, Andrew and Julian on holiday in Dorset in 1937.

Stephen and Joyce Grenfell scriptwriting in Joyce's kitchen.

'How to Cope with Christmas' – Celia Johnson and Stephen in a husband-and-wife sketch.

FIG. 33. WINESMANSHIP: A LITTLE-KNOWN PLOY.

After saying (not of course really having a cellar) "I'll get it from the cellar," enter any cupboard (preferably beneath stairs), *close door*, and make sound with feet as if descending to and (after pause) mounting from a wine-cellar.

ABOVE Illustration by Lt.-Col. Frank Wilson from *One-Upmanship*.

LEFT C.E.M. ('It depends what you mean') Joad.

Francis Meynell, founder of Weekendmanship.

With the Compliments OF

Schweppshire Post

HOME PAGE

COOKERY

WOO HIM

WITH

NATURAL FOODS

Have you tried raw cod sandwiches garnished with a bouquet of shredded turnip?

Serve on a bed of toasted red cabbage if you want HIS eyes to light up.

TEEN-AGE TONIC

Let me be your Uncle

A SPLIT-SECOND SERMON BY DR PRESCHWEPT

From the thousands of letters you have written let me pick one. A simple question. "Why must I relax?" Relaxing is being. Is knowing. Is living. Let the impetus of relaxation come from within out, never from without in. Muscle by muscle. Arms—and remember the bones. LET YOUR TEETH RELAX.

FASHION

for the fuller figger

IF NOT ACTUALLY FAT

A

B

For (**B**) the belt is extended

NEW

Beauté

FOR OLD

Schweppes Appeal

THROUGH SIMPLE EXERCISES

For nose and ears, this is POST'S Bi-manual: With right hand rotate nose anti-clockwise; with left pull out each ear in rhythmic countermotion, allowing it to spring back as *nose reaches upwards position*, so that the two blood supplies may interact.

GARDEN HINTS

'Marquess of Schwepstow'

For those of us who are carrot-minded, E. WILT. *Post's* carrot expert, reminds us of points to look for.

Note, in "Marquess", the high shouldering, absence of "waist", and abrupt taper.

1. Top or "pennant"
2. Shoulder
3. Underwing
4. Waist
5. Tip or "low-point"

'POST' BAG

AN OLD BULB

We have in our home a 1900 electric bulb still working. On it is a picture of the Archduke Otto wearing a sailor suit. Would not gayer, painted bulbs help to brighten our drab world of queues and form-filling?

(Miss) Evadne Schwepperfield

WORTH FOURPENCE

I have just come by a copy of Pilgrim's Progress marked with the date 1883. The price seems to have been 4d. *What is its value now?*

(Address not supplied)

Written by Stephen Potter. Drawn by Lewitt-**Him**

CHWEPPERVESCENCE   LASTS   THE   WHOLE   DRINK   THROUGH

One of the famous Schweppes advertisements.

Stephen's second wife, Heather Jenner, in the Café de Paris in the mid-fifties.
'Stephen's cigarette in the right-hand corner is just going to singe my fur,
a frequent happening.'

The 1953 Stage Golfing Society dinner with H.R.H. Prince Philip. Stephen Potter
is on the far right, and clockwise from him are: Alan Melville, Harold Warrender,
Reggie Seton, Bill O'Brien, Walter Fitzgerald, Ronald Simpson, Anthony
Kimmins, Prince Philip, Capt. Jack Broome, Commander John Wood and Frank
Lawton.

the art of avoiding a hook in a friend's eye or one's own hat or a tree. Stephen latched on to the term 'Spey-casting' and specialized in it. Spey-casting would be his subject whenever he was in fishing company.

At Jack's house afterwards, as they said goodbye, Stephen opened what he thought was the front door and walked straight into the loo. He could not believe that Jack had not arranged this on purpose. 'Masterly!' he said. 'An absolutely masterly ploy!'

With the demise of the *Leader*, and the loss of his first really good salary, Stephen, jobless and fifty, faced the prospect of being a full-time writer. No BBC cushion behind him any more. They would employ him as a freelance, of course, and there were new 'Hows' on the way, a certain amount of reviewing and, assuredly, a successor to *Gamesmanship* which would inevitably be called *Lifemanship*. He was already behind schedule on this book, which was due to be published in October for the Christmas season, and there was an anxious exchange of letters with Rupert Hart-Davis who was a severe editor – Stephen always paid tribute to his work in what he called 'our glorious collaboration', and inscribed copies to Rupert 'for delightful publishership'.

Lifemanship, 'with a summary of recent researches in Gamesmanship', established Station Road, Yeovil, as the head-quarters of the Lifemanship Correspondence College. It intro-duced a number of new characters, concentrating on two of them, Harry Gattling-Fenn and the despicable G. Odoreida. (I have wasted much scholarly research in trying to work out a derivation for this name and am disappointed to find that it is not, as I long suspected, a botanical classification of stinkweed.) Odoreida was perhaps Stephen's greatest creation and he began signing some of his letters to friends 'G. Odoreida'.

The principles of 'one-up' (*Bitzleisch*) and 'one-down' (*Rotzleisch*) are, for the first time, defined, with an ominous compound, *Bitzleischstüsse*. Stephen knew no German but invents it expressively: *-leisch* is somewhere between *leiche* = corpse, and *laich* = frogspawn; *Rotz* = mucus and *-stüsse* is very near to *Stosse* = shock or push. R. Hart-Davis appears in a footnote for his ploy of wearing an old bush shirt, bequeathed to him by his wife's stepfather, whose epaulettes clearly show that he was once a brigadier. There is much fun with OK words like diathesis, mystique, catalyst and empathy. There are chapters on

Weekendmanship, Woomanship ('the sound Wooman is either fascinatingly rich or amusingly poor'), and Newstatesmanship, in which the reviewer Hope-Tipping always takes the quality for which an author is most famous and blames him for not having enough of it. As the non-linguist tends to mock foreign languages so Stephen mocked the prevalent vogue of Rilke and Kafka: he seriously believed it to be 'a monstrous affectation'. Rilking soon became a catchword for this sort of thing and was taken up across the Atlantic by James Thurber.

The technique of ruthless Dedicationship as a means of silencing reviewers was illustrated by the notorious 'To Phyllis, in the hope that one day God's glorious gift of sight may be restored to her'. Among many daunting chapters there is one on 'How to Make People Feel Awkward about Religion', and another on blocking the flow of experts when they are holding forth on a subject about which Lifeman knows little or nothing. One method is *plonking*, uttering a cliché (or repeating the expert's words) in an expressionless voice. The Canterbury Block has become famous throughout the English-speaking world:

Expert (who has just come back from a fortnight in Florence): 'And I was glad to see with my own eyes that this Left-wing Catholicism is definitely on the increase in Tuscany.'
Lifeman: 'Yes, but not in the South.' The Canterbury Block can establish instant one-upmanship in almost any context.

In a footnote Stephen acknowledges that 'World Copyright' of this phrase 'is owned by its brilliant originator, R. Pound'. Reginald Pound, author and sometime editor of the *Strand* magazine, had in fact never met Stephen. The inventor of the ploy, Richard Usborne, author of *Clubman Heroes* and world authority on the life and work of P.G.Wodehouse, who had been assistant editor of the *Strand*, had written an article in *Punch* as long ago as 1941 using the same idea and title, 'long before I knew Potter or had heard of gamesmanship or lifemanship'. He had sent his *Punch* article to Stephen in 1947 when *Gamesmanship* was published. He now wrote thus: 'Dear Potter, – who is this Mr Pound, who claims world copyright for the "Not in the South" gambit? I would like to meet him behind the Fives Court. Congratulations on the book. . . .'

Potter to Usborne, 8 November 1950: 'My God, have I got it wrong? I now perceive with horrifying clearness that I have. . . . I will guarantee complete acknowledgement in the second edition. Of course I would meet you behind the fives court myself but for my old heart trouble. . . .'

'Old heart trouble . . . the old ticker' is a recommended ploy in Golf Gamesmanship and most people who knew Stephen thought of it as such. In fact, Stephen *had* a heart condition; not incapacitating, but frightening. Playing tennis one weekend in Suffolk he had his first attack of paroxysmal tachycardia – rapid heart-beating for two minutes or longer, recurring perhaps for several days at a pulse rate of 160–200.

Lifemanship eventually sold over 96,000 copies in Britain, over 71,500 in America and 6000 in Sweden. What the Swedes made of it we do not know. The Swedish for Lifemanship is *Livsmannaskap*, and phrases such as *Vad ar Plonk?* and *Cogg-Willoughby's anti-sportlinje* certainly look deadpan-funny to an English reader who knows no Swedish.

Among reviews *The Times Literary Supplement* for once entered into the spirit of the thing and praised S. Potter for 'doing for his generation what Samuel Smiles did for his', in the matter of 'getting on'. 'The humour is solemn, the face is poker.' It is the footnotes that keep the fun going. But 'why is it that Mr. Potter has never breathed a word of Lifemanship-Wifemanship? Is it because he knows that even a long-handicap Wifewoman would be more than a match for even a plus-two Lifeman?' The anonymous reviewer quotes the case of W. Darling in *P. Pan*, and the unanswerable counter-ploy of 'Yes, dear, but have you taken your medicine?'

Several reviewers, Margaret Lane among them, contributed 'ploys' of their own. *Time & Tide* hit on the idea of asking Stephen to review his own book. In America, where it was published by Henry Holt, the *New Yorker*, which had not deigned to notice *Gamesmanship*, chose Edith Oliver to review *Lifemanship* (which, in Holt's edition, was subtitled 'The Art of Getting Away With It Without Being an Absolute Plonk'). This was lucky for Stephen: heaven help him if an anti-British-humour man like Wolcott Gibbs had reviewed it. Miss Oliver welcomed the book as 'the second of what might turn out to be, if we're lucky, a series of books on the subject of success'. It was, she was quick to see, a self-portrait: 'You will find him, I hope, genial, encouraging and, provided you are willing to accept the One Down conditions, sometimes genuinely helpful.' The book, she thought, did not hang together so well as *Gamesmanship*, 'but it has more variety, and . . . manages to be funnier'. This is a 'peculiarly English type of fooling . . . in which a writer ridicules behaviour that strikes him as silly or excessive but that doesn't really offend him'; and 'by means of the disciplined and straight-faced style he has devised, he has been able to express great wit and exuberance, and a point of view that is rooted in shrewd observation and goodwill and common sense'.

The *-manship* game was now rife everywhere; Stephen received fan-letters from men all over America, claiming membership of the Yeovil university; they were often given appointments such as 'No. 3 Wisconsin' in the hierarchy of world-Lifemen. One such letter came from Joe Bryan III, of Georgetown, Washington. Joe Bryan is a naval historian, an ex-lieutenant commander in the US Navy, a former associate editor of the *Saturday Evening Post*, sometime member of the Algonquin Round Table, and more recently a biographer of the Duke and Duchess of Windsor. Bryan was made 'US I' and Stephen promised to visit him and bestow the accolade in person if or when he went to America. This was to happen sooner than either knew.

Requests for *-manship* articles poured in, including one for an article on Clothesmanship for the *Daily Express* 'Mantrap' series; all these would eventually be used in books, but already there was a note of weariness in his response: 'I live now in retreat. The remaining years of my life are dedicated to my work as Founder of Games-Lifemanship.' The Duke of Edinburgh, in a Guildhall speech to the Institute of Chartered Accountants, referred to Taxmanship. Adlai Stevenson used the word Brinkmanship in a political speech. Meeting Stevenson at a party Stephen, tail wagging, said: 'I was delighted when you used Brinkmanship to describe the foreign policy of John Foster Dulles.' Stevenson: 'I really can't claim originality for that. It stemmed from *Lifemanship* and all that – invented by that very amusing English writer – now what was his name? . . .'

On Christmas Day 1950 Stephen's mother died, at her Reigate house, nursed until the end by the faithful Minnie. The Potters, all except Julian, were with the Meynells at Cobbolds Mill for the holiday. To Julian in Korea, where he was fighting boredom by gathering botanical specimens (he had inherited Stephen's passion for plants), Stephen wrote: '. . . it is the first unpleasant Christmas I have spent, and it was deeply gloomy . . . The whole of Christmas Eve was a running commentary on the phone from Minnie . . .

about the state of Granny, whom I saw for the last time on Friday, obviously *in extremis*, but not in pain. She . . . died about 4 am on Christmas Day, very quietly indeed – "like a watch running down", says Minnie.' Stephen told no one except Att and Andrew for fear of spoiling their hosts' Christmas; but this had quite the wrong effect, and everybody began to get on each other's nerves. A note of black comedy entered the gloom when it became known that the Meynells' cow Clover was mortally ill and, when eventually they were told on Boxing Day about Stephen's mother's death, they seemed to be grieving for Clover.

Rupert Hart-Davis had been lecturing Stephen about his future. Rupert had warned that, in his opinion, the *-manship* game would not last for more than three books. Already Stephen was in danger of being unable to write in any other style. Could he not find a new vein? To Rupert, now publishing from slightly grander offices in Soho Square, Stephen wrote:

I appreciate very much indeed your letter about my future work. I have been working rather intermittently for the last three months, as you know, on first shots at and plans for more than one book. . . . I do realize that this is the most serious point in my writing career. I feel I am bursting with ungleaned and undigested material, mostly autobiographical. The question is how to use it. Financially also, the question is 'Can I exist by the pen alone?'. . . . Those film rights have not been sold after all. . . . PS I don't really want to write 1000 words on Reviewmanship for five guineas for the Times Book Club Review, whose circulation is 10,000, chiefly overseas, but if you say I ought to I will.

He was experimenting with short stories, which were not his forte, and with an idea for a multi-volume autobiography, based on the detailed diaries he had been keeping since the mid-1930s, in emulation of James Agate's *Ego* series. But he could never have teemed with gossip as Agate had done. Rupert expressed a cautious interest in one experimental volume.

Meanwhile, *Lifemanship* involved him in many things – a possible television series in America, an invitation to address the Oxford Union (always an unnerving experience the first time you do it as a graduate visitor), and a series of 'Lifemanship Lectures' (assisted by Ronald Simpson and other stalwarts of the How Repertory Company) on the BBC Third Programme. There were many new friends. His letters to Julian in Korea (or at base in Japan) are full of news:

I had a rather enjoyable 'How to Go to the Theatre' last Friday. I shall have to get the recording played back to you when you return (hard luck). Mother . . . has made the kind of will that has made everybody feel they have been thought of in just the right kind of way. . . . With luck I shall get my overdraft paid off. . . . I do hope letters are getting through; I write on the average about every six days to you.

John Strachey, now Minister for War, has given a New Year dance in Essex:

Mum and Andrew and I had one or two warming drinks at the big old pub at Chingford which is illustrated in the frontispiece of *Barnaby Rudge*. . . . While we were parking our car John Strachey was walking worriedly up and down and said to us 'Thank God you have come, otherwise I should never be able to explain things' – reason: all the tottering infants of the party had read *Lifemanship* and insisted on being introduced to us. My public seems to be increasingly in the 18-year-old group. I am very complimented at this, and thought, 'Well, 25 years ago I never thought that the War Minister would greet me with "Thank God you have come."' Perhaps this is the highest moment in my life.

Att has had an exhibition at the Leicester Galleries. A gang of young Scottish Nationalists have stolen the Stone of Scone from Westminster Abbey, and Stephen has written a letter to *The Times* on 'Stonemanship'. He has developed a sudden passion for 'old-fashioned standard operas' and 'three glorious French films about a French village'. He is in a panic about the Oxford Union – 'Subject: that this house disapproves of the law and lawyers. I am opposed by Norman Birkett, one of the suavest, most experienced and most appalling cross-examiners in history. Awfully jolly, isn't it. . . . I have to wear tails from Moss Bros.' It is happening *tomorrow* and he has prepared nothing. . . . '*Lifemanship* and *Gamesmanship* are in print again after five weeks out. I gave my last Lifemanship lecture on Monday, with sound effects including Odoreida's high-pitched racket string and the use of the lawn mower to put off your opponent when he is making a break at croquet. . . . It is a very ungolfable winter, rain and wind more than cold. Squash saves my life, and fierce walks round Regent's Park.'

By March there are plans for leaving the Harley Street flat:

Mum and I are starting rather vaguely house-hunting. . . . So far we have only looked at one house in Hampstead which belonged to Romney. Extremely large and £13,000. In spite of the fact that we can't afford more than £6,000 we went carefully over it and decided not to have it because it faced north. . . . Mum wants a large studio and Romney's was almost as big as Up School [at Westminster]. . . . Have just spent the morning in the Press view of the Ideal Home Exhibition at Olympia which I am describing for *Punch* – 'write it how you like'. The most successful exhibits on the whole are the bathrooms, kitchens and W.C.s. . . .

He has been to a luncheon of the Thursday Club, of which Prince Philip was a member,

fostered by that scallywag Baron [*the* fashionable portrait photographer of the decade] which meant that I was drinking for the best part of the day. . . . *Lifemanship* is selling at 600 plus and *Gamesmanship* at 300 plus a week just at the moment, and I am quite well known. Unfortunately by the time you get back nobody will have the faintest idea who I am, such is the fickleness of fame. You will be interested to hear that I have joined Roehampton on the strength of Mother's will, so we shall have one summer at any rate with croquet laid on – if your nerve can stand this game after Korea.

Seventeenth March was Julian's birthday – 'Twenty is rather ancient, old boy. Hard luck.' The house-hunt continues:

We toured the Thames Valley with the vague idea of getting a house rather near Oxford to inveigle you to call on us when you are up. The 'enchanting house of character' usually turns out to be a red-brick horror called 'Dunedin'. . . . 'Wychwood' has been sold at a correct price, I am glad to say, and I shall now be able to pay off all my debts. It will be a wonderful feeling. I shall probably have just as many in a year from now, but I shan't have to borrow money from you *yet*.

Having had 'a series of 3 TV shorts of *Lifemanship* bought over there', and 'I am writing something for *Life*', Stephen planned a visit of about a month to America in May. Raymond Massey was interested in buying the television rights of *Lifemanship*. But first the new house must be bought: pending the surveyor's report, he and Att had practically settled on one which 'beside being Queen Anne is midway between Woking and Moor Park with Roehampton in the offing'. But even the proximity of golf-courses was not enough and London Airport was far too close for comfort. A quick broadcast on botany from BBC West Region, the recording of a voice-over from *Lifemanship* for the Lion and Unicorn pavilion of the Festival of Britain; and he left for America. No Englishman ever crossed the Atlantic with less idea of what he was going to see. He would set foot in the New World with great wariness: but it was the unperceived beginning of a great love affair.

Chapter 11
New worlds

He had left an England where many goods were still rationed, newspapers still averaged six to eight pages and commercial television would not be seen for another four years. Staying at the Harvard Club his first impression was the impossibility of reading American newspapers. The huge headlines, the beginning of five front-page stories, then 'turn to page 63, column 7': 'reading these papers is like trying to read a feather bed'. The decorousness of British papers in the 1950s contrasted strangely with 'five years for Senator accused of bribing Fire Brigade President with girls', and 'fourteen first-grade college girls on heroin charges'.

The second difficulty was the near-impossibility of buying good maps so that he seldom knew where he was. He was soon plunged into almost daily radio and television interviews arranged by Holt, his American publisher, and was bewildered by the multiplicity of stations located in the tops of skyscrapers and reached by breathlessly fast elevators. His first interviewer, at Station WOR, was a sympathetic lady named Martha Stow ('her voice was warm and easy as bedsocks'), who questioned him for forty-five minutes with gramophone records intervening. She was equipped with a remarkably efficient dossier of his entire life – wife, children, Coldstream Guards and all. 'I expect you feel worried about him and proud of him at the same time? – Your son in Korea?' Stephen's reply was interrupted by a commercial – 'Fortescue's Distempers are sold in nearly two hundred shades and one of them is sure to please *you*.' Martha meanwhile briefed him: 'Political, you know. Show the British are in Korea.' Suddenly she is asking about Joyce Grenfell – 'Miss Grenfell is American?' Stephen: 'Well, half – niece of Lady Astor.' Martha laughs. Stephen: 'Why are you laughing?'

Martha: 'Oh, I just like your face! Now tell me exactly how you say "bad luck" when you want to put your golf opponent off?' Stephen: 'Ba-ad *luck*!'

By his fifth day in New York he was asking himself, 'What to do about these drinks? They all drink Martinis (shorts) or Manhattans (whisky base, lots of ice). The Martinis are in fact glasses and the vermouth is often just rinsed in the glass and poured away again, so one is really drinking neat gin double English strength. This hospitality and lack of tennis is getting me down.'

Next day he was the guest of the editorial board of *Fortune* magazine at the Algonquin Hotel – 'five men who wanted to discuss with me their gambits for Businessmanship'. He noticed the one-downness of having a small desk, carpet, room; the man who gets workmen in at night to shift a partition to increase the size of his office; Stephen's Mistakenmanship – 'taking wrong decisions and admitting they are wrong'; the unbeatable one-upness of the chief executive who has *nothing* on his desk – such as 'Fred Wilkie who has *one* telephone across the room which he *gets up to answer*'. Even better, 'Shaver, of Lord & Taylor (expensivest Fifth Avenue shop) . . . has no desk at all.' Henry Luce, owner of *Time-Life-Fortune*, 'with a masterpiece of reticent-humility-of-the-great just calls himself Editor; and there is inverted Christian-nameship, too. Only all *below* the high-ups who work with him can call him Harry!'

On to the 21 restaurant where Ted Patrick, editor of *Holiday*, offered him 500 dollars for 2000 words on Travelship. Here he met a 'sweet little marmoset, white-faced, bald, called Jerome Weidman' (author of *I Can Get It For You Wholesale*) – 'one of those *really funny* US men who instead of bogging everything into a platitude, turns it the other way to a little nest of wit'. They agreed that, just as visitors to London are expected to praise the policemen, so the British visitor to New York is obliged to say 'I think your taxi-drivers are wonderful' for fear of not being a good democratic mixer. Then they fell to the old New York pastime of denigrating Philadelphia and, by the end of the party, Weidman was saying things like 'It's not long since we were pushing westward over the Appalachians,' and 'When I was first in England they gave me a room in St Martin's Lane with a neon light outside it. And I didn't even know they'd got electricity. . . .'

Soon after eight o'clock Stephen, dining at the house of banker

Eddie Warburg in black tie, thought he must be drunk when he found himself staring at Picasso's original *Blue Boy*.

Next day he showed up for a half-hour interview by Louis Untermeyer on television, in a free-for-all unscripted style not yet seen on British television. 'This tiny man', Stephen told his diary, 'never stopped talking and wisecracking in the *boring* American way.' Untermeyer was famous for anthologies of humour. 'A fight, that's what the audience like,' he told Stephen. After introducing 'Mr Potter, whose wit and subtlety you all know,' the hostess, Dorothy Dean, left them to it. Against a background of girls modelling clothes Untermeyer began to attack British humour: 'Our humour is broader, stronger – frontier stuff.' Stephen managed to get in a polite word in praise of the *New Yorker*, then angrily suggested that the Americans had a false idea of themselves as tough; they were really diffident and rather quiet. His final score over Untermeyer was when 'two very young cameramen brought their *Lifemanship* to be autographed'.

With a sense of relief he left New York for Connecticut to spend the weekend with the Raymond Masseys in their New England farmhouse dating from 1711. They were going to advise him on television contracts. Overwhelmed by the grandeur of a Plymouth, a Cadillac and a Ford for the chauffeur, by a beamed farmhouse somehow decorated in Third-Empire style, and by the enormous quantities of food (British stomachs were still rather shrunken in 1951) he astonished his host by insisting on a forty-minute brisk walk on Sunday morning; he also managed to get nine holes of golf at New Canaan. From the Masseys' teenage daughter (at Vassar) he learnt current student terms of abuse: 'He's a *creep* – he's *greby*. The fluff left in your pockets is *nerr*. The scum on a pond is *shlurg*.'

The drink problem was such that Stephen was now pouring Manhattans furtively into pot plants all over the house. Raymond Massey was not yet used to television. In a few years' time he would be accustomed to being hailed in the street, 'Hiya, Dr Gillespie!' after the part he was to make famous in the Dr Kildare series. To teach Stephen about American television the Masseys switched on the Uppie Peppingham Show which turned out to be a parody of BBC television quizzes. 'The American stage Englishman, the American stage Cockney and a "refined" announcer. All American wit, even Benchley's or Thurber's, seems to leave them when they satirize the English. . . . If only they knew how much funnier we are

in real life! The Masseys were embarrassed. "Quite all right," I said
Englishly.' They switched to another channel which was all-in
wrestling. The evening ended with Dorothy Massey saying,
'Stephen, don't you think Americans are less inhibited than the
British?'

He moved on to Boston which, a taxi-driver warned him, was 'out
of date, go-slow'. Here he was the guest of 'typical Bostonian
Charles Morton, literary editor of the *Atlantic Monthly*'. The
Morton family were well versed in Lifemanship. No highballs here:
instead, cheese and sherry, like an English university. 'My piano
playing, politely disregarded in England, is considered marvellous.'
Bostonians, he noted, even *look* English. He explored old Boston,
with its Bullfinch houses, and called in at the Tavern Club which
was affiliated to the Savile in London: 'Chaps have drinks before
lunch, round table eating, billiards after.'

In New York he had been cross-questioned about his connection
with the *New Statesman* which, though pro-Israel, had been anti-
Korea. In Boston his stock shot up when a message arrived: 'Please
ring Sir Gladwyn Jebb.' Jebb, UK representative to the United
Nations, 'is a great British Hero here because of his handling of the
Russians at UNO. Millions watched him flatten out the Russians on
television.' There was a quiet tour of Harvard, conducted by a radio
interviewer who was a Harvard man; and then it was time to leave
for Washington.

He was beginning to doubt whether Americans understood
Lifemanship at all, except for the *Time-Life-Fortune* high-ups. In
Washington they seemed to confuse it with elaborate practical
joking. His first date was with Joe Bryan III, whom he had
appointed US1 in the hierarchy of Lifemen, and whose original
fan-letter had contained that gloomiest of author-to-author jokes,
'I've recommended your book to all my friends and they're lining
up to *borrow* it.'

The Bryans lived in Georgetown, Washington's most expensive
suburb. To Stephen's surprise Joe had arranged a dinner party of
eight men, all calling themselves Lifemen, some of whom had come
over 250 miles to attend it. 'Four of them seem to be in the Secret
Service – CIA – though they call themselves muralists, press
attachés, lawyers, musicians and what not.' They all had one thing
in common, the ability to keep a straight face. Joe had hired a very
dignified coloured butler for the occasion: his name was Kitchener

but he was instructed to answer to the name 'Potter' for the entire evening – and not to smile. 'Potter, will you freshen Mr Potter's glass?' The leg-pull became more and more elaborate; all seven guests had brought copies of *Gamesmanship* or *Lifemanship* for Stephen to sign and then left them scattered on the floor when they went. A parody copy of one of his books with a special dust cover titled *Yankmanship* awaited him in his bedroom and there was a toy tarantula on his pillow.

One of the guests was Squirrel Ashcraft, lawyer and musician, who habitually asked for 'a Martini big enough to pull over my head like a jersey'. Stephen appointed him 'Washington 1'. But the most notable guest was Hugh Troy, 'the Horace de Vere Cole of America', sometimes known as the 'park bench man', famous for his practical jokes. A friend of his filled Hugh's bath with gelatine, which looked like water: Hugh had to bale it out with a spoon. In revenge he went to his friend's apartment, removed all the electric fuses except one so that it would be in total darkness when he returned, then set off an electric fan in a corner of a room and released 200 balloons so that the other man was greeted by soft floppy things in his face. Another favourite occupation of Troy's was riding around on the subway reading newspapers four years old, to watch the effect of out-of-date headlines on passengers sitting opposite. Passing a highway toll gate where the man usually snatched the nickel out of his hand as he reached out of his car, he arranged a dummy arm which came away with the nickel so that the man fainted.

Magnificent, but not Lifemanship, any more than Troy's most famous exploit, the Park Bench Trick. He and a friend (it is always a mystery that practical jokers should have any friends) had a perfect imitation of a Central Park bench made, and were careful to have a bill of sale for it. Entering the Park furtively at about 11 pm they carried the bench towards the exit where they were, of course, arrested and taken to the police station protesting volubly. After a long grilling, being proved innocent of stealing, they were released. They took the bench back to the Park, then tried to take it out again, were again arrested and released. . . . This happened four times in one night until a distracted station sergeant swore that 'next time I'll lock you both up and throw away the key'. Perhaps Troy found the CIA funnier still. It was said in defence of his jokes that they 'caused consternation but never humiliation'.

Joe Bryan discovered that one of the hazards of having Stephen to stay, apart from cigarette stubs setting fire to everything, was letting him loose in a library. After Stephen had gone he found the fly-leaves of many books, including Henry James, Proust, Robert Louis Stevenson and some of his own, inscribed with such generous tributes as 'so glad you took my suggestion for this little thing', or 'based on an idea by S. Potter'. Joe's copy of *Gamesmanship* has two inscriptions: 'To America One, Pioneer of a Continent, from One, on the occasion of his superb hostmanship, 16 May 51' (date of the Potter-butler dinner); and 'To Joseph, but for whose encouragement and warm sympathy during a difficult period, this book might never have been written, from Stephen: Château d'Horizon – Knole – Taormina, 1929–36.'

Not only books, but pictures also received the Potter attention. In Princes Arcade, Piccadilly, Joe had bought for £2 a small head-and-shoulders oil portrait of an unknown eighteenth-century gentleman. 'Who is it?' Stephen asked. 'I've no idea,' Joe said. 'I just liked his face and the way it's painted.' 'We'll soon fix that,' Stephen said, and wrote on the paper backing of the frame: 'Sir James Beaumont the Elder, 1740–1771 (his son was later the friend of Sara Hutchinson, sister-in-law of W. Wordsworth).' Then, as if this were not good enough he added a second fictitious identification: 'J.K.C.Jarvis, 1740–1771, inventor of Jarvis's retractable spool. His name will always be associated with the "Seascale Spool Troubles" (labour disaffection of the 1780s).'

From Washington Stephen flew to New Orleans by way of Atlanta, Georgia (where, for the first time, he saw at the airport lavatories marked MEN: COLORED; WOMEN: COLORED); he stayed in New Orleans long enough to hear some Dixieland jazz and stopped off at Dallas long enough to discover that if you leave open the anti-insect wire-mesh door of your hostess's kitchen the food suddenly becomes full of flying cockroaches. He went to Hollywood to meet Cary Grant who now claimed to be a Gamesman and was interested in making a film of *Lifemanship* (it never materialized). He struck Stephen dumb by saying, 'I'll lend you my spare Cadillac while you're here.'

Stephen sailed home from New York in the *Queen Mary*, 'a vast feather bed of comfort of which I soon got heartily sick. . . . The only exciting thing on board was Noël Coward, and he didn't kill me.' He had plenty of time to observe Ocean Linership – Americans who are so used to transatlantic travel that they don't appear in public until the third day; the style of décor (which he named 'Directress 1933' because it presumably represented the taste of Cunard directors' wives); and the bridge playing of Victor Gollancz and his wife. Much of the time he spent writing an article on London clubs for Ted Patrick's *Holiday*, and day-dreaming that he had been offered a Chair of Social Behaviour at Yale.

Rejoining Att at Aldeburgh for the Aldeburgh Festival he was relieved to be out of the 'too-muchness' of America and to be living in 'two rooms with one cold tap on a blowy sea front with a hole in the linoleum, and only one small newspaper available at the shop'. It was now mid-June. To Julian in Korea:

Mum and I saw a house in Aldeburgh which we have decided to buy. It has got everything. Everything. Including such little etceteras as a beautiful grass tennis court and the fourteenth fairway outside the front drive. . . . Very open Wimbledon this year; nobody knows who is going to win. I got a glimpse of Mottram beating Drobny. . . . You know about Merton being head of the river? Did an old programme yesterday about Oxford in 1939 [an updated version of *Undergraduate Summer*]. Very nostalgic. . . .

The house was the Red House, about half a mile from the sea. Parts of it were sixteenth-century. 'Having bought the house, one's thoughts naturally turn to how to raise the cash, my present problem. . . .' But £6000 was somehow found and Att began redecorating the drawing-room in Venetian red. For her, life was perfect at last – a house big enough to entertain in, above all big enough to paint in; a house she could make beautiful on a shoe-string budget; a house from which Stephen could walk straight on to a golf-course, one he already knew well.

Stephen's fame was now at its height. He was collecting ideas for a new book, *One-Upmanship*. The visitors' book at the Red House was filling up with names of friends associated with the Savile Club and the Aldeburgh Festival: Benjamin Britten, Henry Moore, Gerald Barry, Edward Sackville-West, Dame Evelyn Sharp, Eric Linklater, James Fisher. There were occasional radio programmes in which he took part; and suddenly, in July, a new advertising campaign began to sweep the country in newspapers, glossy magazines and posters. This was the memorable 'Schweppshire' campaign for Schweppes mineral waters, designed, in advertising jargon, to 'reposition' the brand as 'the Rolls-Royce of soft drinks' and destined to run on and off for fourteen years. It began with a picture map of an imaginary English county; and, if it did nothing else, it ensured that no literate English-speaking person could fail to know what the name represented. It was the idea of F.C.Hooper, managing director of Schweppes, developed by Stephen, and contributed to uproariously by all the snooker players at the Savile Club. (That snooker table has a great deal to answer for.) Every advertisement ended with the slogan: 'Schweppervescence Lasts the Whole Drink Through' (except in the autumn, when it became 'How Many Schwepping Days to Xmas?').

The maps and pictures, drawn by the Polish-émigré artist, George Him, postulated an England which contained, within 200 square miles (or rather schweppimetres), a range of mountains called the Schweppenines, a county town called Cirenschweppster, a beauty spot (presumably on the Welsh border) called Schwepps-y-Coed, a race-course on Schwepsom Downs, an Isle of Schweppey, a Schwepping Forest, and a local train called the Schwepton Belle. You could spend hours discovering fresh jokes hidden in odd corners of the map – tundras, locusts, limits of Arctic ice, limits of decency. There was hardly any awful word-play of the *1066 and All That* kind which could not be fitted in somewhere. Schweppshire was topical when required: the Festival of Britain led to a consideration of 'curious customs at Schwepherd's Bush'. 'Sport in Schweppshire' took the reader to the Royal Mid-Schweppshire golf club; literary masterpieces included *The Schweppshire Lad*, stately homes boasted that 'Queen Elizabeth Schwept Here', and there was a splendid burlesque of country newspapers in the *Schweppshire Post*.

As time went on, and Stephen's invention was obviously flagging, Schweppshire boasted the world's leading players of the poly-omnipanhorn, a wind-instrument with several mouthpieces for 'group creation', a 'reinhibiting centre for Depsychoanalysis', and a dress-designer named Schwepparelli. It earned Stephen £1000 a year while it lasted, and it gave him a new sense of wonder as he gazed at a huge hoarding in Piccadilly bearing a map of Schweppshire: 'To think that half an hour's work by *me* results in something millions of people stop to look at!'

He was now in regular correspondence with Joe Bryan: the two men, apart from the bond of Lifemanship, shared the same kind of verbal humour; early in 1952 Stephen joined Joe and a small bunch of Americans in an all-male holiday in southern Spain. It is no use avoiding the fact that several of them, Stephen included, were slowly and for various reasons drifting apart from their wives: hence the atmosphere of irresponsible bachelordom that pervaded this vacation. Only James Burnham, Professor of Philosophy at New York University and author of such weighty works as *The Managerial Revolution* and *Suicide of the West*, had his family with him. He was, however, enough of a Lifeman to want to upset any attempts at photography. Thus, when the party explored Granada, which is some 2200 feet above sea-level and can be savagely cold in winter so that the very Fountain of Lions in the Alhambra was frozen solid, he and Joe whipped off jackets and ties so that the rest of the party appeared hopelessly overdressed, like foreign statesmen at an international conference.

They all shared the same apartment at the El Remo at Torremolinos, which was then a charming fishing village populated largely by painters. Visiting Americans, all writers, moved in and out, among them John Steinbeck and Mackinlay Kantor. In the evenings they played Scrabble, then the latest thing: being a word game it was not difficult for Stephen to win every time, quoting the *Oxford English Dictionary* and a number of imaginary authorities whenever he was accused of inventing a word.

At Malaga Airport, when Stephen arrived, Joe Bryan demonstrated a degree of Oneupmanship which completely silenced Stephen: it took advantage of Stephen's greatest weakness, his inability to cope with foreign languages. Joe had once learnt a little Spanish; but now all that remained were a few Spanish proverbs he had learnt by heart. Hearing that Stephen's plane was likely to touch down about three quarters of an hour late, he conveyed to the airport manager, Señor Murube, the fact that a most distinguished British *littérateur* was on board – he really ought to be given VIP treatment. On arrival it seemed to Stephen that Joe had the whole airport, indeed all Spain, under his thumb; for there he was, giving orders to Murube and everyone else in 'liquid Castilian'. What he was actually saying to them, striking suitable attitudes, was 'All is not gold that glitters,' 'Least said, soonest mended,' and 'There are but two families in the world, as my grandmother used to say, the Haves and the Have-Nots.'

Joe Bryan was, and is, a natural Clubman: he belongs to four clubs in America and one (Buck's) in London. He became a regular guest at the Savile Club where he learnt Savile Snooker, never having played any kind of snooker before; he took very quickly to the Savile game (which I have heard of but never actually seen) of rolling a penny down the groove in the banisters of the main staircase. He was also lured by Stephen into country walks with a botanical commentary all the way along. It was some time before he realized that Stephen was making up all the names, both English and Latin: 'Maiden's Milk', 'False Goat's Breath', 'Adam's Beard' and the Great Stinkwort (*Odor Odor*).

Back in Aldeburgh Stephen entered into the life of the festival town with enthusiasm. To Julian, now out of the Army and at Christ Church, Oxford, he wrote in May: 'The house is looking and being particularly gorgeous at the moment, and the Potter-Britten-Pears axis is in full swing – although Ben's tennis elbow unfortunately is bad for his conductor's wrist. . . .' Benjamin Britten and Peter Pears were frequent guests for tennis at the Red House: at that time they were living at a house on the sea front. Friendship with the leading young composer of the English-speaking world was enormously satisfying for Stephen; but it was rather one-sided. Britten was unimpressed by Stephen's musical conversation and did not respond to his kind of humour.

A new guest at the Red House was Edward Lydall whom Stephen had met at a drinks party in London just before Christmas. He appears in *Supermanship* as 'Edward of Albany' for reasons which will become apparent. For a man who sang the *Lieder* of Schubert and Hugo Wolf with great gusto he had an unusual background – the kind of Establishment-Man-of-Action background with hint-of-Secret-Service which Stephen greatly admired. He had been a district administrator of headhunting tribes in Assam; had done relief work in the Quetta earthquake of 1935, and had served on the North-West Frontier, dealing with the Pathans of North Waziristan during operations against the Faqir of Ipi. He had been Secretary of the British Legation in Kabul; President of the Manipur State Durbar ('roughly equivalent to Prime Minister,' he explains modestly) during the siege of Imphal by the Japanese, and player of Manipuri polo; negotiator with maharajahs during the post-war hand-over of power. He was a barrister, moreover, who became marine-law adviser to Shell and author of two highly entertaining volumes of autobiography. . . . But none of these, for Stephen, was the most fascinating thing about him. What stirred

Stephen's imagination was that Edward Lydall lived in Albany, those exclusive bachelor flats (which you must call *chambers*) where Raffles the Gentleman Crook had once lived, and where J.B.Priestley and Terence Rattigan still lived.

Lydall was aware of this: 'Stephen was always very conscious of his rather dim suburban origins, though making no secret of them and laughing at himself the while.' There was a certain amount of latent Lifemanship in Edward Lydall: 'Stephen asked about a photograph of a much-bemedalled military figure in my sitting room. "Oh, that," I said in my best throw-away manner, "that's Field-Marshal Lord Ypres – alias Uncle Jack." Stephen laughed: "I *do* wish I could say things like that!" – but really meaning it.'

Edward Lydall, a shrewd observer, was present at a lunch party at Lord Mancroft's where there were, if anything, rather too many wits. Whether it was a good idea to invite Stephen and Peter Ustinov to the same party, each being accustomed to hold the floor, is debatable; what could not be mistaken was Stephen's 'pleasure from reminding himself that local boy had in fact made good' as he 'exchanged sallies with his fellow "personality" across the table for the delectation of us ordinary mortals'. In Ustinov he recognized a talent he could not equal, 'nevertheless he could slap down people when they bored him, and I remember Gerald Barry, of Festival of Britain fame, who was rather full of himself, being firmly told: "We've already had this conversation once this weekend." '

This was at Aldeburgh, on Stephen's own ground. The Savile Club too was his own ground. Stephen had a tendency to divide people up according to the subject in which they were supposed to have specialized. Thus, Jack Hargreaves's subjects were: fishing, veterinary surgery and country life. One day at the Savile, seeing Stephen and Sir Arthur Bliss in deep discussion about music, Hargreaves, a tolerable amateur violinist, contributed a mild opinion and was given the Potter slap-down in such a manner as to exclude him from the conversation: 'Not really your subject, old boy, is it?'

Edward Lydall's first visit to the Red House was for the Aldeburgh Festival in June 1952. ' "We shall expect you at one o'clock sharp," Stephen told me. "Whatever you do don't be late." Driving furiously I managed with some difficulty to arrive on the dot to find Stephen playing a very serious game of croquet with Eddie Sackville-West. He gave me a distant wave and continued playing for another half hour. I asked him afterwards what the hurry had been and he seemed surprised at my not having recognized a routine bit of Lifemanship.'

'Stephen was a frequent visitor to my chambers, K.1 Albany,' Edward Lydall continues. 'My copy of *Gamesmanship* is inscribed "To Edward for delightful K.1-manship', and I was awarded the "Gameslife Regional ranking" of Albany 1 (world ranking 9).'

In due course Edward Lydall, already a member of the Oriental, was put up by Stephen for the Savile Club where almost everything Stephen did was construed as a ploy. 'I remember standing with him at the bar when, with a too expansive gesture, he knocked a fellow-drinker's sherry over his (the other man's) tie.

Stephen (who did not know the man): "My dear fellow, allow me to buy you another sherry."
Flustered fellow-drinker: "No, no, allow *me*. . . ."'

Lydall was thus well prepared when, in K.1 Albany, with a similar expansive gesture, Stephen knocked his own pint of beer on to the floor. 'My dear Edward,' he said, 'you must allow me to buy you a new carpet.' Knowing that he was unlikely to get any such thing Lydall suggested that they should lunch together on a don't-give-it-a-thought basis. 'This ploy,' Lydall says, 'earned me a mention under "Lydall's Reproach" in *One-Upmanship*.' Lydall also makes an appearance in *Supermanship* but gets hopelessly confused with another character named Edward Brick, who is Supertown in the town-and-country argument, but gets the best of both worlds because town has a tendency to spend weekends with country rather than vice versa.

However, Edward Lydall, on ceasing to be a bachelor, exchanged Supertown for Supercountry in the form of a Sussex farmhouse. Driving Stephen down from London for the weekend he lost the way. Stephen refused to believe it was not a ploy: 'You were very successfully giving the impression that normally your chauffeur drove you!'

On one occasion the kind of thing that usually happened to the forgetful Stephen happened instead to Edward Lydall. He had just given Stephen dinner at the Oxford and Cambridge Club and they were going up to the billiard room, glasses of port in hand, for a game of snooker. 'In the middle of the first game', Lydall says, 'it suddenly dawned on me that I had got my dates mixed up and that I should at that moment have been attending a banquet at the Cyril Rays!' Dinners given by Cyril Ray, a wine connoisseur, and his wife Elizabeth, an eloquent writer on gourmet cooking, were not to be lightly missed. 'Leave this to me!' said Stephen and accompanied Lydall to the Rays'.

' "Terrible thing!" Stephen told my host. "Car broke down the other side of Colchester!" ' To Edward, out of the corner of his mouth, he whispered: 'Don't forget – Colchester.' Pressed to dinner, which had now reached its penultimate course, Stephen politely refused: 'Must get back to Colchester.' He left Edward to eat his second dinner that evening.

Social life, as so often with Stephen, was interfering with work. He made only two radio appearances in 1952, one of them in his own burlesque 'Salute to the BBC', in which he exploded the general solemnity of the BBC's celebrations of its thirtieth anniversary with Salutes to the Governors, Salutes to the Heads of Programmes, Salutes to the Engineers, Salutes to the faceless administrators – with fanfares, marching feet, and military music galore, mostly Elgar and Bliss. Later in the year, just before the publication of *One-Upmanship*, he gave a lecture on Woman's Hour, on *Wifemanship*. But he was uneasy. Much depended on the success of *One-Upmanship*: was the vein worked out? If so, what was to take its place? A nervous letter to Rupert Hart-Davis: 'Bad news. Shrewsbury School Debating Society. The motion "That Lifemanship is more important than Life" was defeated by 95 to 65.'

One-Upmanship, when it appeared in October 1952, was prefaced with the usual acknowledgements and the mandarin dateline: 'Regent's Park – Vicenza – Aldeburgh', after a manner favoured, in his youth, by Compton Mackenzie and other must-live-abroad literary figures of the 1920s and 1930s. It also thanked the editor of the *Lancet* for 'permission to reprint', which looked like a spoof but wasn't. Indeed, Doctorship is the largest chapter in the book. He enumerates the four main types of doctor who practise 'the art of getting one-up on the patient without actually killing him', including the specialist who achieves eminence by saying, 'Alas, we don't know.' Patients suffer from the 'natural one-downness of the unclothed'; also from the kind of doctor who asks the patient about his symptoms while obviously not listening and examining other parts of the anatomy; and the 'intensely annoying ploy of treating the patient as if he were as ignorant of all anatomical knowledge as a child of four', referring to blood corpuscles as 'white fellows' and 'red chaps'. The only counter-ploy against this is to say something like, 'I am, I suppose, right in calling you Doctor?'

Stephen, all his life, was fascinated by doctors and diseases, combining this with an unusual squeamishness about actually seeing the results of illness. His chief medical crony was Doyne Bell, a paediatrician at Charing Cross Hospital and chairman of the membership committee at the Savile Club, about whom he had produced a radio feature in the series 'Professional Portraits'. Too impatient to acquire a sound working knowledge of medicine Stephen yet treasured isolated facts: half-seriously, he told a journalist, 'I take lots of technical magazines, especially the *British Medical Journal*. I've learned a special vocabulary of about fifty words and now I can shine in almost any scientific argument.'

From Doctorship the book moves on to Businessmanship which is clearly influenced by the author's luncheon with the directors of *Fortune* magazine in New York, and Committeeship, the 'art of coming into a discussion without actually understanding a word of what anybody is talking about'. Litmanship (borrowing from *The Muse in Chains*, fifteen years before), 'the art of knowing about English Literature without actually reading any books', leads on to a dreadful house-party at which old boys of Yeovil Correspondence College come back for a refresher course; and a chapter on Carmanship, the star of which is Godfrey Plaste, 'a ferociously selfish driver' who, having overtaken at the wrong moment (and possibly on the near side), waves cheerily to the driver he has overtaken in what has become known as 'Plaste's Placid Salutation'. I am told, by various observers, that Stephen, a long-distance driver of high endurance and reliability, but fairly dangerous if daydreaming (like Thurber's Walter Mitty), occasionally used Plaste's Salutation himself. Having learnt to drive in pre-Highway Code days he deeply resented back-seat driving which he countered by leaping out of the car and saying to his critic who was sometimes his wife: 'Right. *You* take over.'

And so, by way of Birdmanship (owing something to Sir Peter Scott) and Troutmanship (owing everything to Jack Hargreaves and containing a number of private jokes likely to mystify Average Reader), through Clubmanship (to be a Clubman, you must belong to at least *two* utterly different clubs, posing as a soldier in the Arts and an artist in the Military) to Winemanship. Nobody who chain-smoked as Stephen did could possibly have a true palate but he loved to have wine catalogues scattered about the floor of his study and he understood the theory of his subject; as with 'Not in the south' he provides the Lifeman with an unanswerable remark about a wine: 'Too many tramlines.' Only a cad like Joad would then rejoin with a 'What precisely do you *mean* by that?'

'There is no doubt of the man Potter's ingenuity,' said *The Times* ponderously 'and it is this that makes him so dangerous an influence in modern life. He has given to the civilised world, not a new word, but what is in essence a new language. . . . He has brought about a state of affairs which leaves no word free from the terror of having that ominous ending -*manship* tagged to it.' Like modern advertisers he is 'frightening the world into believing that, unless something or other is immediately taken, decay will set in from head to foot'. He is 'keeping up a game, which should have exhausted itself in two or three thousand words, with astonishing zest and fertility of invention'. Nevertheless, 'there are times when the orotund phraseology . . . suggests as much Potter, G., of Hogsnorton, as Potter, S., of Yeovil'.

There were not so many reviews of *One-Upmanship* as for its predecessors. Potter to Hart-Davis: 'Funds *urgently needed* for my Society for the Suppression of New Authors.' And, 'I am told on the highest authority that you think Dickins & Jones is an OK place for me to go and sign books, and I shall hold you completely responsible if this form of publicity turns into anti-publicity for the sake of selling a hundred books or so, and bearing in mind that I am basically a serious author of the T.S.Eliot type, as my future work will show.' (Is it a leg-pull or, getting understandably bored with the -*manship* lark, does he really mean it?) '. . . I do ask you most seriously to consider that you are piloting your author dangerously near the perilously un-OK seas of Eastern Oxford Street'. This refers to his unwillingness to sign copies at Bourne & Hollingsworth; he did in the end oblige but was plagued by customers who, instead of buying *One-Upmanship*, brought him old copies of *Gamesmanship* to sign so that they could boast for ever after that they had outwitted the Founder.

'*One-Upmanship* is going very well,' Stephen wrote to Julian who was now at Oxford, 'and another ten thousand making a total of fifty are on order from the printer. But no ancillary gambits [film and television rights] have progressed at all.' *One-Upmanship* in fact sold over 71,000 copies in Britain and over 57,000 in America (in each case less than *Lifemanship* but still a relative best-seller).

There now came a lull. To Rupert Hart-Davis Stephen wrote in March 1953:

I must talk to you very soon about the possibility of a mid-autumn book [allowing himself and Rupert six months from start to publication!] – I have been doing a fair amount of work on my diaries – doing one bit from 1936 and one bit from 1940, for instance, with the idea of showing the result to you for your comments. . . . However, in the last fortnight I have been completely absorbed for the first time in my life in a Story with a Plot. In fact, the plot is the best thing about it at the moment. I seriously think this is the best bet for an autumn book. It is a light theme but seriously treated. . . . I have always hoped my fifties would be the time when I really started writing. Perhaps this is it. Perhaps it is not. . . . I have great hopes of my book of Collected Criticism with lots and lots of new and rewritten stuff, but this cannot be for the autumn. I think whatever happens I must write this novel first.

He adds, without a trace of humour, 'the basic situation is connected with golf'. Unfortunately the masterpiece has not survived.

There is another idea which he does not mention. A publisher, Max Reinhardt, had suggested that he edit, with connecting commentary, an anthology of humour: mainly, of course, English humour. It would one day form the basis of hectic lecture tours in America. For this he enlisted the help of his old friend Lionel Millard. In May 1952 he had written to Lionel:

Will you spend the time you have during the next fortnight exclusively on the Humour project? What it looks like now . . . is an evolution of British Humour, i.e. what sort of things we laugh at and why. . . . Besides keeping a general look-out for samples as widely-ranging as possible, you might think out such headings as Puns, and when did they come in. When did we stop laughing at hunchbacks on the stage is another pregnant theme. When did the A.A.Milne 'Edwin and Angelina were the names of our two favourite ants' start?

Three months later the project seems to be taking shape: 'We have got really to make a compromise between the two aims of (a) historical completeness and (b) a book which is complete in itself without the historical interest.'

Stephen's private life was now in two halves: Heather and Att,

London and Aldeburgh. There are various reasons for making new friendships and one of them is that the new friends are in the same situation as oneself. Stephen had met Jack Broome through Ronald Simpson and the Garrick Club and all three men belonged to the Stage Golfing Society. Ronald Simpson's marriage was firm: Stephen's and Jack's were not.

Captain Jack Broome, DSC, had commanded the famous PQ17 convoy, twenty-five square miles of ships, British and American merchantmen carrying tanks, planes and supplies to Russia in the Second World War. By an error it had been thought at the Admiralty that Germany's last great battleship, *Tirpitz*, was about to attack it. The convoy, ordered to 'scatter', was an easy prey to German aircraft which sent twenty-three merchantmen to the bottom of the Barents Sea in the Arctic Circle. Eleven got through to Russia. It was, in Churchill's words, 'one of the most melancholy naval episodes in the whole of the war'. Stephen admired Jack Broome as a man of action and was impressed by his DSC and his versatility.

Broome had joined the Navy at fourteen and gone up to Cambridge in 1922. He was a skilful and irreverent caricaturist and soon became art editor of *Granta*. He claims responsibility for the magazine's most notorious headline, which was extremely shocking for 1923: 'Don Says May Week is All Balls.' He was also at the centre of the famous Tutankhamun Rag in which an effigy of the Pharaoh was buried and disinterred at the underground lavatory in Market Square. Having thus distinguished himself – it was the kind of background Stephen loved – he returned to the Navy as a submariner. He was now, in 1953, editor of the *Sketch*, a companion glossy magazine to the *Tatler* and *Illustrated London News*. As he had to be his own dramatic critic this qualified him for the Stage Golfing Society.

Jack Broome and Stephen played level, both having at this time a handicap of ten, and both were members of Moor Park and Woking. But it was at Walton Heath, on a winter's day in a biting east wind, that Stephen felt one-down playing with him. Stephen wore bulky, restricting, warm clothes, including a golf jacket that spoilt his swing; but Jack, in an open-necked tee-shirt, appeared to be wearing very little underneath. Stephen, who prided himself on his hardiness, was perplexed. At Sunningdale he had used his 'squeaky trolley' ploy; at Woking, on a steep slope up to the green, his 'old ticker', walking in zig-zags to lessen the gradient; but now he was put off to the extent of losing the game by four holes. Jack Broome was in fact wearing two layers of silk underwear, socks and sawn-off socks as mittens. 'The all-silk tip came from a bomber pilot I had flown with. I instantly adopted his theory that clobbering yourself with thick heavy clothes restricted your mobility, comfort and ultimately your circulation. "Insulate with thin layers," he advocated. My next layer was a pair of silk pyjamas with a jumper – *not* button-up – top.'

At the Stage Golfing Society dinner that year, in the company of Frank Lawton, Alan Melville, Anthony Kimmins, Ronald Simpson and other actors and barristers, Stephen met, for the second time, another naval figure he greatly admired, Prince Philip.

Another distraction from worry, especially worry about the conflicts of his private life, was provided by what Stephen calls, in his diaries, 'flirtations'. They happened all through his life, usually when the girls concerned were in love with someone else and it was all going wrong, or when Stephen himself was in a similar situation or had had some career disappointment. There is no evidence that 'flirtation' meant anything deeper than a bubbling atmosphere of laughter, talk and a kind of Noël Coward dialogue. Often the girls were invited to Aldeburgh as friends of the family. They were usually tall, blonde and half Stephen's age. There had been one or two at the BBC. There had been another during his time at the *Leader* magazine. Waving goodbye to his colleagues at Hulton Press he had ushered a tall blonde into a taxi and struck a theatrical attitude, saying, 'We've both decided it can't go on any longer. We're going to the Savoy to break it off amid tears and laughter.'

'One of my greatest pleasures,' he had told his diary on 4 January 1945 (and it sounds as if 'meet more pretty girls' was a kind of New Year resolution),

which I have been having one or two goes at lately – is going about with a beautiful and intelligent woman – in this case Peggy Scott . . . we chatter for an hour hard – and I ask her about her 'coronet lunch' with Bert. [The fact that she is admired by the Duke of Norfolk obviously adds to her attractiveness.] I don't know why I like it – but if she's nice and handsome it's like an hour in the sun at the seaside, or walking along the front up to Splash Point. I steer her to the Leicester Gallery where there is a private show of John Piper. . . .

He is delighted to be able to show her off to the fashionable crowd, among whom are G.B. Stern the novelist, his old friend Gwen Herbert, Robert Speaight the actor, Stephen Spender ('very laughing and noble and yet beginning to look slightly moulting') and Sir Osbert and Edith Sitwell: 'The Sitwells are presiding as if it was *their* party . . . he gives me a dignified greeting. . . . Edith, sitting, tells how G.B. Stern has just been mistaken for Mrs Patrick Campbell. . . . I tell Peggy what to say about the pictures but I think she knows plenty. . . .' He had hoped that Peggy (Margaretta Scott) might appear in a play he had written; but the Tom Arnold management had rejected it.

He had known Doone Beal since his wartime days at the BBC where she had been a Junior Programme Engineer which meant anything from sound effects to choosing incidental music. Doone, now Lady Marley and a well-known travel writer, not only fulfilled his 'nice and handsome' criteria but was also a good golfer. 'To me, at twenty,' she recalls, 'he represented total sophistication. He was full of interest and sympathy, he had a kind of "life force" that I found wonderfully stimulating. And it was flattering to be taken seriously by an older man.'

To Elizabeth Jane Howard, the novelist, he was always the lovable 'funny man' she had known in childhood. 'He had, in his fifties, a young man's idea of a perfect day – tennis, and perhaps swimming too, at Hurlingham, followed by dancing to Carroll Gibbons at the Savoy in evening dress. His energy was tremendous – not easy to keep up with.' At Hurlingham Stephen wore a smart blazer; for younger girls, it seemed, he had an idealized self which needed to be uncharacteristically well dressed as he would like to have been in the twenties and thirties – for which he had recurrent bouts of nostalgia. One or two members of the Savile noticed it. 'You look very distinguished today,' one remarked to him. 'Distinguished from what?' Stephen snapped, and made for the snooker table without waiting for a reply.

Elizabeth Jane Howard, like Wynford Vaughan-Thomas and many other pianists of the required standard, was pressed into the famous duets on one piano: if it wasn't Bach organ music arranged for two pianos it was four-handed versions of Beethoven symphonies. Stephen's favourite was the slow movement of no. 7. She also took her place in the Lifemanship hierarchy. Having written him a bread-and-butter letter thanking him for an evening out, using *his* headed writing paper, not hers, she was appointed 'Marylebone One'.

Major 'public appearances' were not many; Stephen was perhaps unwisely accepting too many badly paid or unpaid invitations to address student audiences – the laughter which started as soon as he had uttered the words 'Mr Chairman' or 'Mr President' was reassuring. One he never forgot was at the London School of Economics where he addressed a packed meeting on Oneupmanship. About halfway through an elegant, rather un-LSE, young man entered the lecture theatre and interrupted the proceedings to ask very politely: 'Would Mr Potter be kind enough to give me a summary of what he has been saying so far? I had an important engagement elsewhere and I've only just got here.' Amid general laughter and applause Stephen gracefully conceded defeat.

A more serious 'Lit.' lecture was given at Dartington Hall in August 1953. 'Getting a lovely dose of the wonderful atmosphere of progressive 1925-ness gone slightly to decay,' he wrote to Muriel, 'all slightly faded and crumbling.' And the following month he did a programme of chosen music in a radio series called 'I Know What I Like'. But he still lacked regular employment; was still working on ideas whose future was uncertain. Fame, he was discovering, did not automatically bring solvency.

Probably the most enjoyable occasion of the year for him was giving away prizes at Muriel's school in November. Muriel, now fifty-nine, was due to retire in a year's time. She had built up South Hampstead High School into one of the best girls' day schools in the country, widening the curriculum by introducing biology, cookery, economics, civics and current affairs, and giving the school a new academic standing. She had introduced a biennial Festival of Art, Music and Diction; the school had produced a number of actresses, among them Lilian Braithwaite and Gwen Ffrangcon-Davies; in Muriel's time it produced Glynis Johns, Miriam Karlin and Stephen's god-daughter, Angela Lansbury. She had somehow, during the War, run a school in two parts, separated by nearly thirty miles, one half of it having been evacuated to Berkhamsted to accommodate the Auxiliary Fire Service. Hampstead was full of refugees from Nazi Germany and Muriel had instituted combined Christian and Jewish religious studies and joint prayers.

Muriel, always the Good, even Great, Headmistress, had watched her young brother's progress with mingled pride and misgiving. At this time, in late 1953, she was sorting through her collection of family letters and making voluminous notes for Stephen's projected autobiography. He habitually sent her untidy drafts of his books for criticism which she dispensed with a kind of tactful severity. She was quick to pounce on Americanisms, suburbanisms like saying *ladies* instead of *women*, and some of his own less happy neologisms such as *vomitty*. Occasionally they had argumentative rows which Stephen called 'having a good clear-out with Muriel'. Now, in her last year at South Hampstead, she had invited him to preside at speech day. (She had already had Joyce Grenfell who astonished the school by doing one of her sketches.)

Stephen began his speech absent-mindedly by saying 'Of course, I was taught English by Sir Walter Raleigh,' which was received with gales of laughter until he explained that the name had been shared by two great men; he went on to say in all sincerity that he 'owed his love of literature' to Muriel's 'guidance and example'. He recalled meeting an Old Girl who had asked him: 'Are you really Stephen Potter?' Stephen, bracing himself for gushing admiration, said he was, but was cut down to size when the Old Girl said, 'Oh, I'm so glad to meet Miss Potter's *brother*.'

To Muriel next day he wrote: 'I must send you a letter to tell you how much I enjoyed coming up to Hampstead and how extremely proud I was to be some kind of help to you. . . . If ever you want any support or help on any occasion of any sort in the future, do for heaven's sake remember your bro.'

Chapter 12
Division

The winter of 1953–4 was severe, most of all on the East Coast. Stephen to Muriel, after she has sent him his usual birthday cheque:

The older I get, the more delightful actual solid cash is to receive . . . it is really absolutely sweet of you to send it. We are standing up to the cold, though not all of the plugs are quite in working order. During the day I don't much move outside my study which has central heating, a log fire and an electric stove. . . . I think there is only one person who ever thought I was extra special beside yourself, and that was my friend Edgar Lansbury; and as he is dead it is absolutely essential that you should go on having this opinion. I won't tell you the truth till I am at my dying gasp. . . .

I have just finished the book on the English Sense of Humour, and following my usual practice on these occasions I am spending a fortnight on a film script which will almost certainly prove abortive. . . .

Musical life at Aldeburgh, however, goes gently on: 'On Friday we are rehearsing for the Music Club Bach Cantata, and I am singing bass with Martin the chemist, Att is singing alto, Ben [Britten] is playing the viola and Peter [Pears] is (very badly) playing the piano. The menace is Mrs Y—, who has a nice soprano voice which unpredictably goes treble strength, and everybody starts to giggle.'

Muriel's good opinion would, in the next few months, have its greatest test. Whatever happened to Stephen's marriage, the world, and Muriel most of all, would blame him. How much she knew or guessed it is impossible to say. Visiting Julian at Oxford for Eights Week, he took Heather with him. 'I'm bringing that nice Mrs Cox,' he told Julian.

Sense of Humour was published in the awkward month of July when prestige books which are too early for Christmas are not expected to become best-sellers. It is a highly organized work of criticism, a kind of connected anthology which seeks to embrace all the humour in English literature and drama and relate it to all known theories of laughter. It is Stephen being scholarly but also coming dangerously close to the kind of Eng. Lit. criticism which he had mocked in *The Muse in Chains*. The book is divided rather portentously into The Theme, Funniness by Theory, The Irrelevance of Laughter, The Great Originator (Chaucer, of course), The Theme Illustrated, and so on.

Stephen postulated 'The English Reflex': humour is a special English thing: 'Most people who deliberately make humorous remarks have *no* humour in the special English sense.' Moreover, 'the day of English humour is declining': *Punch* is getting acid after eighty years of alkali. But this only applies to the middle class and above, and he quotes Taine's *Notes on England* on the 'grim savagery and gloom' of Cockney humour, such as Sam Weller's ability to make tragedy ludicrous: 'It's over and can't be helped – as they always say in Turkey, ven they cuts the wrong man's head off.'

In the days of Hazlitt (on the English Comic Writers) and Leigh Hunt (on Wit and Humour) the 'English Sense of Humour' cult had not yet begun. When *did* it begin? The question is never satisfactorily answered. With Bergson, he analyses *Le Rire*; with Freud, Wit and the Unconscious. Louis Cazamian, of the Sorbonne, found humour as early as *Beowulf*. At what point did 'laughing *at*' become 'laughing *with*'? Perhaps J.B.Priestley, in *English Humorists* (1929), had come nearest to a workable analysis – and he approached humour with an enthusiasm which critics seem to have lost. Priestley's own humour is based soundly on observation of character.

We laugh, Stephen finds, only in company (really?). We laugh at things because they are familiar, or again because they are *un*familiar. Only a few centuries ago 'we laughed to see a lunatic on the end of a chain, or a bear tied to a post and bitten to death by dogs'. Now 'we pride ourselves on laughing at our own idiosyncrasies'. We laugh loudly when we are unsure of ourselves; with relief after escaping physical danger; at funny hats; at sex jokes. 'We do not laugh at sex jokes if they are not funny, unless other people are present' – say, in a music-hall audience. 'We laugh even at bad sex jokes if we are young and virginal, to show we are not young and virginal.' Laughter is mainly release; but humour can have a poker face (like all Stephen's own humour).

Humour needs gentleness and 'seeing both sides'; thus Professor Walter Raleigh had spoken of the 'china blue eye' of Chaucer. And, after Chaucer, humour does not really reappear for 300 years. The awful wordplay of Shakespeare's clowns and the enormous footnotes that have been written about them, and Ben Jonson's *Comedy of Humours*, have nothing to do with humour. Was the new Age of Humour born with Addison and Steele? Swift is savage, Fielding is comic, Goldsmith is a buffoon – and Stephen elects Sterne the first great humorist of the eighteenth century. Boswell, often ragged by Johnson for lacking humour, has yet the humour of observation: 'To avoid any appearance of servility, he whistled as he walked out of the room, to show his independency.' So to Lamb, the first completely conscious Sense-of-Humour Man; and Dickens, paving the way for modern humour; and – surprisingly – Shaw, as the climax of the age of English humour. Humour is seen to contain elements of good manners and sportsmanship.

Stephen's 'personal choice' of humour includes the unintentional humour of McGonagall's verse and a car instruction manual, a connoisseur's collection of 'unnecessary footnotes', old Victorian advertisements, Hugh Walpole's letters to Arnold Bennett, the wartime radio romp 'ITMA', the crossword puzzle clues of Torquemada in the *Observer* ('evading the issue' = birth control; 'S.O.S.' = naughtinesses; 'Heggs' = exasperated), Edward Lear's insects (*nasticreechia Krorluppia*), the hilarity, to English ears, of foreign translation (*Hasenfamilie Plumps* = Flopsy Bunnies), the spoof-exam papers from *1066 and All That* ('Do not attempt to write on both sides of the paper at once'), Peter Ustinov's vintage collection of clichés of stage dialogue, James Agate's account of a grand piano that was too big to get into the Concert Hall at Broadcasting House. . . . The conclusion is that 'Observation is the secret of the English Sense of Humour'; *The Diary of a Nobody* is 'the greatest work of humour since Dickens'; and, on the way, we have met all the Potter enthusiasms and reminiscences of all his life's reading.

In this 'personal selection' there are strange omissions – dangerous in anything of an anthological nature. What, no early Evelyn Waugh? the reader exclaims crossly; and Stephen's reply is 'No, because I was a Huxley man.' What, no Sydney Smith? No Disraeli? No Wilde? But these are classified as wits, not humorists. No Wodehouse? No Peacock? No Jane Austen, even? The book contains riches and is still a splendid selection to disagree with. Norman Shrapnel, in the *Guardian*, hinted nastily that it might all have been 'designed to show how much funnier Stephen Potter is'. Raymond Mortimer, in *The Sunday Times*, lamented his inability to laugh at many of the examples quoted. 'Perhaps', he ended, in a sly dig at Schweppshire, 'perhaps my Schwense of humour is defischwent.'

To Rupert Hart-Davis Stephen sent a copy inscribed: 'Dear Rupert, – You may find one or two of the extracts new to you and amusing. The Introduction you must read at the rate of 2 pages a day for prep.' Earlier he had written a rather embarrassed letter to Rupert explaining that 'there has to be this pause before the next Potter-Rupert book. I am dashing off ['wrestling with' would have been more accurate] a small collection of humour . . . long promised for Max Reinhardt. I am against anthologies of humour as a class, so I don't think you will be sorry to miss that one! . . . Decks will soon be cleared for these great lit. works, the dates of which future lit. students will be required to know for Matric.'

The book sold nearly 9000 copies in Britain and under 5000 in America: not impressive sales, by the standards of the *Games/Lifemanship* books, but it was not addressed to a comparable readership. It gave him material for future lecture tours, however, which certainly produced more financial reward than his book royalties.

Sense of Humour had been written during a year of 'harrowing personal events' as he put it in his diary. There had been a symptom of this during a weekend at the Red House when Stephen, playing 'acrimonious bridge' in which he was partnered by a very distinguished lady civil servant, revoked. She, being dummy, asked at the end of the hand, 'Had you no hearts, partner?' Stephen flew into a sudden, uncharacteristic rage: 'Why can't you keep your —— ing mouth shut?' The game, and the weekend, broke up in disorder.

His refuge, as always, was the Savile Club. J. W. Lambert of *The Sunday Times* recalls a morning 'in the rather gloomy room facing Brook Street'. The two men, though they frequently broadcast together, were not close friends. 'Stephen came in and pottered restlessly about. . . . The usual grunted greetings passed between us.' At length Lambert asked, 'What's up? You seem a bit *distrait*.' Stephen replied that he was worrying about his marriage and thought he was 'probably going to leave his wife Mary [Att] and set

up with someone else. He must have been under considerable
pressure to have said this, since we were not at all on such
confidential terms.'

By the beginning of 1955 it had happened. On 4 February
Stephen wrote Muriel his usual birthday thank-you letter, adding:

I miss Att and Aldeburgh constantly – love seeing Att as I do almost once a
week. . . . I am also at least as much in love with Heather as ever, and she has
shown new powers of being able to share my life . . . and accept my
celebrated shortcomings. . . . It seems to me still that I did the right and
only possible thing, according to my perhaps strange standards, so far as the
total happiness of the world is concerned.

A temporary escape presented itself: a six-week tour of America to
collect material for commissioned radio scripts, articles and a
possible book on American golf Gamesmanship. Out on the *Queen
Mary*, back on the *Queen Elizabeth*, first class both ways. On the
outgoing voyage Heather came with him. They sailed on 10 March,
arriving on the 14th. For the next few weeks Stephen lived in a blaze
of publicity such as he had never known in Britain, most of it
organized by Holts, his American publishers, who could even get
him tickets for *The Pajama Game*. New York papers were full of the
Mickey Jelke living-on-immoral-earnings case, the romance of
Princess Margaret and Peter Townsend, and any available detail
about Winston Churchill. Disc-jockeys recommended songs
'because Princess Meg is fond of them', and when the divorced
Anthony Eden became Prime Minister the New York *Mirror* asked,
'Will This Ease Way for Meg?'

Stephen lunched at Sardi's with Francis Brown, literary editor of
the *New York Times*; he met his old friend Commander Ted
Whitehead of Schweppes, who took him and Heather to the Stork
Club and El Morocco. By the 'incredibly unbusinesslike' Nebula
Airline he flew to Augusta, Georgia, to see the famous golf-course
designed by 'little Bobby Jones the Great . . . greatest world golfer,
now paralyzed below the waist, living beside it and riding over the
course in an electric chair'. He noted the 'wittily-placed water-
hazards', and the fact that each hole was named after a flower.

At Palm Beach he watched the Pro-Amateur Competition at
Seminole; then, window-shopping on Worth Avenue, noted 'loo
seats with pictures of poodles on them' and nylon underpants with
pictures of ants on them. On to New Orleans where he saw a strip-
show, did *not* dine at Antoine's but drank *sazarac* (whisky, in a glass

rubbed round with absinthe) and heard 'Snookums Mathews playing Dixieland'. He was, he admitted, 'doing' America 'at ten times the speed of an American doing Europe'.

In Washington he recorded (in a letter to Muriel) his astonishment that the Senate was even more disorderly than the House of Commons: 'As the speaker speaks, everybody talks animatedly and quite loudly about other things to everybody else.' He 'felt proud' of the Lincoln Memorial and uncomfortable at the Washington Memorial which was 'so sacred' that there was 'a complete absence of loos'. He stayed for some days with Hugh Troy, the park-bench joker, noting how many of the Troys' friends seemed to work at the Navy Office which was presumably a cover for the CIA. But the high spot of Washington was Burning Tree, Eisenhower's golf-course, to which Stephen was driven by Phil Graham, owner of the *Washington Post*. Burning Tree, which struck him as 'rather like Woking', gave Stephen a Gamesmanship idea – the 'celebrated member ploy' by which guests are made to feel that the President is playing just behind them.

Back in New York there were more press and radio interviews: one, with Clifton Fadiman and television star Henry Morgan, was an extempore conversation on 'if I had six months to live'. Another, for which he had to get up at 5.30 am, was on the early-morning television programme 'Today': a routine interview on Gamesmanship, eight years after the book's publication. He went up the UN building and down to Harlem; listened to serious jazz at Birdland, and visited the Metropolitan Museum of Modern Art; and then, arranged subtly by the old-girl network of New York hostesses, Stephen went to the 'most famous, most beautiful, most difficult' golf-course, Pine Valley, near Philadelphia. Here he found himself playing with the president of the club, was overawed, played badly, and lost.

On 6 April Heather returned to London. Stephen wandered aimlessly about Broadway, felt suddenly alone, and wrote to sister Muriel: 'I don't know whether I feel too much or not enough, whether I am weak or strong, right or wrong. . . . Att divorced me on April 1st and then shook off the atmosphere of the law courts by going to look at some reviving pictures at the National Gallery. . . . We both expected it not to happen till July.'

There was another interview on *Gamesmanship* by Dave Garroway; dinner with Victor Gollancz, both as guests of the New

York PEN Club; lunch at the 21 with Al Wright of *Sports Illustrated*; a glorious 'weekend in the country with the Raymond Masseys; and a meeting with "my old acquaintance Alistair Cooke" ', whom he watched recording some of his talks, admiring the 'getting-on-with-it professionalism and lack of loose ends' of 'The Good Journalist' – something Stephen himself would never be. He visited the Stock Exchange, and a baseball match (Giants *v.* Dodgers) with Walter Cronkite, and had dinner with Bennett Cerf and George Kaufman; then, since he was due to sail for England next day, a typical Potter last-minute rush, with no Heather to take care of the organization – sitting up all night writing two articles, one on Reviewmanship for the *New York Times*, the other on Golf Gamesmanship for *Sports Illustrated*, dictating each next morning to a secretary at the office concerned, literally running about New York because the traffic was too thick for taxis. All his money was spent so he had to ask his publisher, Henry Holt, for a loan to be stopped out of his US royalties.

Yet somehow, between articles, he found time to write to Muriel in answer to her criticisms of him: 'Brilliant girl! You are utterly right in your diagnosis. Late in growing up – and there is a *chance* that all this may do the trick . . . though I don't know whether anyone in a tidal wave can really congratulate himself on the course he is taking. . . .' On the homeward *Queen Elizabeth* he looked at the passenger list and saw the name of 'my old acquaintance and occasional golf opponent Lady Astor'. Her first words to him were, 'I hear you've been making a fool of yourself again [meaning his remarriage] – my friends are all lunatics – and you say you've been playing on golf courses, and that's *work* ?' Walking round the ship with her he was embarrassed by her gratuitous advice to total strangers, especially mothers: 'You ought to play with that child more. It doesn't know what to do.' At Southampton Nancy Astor and Stephen posed with three Salvation Army people for news pictures. Pointing to Stephen, Nancy said, 'That's the one whose soul you ought to save.'

On 15 May he wrote an embarrassed little letter, in the Savile Club, to Muriel: 'Heather and I are getting married next Friday the 20th at Chelsea Registry Office, extremely non-publicly and with only about three people present.' But newspapers keep tabs on all West London registry offices and reporters were not slow to quote Heather Jenner's book, *Marriage is My Business*, to point out that she had arranged 5000 successful marriages and to suggest that she herself had been hooked by Stephen's Woomanship, in particular by the 'chipped glasses or Oddsox Ploy', i.e., the endearing sloppiness that is said to arouse maternal instinct.

Stephen was now broadcasting again fairly regularly and his abrasive voice was especially well known on 'The Critics', a weekly review of the arts, in which he usually covered radio. J.W.Lambert of *The Sunday Times*, who sometimes chaired the discussion but generally covered drama, has described the Potter technique on this programme:

He was never backward in seeking means to make a fellow-panellist feel at a loss. In my case this usually took the form of getting my name wrong. Instead of referring to me as Jack Lambert, the usual procedure after the initial reference to J.W.Lambert, he would often (on one occasion, I remember, three times in one programme) refer to me as J.S., J.R., W.J., even R.S. (a wonderful confusion – R.S.Lambert was the name of a pre-War editor of the *Listener* who was a sceptical student of psychical research) – anything but J.W. Because we were all very good-humoured, I don't think I was much thrown by this.

There is even a possibility that Stephen, notoriously bad at remembering names and faces, may have genuinely got the initials wrong. Anyway, Lambert occasionally hit back by referring to Stephen as 'P. C. Potter'.

The name of Samuel Beckett was, in 1955, known to only a few people. When, on Sunday, 24 August, 'The Critics' discussed *Waiting for Godot*, just produced at the Arts Theatre Club, Stephen did a public *volte-face*, his own hatred of the play overwhelmed by the majority opinion against him. Lambert began by outlining the plot: 'Two filthy tramps sit by the roadside, waiting for Godot, passing the time as best they can, quarrelling, making up, day-dreaming, sleeping. Who is Godot? . . . Godot is what you will, or rather what you wish for – every man's secret and hopeless hope. . . .' He found the play 'wonderfully successful – tremendously funny, deeply sad'.

Paul Dehn, the film man, thought it would create 'a minor revolution in the theatre'. Colin MacInnes, the art man, said he 'could have gone on listening to it for ever'. G.S.Fraser, the book man, thought it 'a play of profound religious symbolism' – the tree on the stage obviously stood for the Cross. . . .

Stephen, despite being bound by his classical Eng. Lit. background, threw away his prepared notes:

I've been silent so far because an extraordinary thing has been happening to me. . . . For the first time on record my opinion has been somewhat changed by the opinions of the other critics. [Laughter] I thought it was a masterpiece of production – beautifully acted . . . a very refreshing change from the average West-End play where, as I think Shaw used to say, 'a series of milliners' and tailors' advertisements sit on a set of upholsterers' advertisements'. But I didn't at the time appreciate the depths of the symbolism. . . . I thought the play had no real centre – it's exactly like Peer Gynt's onion. . . .

Lambert (getting his revenge for months of wrong initials) said, 'That seems to me practically the whole point of it.'

A short holiday in the south of France with Heather, her children and Julian, and Stephen was ready for America again. This second visit of 1955 happened because Stephen had chanced to mention to Bennett Cerf, of Random House, that he was returning in October to give a lecture at the Institute of Contemporary Arts in Washington. 'Only *one* lecture?' Cerf said incredulously; then spoke into one of the many machines on his desk: 'Get me Bob Keedick.' (Stephen loved to imitate this: he would pick up any telephone anywhere and bark into it, 'Get me Beirut,' or Canberra, or Buckingham Palace.) Bob Keedick, who stood 6ft 7ins high, was a lecture-tour arranger. So began the breathless life of Potter the Lecturer, seeing America even faster than before.

He was to speak in Washington on the dangerous subject of 'English and American Humour Compared'. He was extremely nervous. ('Edith Sitwell and Aldous Huxley are to follow me next month.') 'Keep it gay, keep it light,' advised Robert Richman, secretary of the ICA. 'Speak slowly or they won't understand you.' At the last moment a journalist from the *Washington Post* appeared and took him out for an unwise last-minute drink. In the lecture hall Stephen was appalled to see several members of the League of Washington Gamesmen: prominent among them were Hugh Troy and Joe Bryan III. Washington, even in October, is hot by English standards and Stephen's glasses steamed over so that he could not read his notes. At the end Hugh Troy stood up and asked, 'Would the lecturer please tell us why he is appearing in costume?' (That is, dressed like an American, not in the American idea of English clothes.) 'It is surely considered proper,' Stephen retorted, 'when

visiting foreign countries, to follow the customs of the aborigines.'
Polite laughter. Next morning the *Washington Post* carried the
treacherous headline: 'POTTER (UGH! WHAT A BORE) STARTS
ON ANOTHER LECTURE TOUR'.

Joe Bryan organized another Gamesmanship dinner; there was
Sunday lunch at Dean Acheson's with Sir Oliver Franks, until
recently British Ambassador to Washington, and an evening of
terror when Mrs Hugh Troy choked on her dinner and was escorted
by Stephen to hospital in a police car at 75 mph, sirens howling;
then he left for New York. This time Heather was not with him and
he was lonely. He appeared on Alistair Cooke's television
programme, wrote an article for *Holiday* on London clubs, and
lunched with Al Schacht, baseball player and restaurateur. . . .
Then he went on a long journey to Ohio in one of those 'chapels of
peace', a 'roomette' in a main-line train where he was looked after
by an elderly negro waiter who kept saying 'I've got more'n I kin
do.'

His next lecture was at Oberlin College near the beautifully
named town of Elyria whose derivation was a philological defeat for
him. His lecture was delivered in the College chapel to a responsive
student audience among whom was a tall middle-aged negro in a
tuxedo: it was Duke Ellington whose band was the next 'turn'.
Stephen's lecture was free but the Duke cost a dollar. Pausing only
to play a round of golf with an Oxford graduate who was teaching
the organ at Oberlin he moved on seventy miles to a women's club
lunch at Canton: a failure – they took it all seriously and there were
no belly-laughs of the kind he was able to get from students.

He had chosen a roundabout route to Vancouver, his next
destination, via Cleveland and Toronto, because he wanted to see
the Great Lakes from the air (a marvellous experience of which
supersonic and stratospheric air travel has robbed us for ever); also
to satisfy a boyhood ambition to ride on the Canadian Pacific
Railway, looking out upon endless prairie (and going without a
drink for two days while crossing the 'dry' state of Alberta),
followed by the grandeur of the Rockies, all seen from an
'observation dome'. Welcomed at Vancouver by a Professor
Binning of the University of British Columbia, Stephen felt, in his
studio, a sudden nostalgia for Att, engendered by 'the stimulating
smells of Chinese White and Yellow Ochre, in which, for a quarter
of a century, married to an artist, I lived myself'. The lecture, given

to students while they were eating their sandwich lunch, was, as nearly always with his student audiences, a success.

By train to Portland, Oregon: a journey marred by two Potter proclivities, starting too late for the station and forgetting that, to re-enter the USA from Canada, he needed his passport which was packed in one of his two large battered suitcases, both of which had to be searched in three minutes to find it.

The lecture at Reed College, Portland, was to a wary audience, very Gameslife-conscious, of mixed students and teaching staff: he got his biggest laugh, unintentionally, by the wrong word-order of a sentence: 'Our *Punch*, like Reed College, was once highly progressive. Later it became pompous.' There was a good deal of attempted out-gambitting and Stephen was ignominiously floored by a Cambridge-trained philosophy tutor with the question: 'How can a school of philosophy flourish without at least one neo-Hegelian?' It was one of those few remarks which could not be countered with 'But not in the south.' However, various dons and their wives were appointed Oregon (East) I and so on, in the World Lifemanship hierarchy.

He had been told by a Reed student that his next place of call, the University of Portland at Eugene, centre of the lumber industry, was 'a sort of playground'. Here he was one-upped by the English professor, Robert D. Horn. Talking about bad poems Stephen quoted the anonymous 'Think of Three Hundred Gentlemen at Least', written in 1704 in honour of the battle of Blenheim.

Horn: 'As a matter of fact, you're misquoting it.'
Potter: 'But I got it out of Macaulay.'
Horn: 'He misquotes it too.'
Potter: 'Does anyone know who wrote it?'
Horn: 'Well, yes,' and he gravely produced a first edition, 'I think it's the only one in existence.'

Stephen took the next few days as holiday, typically cramming every possible experience into them. Sacramento, California; then a taxi-tour of San Francisco; finally a long-awaited flight to Las Vegas, 'this comic little hell of time-wasting and gloomy hypnotised squint-brains . . . laid bare under the eye of a sarcastic God'. Should he one-up everyone by *not* gambling? At least nobody before him had ever gone out into the desert to find botanical specimens. In the end gambling *did* get him, in a spirit of scientific inquiry, as he tried, by telepathy or telekinesis in the J.B.Rhine style, to *will* a coin or a ball or dice to come up with the right numbers. He found that it works, until your will-power gets tired, and ended up $25 to the good.

He went to Phoenix, Arizona, to be entertained by friends of San Francisco friends, and to play golf on the beautiful Paradise Valley course where the hazards include cacti to one side and rattlesnakes to the other; and so to New Orleans, his third visit. Here the lecture, to a mixed audience of town and gown at Tulane University, in a half-empty auditorium, was a hollow flop. He was consoled by golf, especially by his successful ploy of showing more attentiveness to opponents' wives, in picking up their holed putts and golf-bags for them, than their American partners or husbands did. And he had time to absorb some of the weaknesses of American primary education – 'play education', 'doing things' rather than being able to read or to write a grammatical sentence in your own language – and a complaint from a child at school in England after beginning its education in America, 'Why do we have those nasty *lessons*?'

In Kansas City all was success: a fifty-minute talk to 2000 students, loudly applauded, was followed by a faculty dinner for 150 people whom he was invited to address on anything he liked. Largely improvised, his talk developed into a discussion of 'Small Differences between the United States and Great Britain': language, pronunciation, intonation; democratic attitudes; food, comfort, elections; the different meanings of the word 'provincial'; competitiveness; and the perils of the phrase 'Anglo-American Relations'. At the end of it all, a solemn little man – presumably the Hugh Troy of Kansas City – stood up and asked: 'What is the chief difference between the English and American way of making love?' (Think fast, Potter.) 'The English are more romantic, the Americans more hygienic.' Tremendous laughter.

In Chicago he made the round of various friends, many of them introduced through Joe Bryan III. He noted his chief impression: no gangsters but lots of picture galleries and private collections of Picassos and Klees. Socially Stephen put his foot in it only once: he said he loved New Orleans jazz.

We shall never know at which Middle-West town Stephen was introduced to a women's club thus: 'I expect a lot of you think that the English have no sense of humour. But wait till you hear Mr Potter.' Something of the kind happened at the University of Illinois, Urbana – another 2000-student lecture where all went well and vociferously. Stephen says little about it in his diary but fortunately we have an eye-witness anecdote from one of the students:

As I recall, the head of the English department introduced Mr Potter with the remark that he had never understood English humour and sometimes doubted its existence. The professor illustrated his view: he had heard someone telling the old joke about the male robin who, upon finding a brown egg in his nest, inquired of his wife regarding this phenomenon. She replied that she had done it for a lark. The professor remembered having heard the joke retold later by a Briton who told it intact, except for the tag line, which became: 'I did it for a sparrow!' This, the professor insisted, made it difficult to believe in English humour. . . . Mr Potter took the podium and acknowledged the introduction with: 'Thank you, Professor. I'm terribly sorry that you didn't get the point of the sparrow joke.'

Urbana, Stephen discovered, was also a centre of the educational theory industry, where, as qualifications for teaching, academic attainment came a long way behind knowledge of such things as 'Cultural Upset and Reintegration', and 'Refined Social Knowledge and Insight'. And among many practical courses was one on Dry-Fly Fishing.

Back in New York he looked up the Raymond Masseys who took him along to Tyrone Power's for dinner. He was stunned to see, on Power's bookshelves, 'six huge folio volumes of Steevens's eighteenth-century edition of Shakespeare'. He visited New York clubs and an American football match at Princeton, all under the aegis of Joe Bryan III, and played tennis over a weekend at Ted Patrick's on Long Island before a lecture at New York Town Hall.

A dinner party in Washington was given for him by Robert Richman, with the British, Peruvian and Indian Ambassadors present, Walter Lippman and a Chief Justice; there was another party at Hugh Troy's to meet Herblock, the *Washington Post* cartoonist; and on, by air, to his final lecture at Duke University, North Carolina, where Humour, ESP and Las Vegas were successfully tangled up and Stephen at last got to meet Dr Rhine himself. He felt he had been in the presence of a 'Galapagos Islands, orbit-of-Mercury scientist'.

Arriving back into the late November drizzle of London Stephen was plunged into the muddle of temporary accommodation that is so often the by-product of sudden remarriage. His and Heather's first home was her small flat at 3 Herbert Crescent, off Sloane

Street. There are few hardships for a writer worse than a party telephone line; this one was shared with a lady who organized debutante functions. Only slightly less uncomfortable, but far more fragrant, was the next flat, a furnished maisonnette in Sloane Street above Chelsea Flower Gardens, a flower shop owned by Mrs Thelma Cazalet Keir, MP. Much housing in fashionable areas of London was still in bad repair more than ten years after the War, and 12 Sloane Street was one of them. It is described by Stephen's secretary of that time, twenty-three-year-old Jeanette Henderson, as 'one of those tall, narrow Chelsea houses, excessively inconvenient, with dining room and kitchen on different floors. Stephen's "study" was the back part of the drawing room, shut off by double doors.'

Despite the flower shop, the flat was not always fragrant. 'Stephen had absolutely no sense of smell,' Heather recalls. 'We overlooked Sloane Street by a bus stop and if you opened the window the whole place smelt of diesel and petrol. Next door was a tobacconist with a bell which rang when anybody opened the door. The whole house was rickety, the banisters fell out like daisy petals and it was always wise to test a chair before you sat on it. The plumbing was also terrible.' The kitchen equipment seems to have been fairly ancient, since 'the geyser blew up in Heather's face'.

Miss Henderson, an observant secretary, found her employer alarming at first ('due to thick lenses, I think – they made him look as if he was glaring'). Stephen's clothes seem to have improved about this time, perhaps owing to Heather's influence: 'Dark blue shirts, red ties or Leander tie, brown suede shoes, very well-cut grey suits marred by cigarette ash and burns.'

Jeanette's was a lonely job. Much of the time Stephen was in America, sending home sheaves of diary notes which eventually became *Potter on America*, and Heather was in her office running the marriage bureau. 'The job could well have been part-time, but they wanted someone to be around to man the telephone.' One or two of Stephen's secretaries had been infuriated by his vagueness to the point of throwing things at him but not, apparently, Jeanette. She found him

extremely nice, kind and good about afternoons off, etc. Was mildly annoyed when I made a nonsense of some invitations to the Christmas drinks party. Not at all fussy about typing mistakes, layout of letters, etc. . . . Always ready to say he was sorry, quite un-devious and never pushed his great knowledge down one's throat. . . . manuscripts and articles dictated with great speed and fluency straight on to typewriter. The rare letter taken down in shorthand, but this very seldom. Mostly he scribbled on letters the gist of what he wanted to say in reply and left the rest to me. . . . He was very restless, used to pace up and down, go in and out of the room.

Organizing Stephen for foreign travel was never easy: 'I always kept his passport and vital travel documents in my desk and gave them to him only when the taxi was at the door, otherwise he lost them and there was a frenzy.'

Jeanette found him 'seldom the same two mornings running. . . . One morning he would be distant and hardly seemed to realize one was there, and the next day be his usual self.' She had the impression that he was worried about money, that he felt he wasn't doing well enough on 'The Critics' radio panel, that he wasn't getting (for him) enough exercise, that the pressure of keeping up the flow of invention for the Schweppshire advertisements was getting him down.

Stephen always reacted badly to any alteration in his copy. Some of his made-up names for Schweppshire characters were so near to those of real people that the advertising agency, fearing libel, struck them out. All these were disciplines generally accepted by professional copywriters and journalists. With Stephen they rankled: the adulation, high fees and freedom he had known in America, with the Sardi's-21 Club life-style, had unsettled him. Nor had he any really clear literary plans beyond making his American diaries into a book for Rupert Hart-Davis's Christmas list.

At least the accommodation problem was soon to be solved by moving to a detached Regency house in Hamilton Terrace, St John's Wood, a road believed by the press to be inhabited by millionaires. But before that there was a motoring holiday abroad: it was as if he expected travel to provide diary material for ultimate processing into books. Heather was now pregnant; but this did not deter them from setting off on a long overland journey to Italy. On the contrary, Heather's doctor thought it would be good for her circulation to go south. Before leaving, Stephen scrawled, on a leaf torn from a notepad, a sort of will, addressed to Rupert Hart-Davis: 'Dear Rupert, will you *please* be my literary executor?'

They took in Avignon, St Raphael, Pisa, Florence, Rome and

Naples, the Auberge des Pyramides at Vienne, and Paris on the way back. Under Heather's influence Stephen was becoming, in his fifties, the Sophisticated Traveller. In Italy it was sunny but cold. A postcard, from Florence, to Joe Bryan: 'Ah, Firenze, *bella Firenze* at last! It's everything my dreams told me it would be, but some of the fairways are rather shaggy, and the long fifteenth really should be a par-5.'

Naples was a success, though it began badly with the only really uneatable meal of the trip – some pizzas, 'like a brick', Heather's diary records. Stephen had had a lifelong desire to photograph the crater of Vesuvius. He refused the help of guides, making them very angry indeed, and drove all the way to the top in his car. On the way down again he became hopelessly entangled with an Italian funeral cortège which scattered in terror.

To Rupert Hart-Davis, on a postcard showing a distant view of Vesuvius: 'Your parcel with notes received. Your suggestions [on the forthcoming book about America] very useful, will be faithfully followed – especially what I say about Heather, who happens to be just about the most delightful travelling companion imaginable on this earth in (a) fair weather or (b) foul (it is foul at this moment). I am always afraid of being soppy about her. Yours eternally, S.'

At home in London, after a month away, he wrote sister Muriel one of his rare eight-page letters (on stationery pinched from the Francis Hotel, Bath, and Broadcasting House) recalling that 'the Arno latitude' had been 'visited by Stephen and Muriel Potter near the start of their distinguished careers, through the delightful generosity of M. Potter which did much towards the general waking up of S. Potter'. He was looking forward to the birth of his and Heather's child – 'having seen H. with her two children, I know what a gorgeous mother she is'.

He was still lunching with Att about once a month and occasionally visiting Aldeburgh. The Red House was obviously too big and expensive to keep up and a tidy, if temporary, solution was eventually devised by which she simply swapped houses with Benjamin Britten who had been living in Crag House on the sea front.

In June, Stephen did a brief stint as 'Guest T.V. Critic' of the *Evening Standard*. This was still stay-at-home stuff but it had the spur (always necessary for Stephen) of having to work to a deadline, and fast. His most perceptive articles were on Popov, the Moscow

Circus clown, and Jack Benny: 'Benny has only one joke: the question is asked hopefully, expecting the answer Yes – and back comes the answer No.'

In August, only three weeks after moving into Hamilton Terrace, Heather gave birth to a son who was christened Luke. Stephen, rejuvenated by new fatherhood, would spend the next few years watching his son's development, excitedly reporting his first words and sayings to Muriel. As with Andrew and Julian he would conduct part of Luke's education at home.

Potter on America, published in December 1956, was an unknown quantity. It was not in the *-manship* genre: would it succeed? Stephen to Rupert Hart-Davis: 'Dear Rupert, I thought all those advertisements looked both good and eye-catching. Excellent. It won't be your fault if the book doesn't go. As soon as we have a little concrete evidence about what the great world really thinks of this particular line, I hope you will come up here for a long meal and talk about future books.' His signed copy for Rupert was inscribed 'To Rupert, whose usual most glorious collaboration is actually, in this book, by a rather decent gesture, acknowledged in print. Love from Potter.' Collaboration presumably meant the fairly ruthless editing which Rupert performed on much of Stephen's work.

The Times reviewed the book with two other more solemn books on America, but leading with *Potter on America*. Stephen was, it said, 'a late starter' in the field of United-Statesmanship – he 'runs off with the Stars and leaves his fellow-travellers with the Stripes'. He is a 'deft diarist', however, and, like Coleridge, 'reflects on his own reflections', and there are plenty of what Americans call 'insights'. He has obviously fallen for 'the lavish book world of New York' where 'the slight loneliness, minor discomforts and feather-weight disasters are absorbed in and counteracted by a huge superficial satisfaction'. Mr Potter 'tells stories of the great with neither impertinence nor adulation'. The reviewer likes best of all Stephen's story, apropos the erroneous idea that Harry Truman speaks and does everything off the cuff, of Dean Acheson pointing to his own head and saying: 'Do you see all that grey hair? That's Truman's spontaneity.'

Kenneth Harris, in the *Observer*, perceived the book's literary quality: 'the extraordinarily truthful but economical way in which Potter hits off a scene or situation' in phrases like 'those long, pale, slack, graceful American boys' (they were a television camera crew) and 'the quality in the English voice which Americans dislike, the English habit of speaking in echoless, matt voice, from the front of the face only, dropping syllables out like bits of gum with the taste sucked out of them'. And *The Sunday Times* liked the book for 'throwing a flood of light on the manners and customs of the Americans'; sooner or later, 'every well-known author seems to write a book about America. Mr. Potter has done it for the best of all reasons, because he loves the country.'

Potter on America sold 12,250 copies in Britain and a disappointing 3575 in America. Why? Was it the egotistical diary-form? Was there too much high-level name-dropping, or did America, in the year of Suez, simply resent being written about by an Englishman whose observations may have seemed patronizing? Or was it simply that Potter on -*manship* was OK but Potter on anything else was out of character? Much that Stephen found strange or exhilarating in America has since arrived in Britain, and much is now dated; but the book remains a fresh, if over-personal introduction to our so-called cousins.

He was worried enough about the book to write, after Christmas, to Muriel, now living in retirement at Rottingdean, trying to get her opinion of it. 'Gameslife I can rip off at 100 miles an hour, sometimes with very few corrections – but anything else. . . . This one was practically written three times and could have done with a fourth.' He was still basing his literary plans on autobiography, the raw material for which was his diaries, scrawled in red ink in foolscap-size day books which he carried with him everywhere. There are those who maintain that diary-keeping is the antithesis of creation, that it is almost an excuse for not writing books. Stephen might have reflected that his admired Arnold Bennett wrote a million words of his journals over thirty-five years in addition to all his books. Now, he tells Muriel, he is contemplating 'a book of characters – Mother, probably; Andrew aged 6 perhaps; Edgar Lansbury; one of my masters at Westminster and so on'; and he sends her a sketch of Uncle Willie as a sample. Would it, he asks, interest anyone 'outside ourselves'? We do not know her answer. The idea would have had to be conceived on the level of Harold Nicolson's *Some People* to succeed.

Chapter 13
The oldest young man

America again came to his aid. In February 1957 he set off on
another of Bob Keedick's lecture tours – an exhausting one,
sometimes two lectures in one day. The plan this time was to earn
most of the money in the first month (helped by the fact that, as
literary lecturers were 'culture', they were not taxable in America);
Heather would then fly over from London and together they would
complete the tour with extra-curricular excursions. Keedick was
marvellously efficient, giving him 'green sheets for each lecture,
telling me what train or plane to catch, whom to ring up, type and
size of audience, whether to wear "tux" or "informal" '. First, a few
days with Raymond and Dorothy Massey in Connecticut: 'They
disagree *without break* – and if one goes away, the other is lost.'

Everyone was criticizing Anthony Eden and Suez while
deprecating John Foster Dulles; but the main topic was Prince
Philip about whom there were scandalous 'revelations' in magazines like *Confidential* – he was said to have a mistress. 'It made me
angry,' Stephen told his diary, 'because of his personality and fine
work of democratizing the monarchy a bit.' There had been similar
references to Philip's membership of the Thursday Club as if it
were a sort of orgy. Again to his diary he confided: '*I* am a member
of that faintly interesting *men's* club which meets for lunch at
Wheeler's and there are *no* nautch girls. . . . "If he does anything to
harm that wonderful girl . . ." Dorothy keeps saying.'

The first lecture was at the Massachusetts Institute of
Technology, to 1250 students. He was given dinner by four of them,
who said: 'We are typical. We all make our own radio sets, have the
same classical records (*Brandenburg, Jupiter* and so on). No swing
here.' Despite their seriousness they laughed uproariously at his

jokes and the lecture was a great success. Then he flew to Buffalo where he was greeted by a man who said, 'Don't suppose you've even heard of Buffalo before,' which he answered by singing 'Shuffle Off to Buffalo'. The great thrill of Buffalo was picking up a Hertz self-drive Belair Chevrolet (no gears, and power steering) to get to his next few destinations. A dull lecture to a teachers' college at Fredonia, a small town beside Lake Erie; then an all-night drive through snow, confused by bad signposting and misdirection from a policeman, to Syracuse, taking seven and a half hours to cover 240 miles, and arriving in time to snatch an hour's sleep before the next lecture – a morning one to 300 College of Forestry students: 'Perfect listeners, and enough laughter to make me have to cut 30 per cent.'

Next he drove a short distance west to Brockport, his first experience of 'the joys of the State Thruway'. Here he gave a bad lecture, due largely to the unstimulating effect of his host's 'Californian burgundy mixed with some wine I had made myself'. There was another night drive in snow to Oswego on the frozen shores of Lake Ontario: another morning lecture ('Ah, God, 10 a.m. is not the hour for light touches'), received with 'polite, puzzled smiles' and accompanied by 'ping-pong-pang noises from the bursting central heating system'. On, after lunch, to an art teachers' college at Geneseo – 'O ameliorating Arts! . . . a *good* lecture, after two bad ones'. Here Stephen was treated to the fashionable 'hate joke', a kind of refinement of Charles Addams: 'Yes, but what did you think of the *play*, Mrs. Lincoln?' Next he drove fifty miles to Rochester to catch the midnight train to New York; a few hours' sleep and, in the afternoon, a commuters' train to Bethlehem, Pennsylvania, to the famous golf centre of the Saucon Country Club where his host turned out to be an American Old Etonian with a fine collection of Hardy first editions. Back to New York for a talk to the Young Men's and Women's Jewish Associations, Stephen visited NBC studios where the original version of 'What's My Line?' was in progress, featuring Bennett Cerf (Stephen's new American publisher), Ginger Rogers (Cerf's wife's cousin) and the impresario Mike Todd. They all dined together after the show, their taxi having been mobbed outside the studios ('these people are the Royalty of the U.S., and there was something very Princess Margaret-ish in the angle of Ginger's arm, waving to the crowd, as we drove off').

He was up till 4 am preparing his Washington lecture (on English literature this time, not humour which had flopped on a previous visit); two hours' sleep, then to Idlewild airport to meet Heather ('glorious H') and fly with her on to Washington. Back in New York, Stephen broadcast with Clifton Fadiman and Bennett Cerf on 'Lecturing', and they were guests of honour with Ginger Rogers, Alistair Cooke, the Budd Schulbergs and the Oscar Hammersteins at a full-dress dinner given by Bennett Cerf. 'I expected Mickey Mouse to come out of the floor,' Heather says.

The Potters then flew to Palm Beach for Stephen to rest; he was extremely tired and this may have been the reason for his having caused a certain amount of consternation at a Washington party. Buttonholed by a woman who insisted on telling him about all her ex-husbands, one after another, he looked at her fixedly with wide-open smiling blue eyes, as if fascinated. People who knew him well knew that this stare meant, 'I am bored, I am not listening to a word you say, I am miles away.' At a suitable pause in the narrative he asked, 'And have you never married?'

The tempo of the lecture tour, in which tourism became more important than lecturing, now grew, if possible, even faster. In San Antonio, Texas (dry, in the drink sense), Stephen addressed a women's club whose members wore hats and white gloves. In Albuquerque, New Mexico (wet), they suddenly realized that Tom Lehrer was in the audience. At Santa Fé, Stephen, remembering that Taos was only seventy miles away, could not resist a D.H.Lawrence pilgrimage, and was rewarded by a meeting with Spud Johnson, believed to be the original of Villiers in *The Plumed Serpent*, and still indignant about the 'lies' Lorenzo wrote about him. Spud (or Spoodle) Willard Johnson, editor of a strange experimental magazine called *The Laughing Horse*, had, with Witter Bynner, been Lawrence's guide round Mexico in 1923, beginning with the bullfight which figures in the opening pages of *The Plumed Serpent*. A small man in a skin-tight sweater, with pale face and cropped hair, he was rising sixty.

In California, which Stephen had visited only two years before, he could pose as guide for Heather, a role he perhaps carried to excess. Stephen: 'See that over there? It's a cinema.' Heather: 'Yes, I know – it has MOVIE HOUSE above it in lights.' At least he could really show her round San Francisco, which he had 'done' in one day by taxi in 1955; this time the sightseeing included Mrs Potter

Russell's famous collection of Impressionists. They took a 600-mile flight north to Pullman, Washington, for a lecture and an informal talk to a women's club at Chico, in the foothills of the Sierra Nevada (no hats and gloves this time – after all, it *is* California); then to Carmel, to a motel with the splendid name of The Tickle Pink. Carmel was a little suspicious of visiting Englishmen: Randolph Churchill had just been there, drunk and generally upsetting everyone.

Here he took enough time off to keep his neglected diary (as usual in red ink) and send a great swathe of it to Muriel in Sussex. He was travelling so much and so fast that his diary at this point degenerates into notes for future reference – the observation is not 'written up'. Moreover he was now so at home in America that he was beginning to lose the 'innocent abroad' touch that makes for detailed observation of the simplest things seen for the first time. When he wrote to Joe Bryan from Florence, mentioning nothing but the golf-course, he was leg-pulling; now, from Carmel, he wrote to Muriel: 'I've just achieved a life ambition and have played the Cypress Point Golf Course' – and he meant it.

During the next weeks, however, Cypress Point was to face a lot of competition – Las Vegas, where Stephen now considered himself a veteran at the Desert Inn and the Golden Nugget; the Grand Canyon; the Hoover Dam; and Phoenix, Arizona. Here he and Heather stayed at the Arizona Biltmore which jealously guarded its reputation of being 'the most expensive hotel in America'. Stephen's luggage, held together by long straps, always caused consternation at Biltmores. Most hotel bookings related to lecture tours were efficiently made by Bob Keedick; but, left to himself, Stephen never booked: 'He thought it unsporting,' Heather explains. This sometimes landed him with no choice but the most expensive hotel in town. They took tea with Mrs Wrigley, the chewing gum heiress, in her house filled with portraits of the Royal Family; played bridge and golf with Henry Luce and his wife Clare. Stephen had met Luce in New York in the early days of Lifemanship but, in the company of his wife, he was not an easy conversationalist. Heather did her best with him when instructed by Stephen: 'Talk to Henry – he's shy and a little deaf.'

One lecture not on the regular schedule was at the invitation of an artist named Fred Cabotick with whom they stayed at an Indian village between Albuquerque and Phoenix: a collection of tin-roofed shacks inhabited by cheerful people wearing blankets. Arizona has more Indians than any other state and, to these particular Indians, all Englishmen were 'John Bull'. There seemed to be a feast or carnival on – why, it took some time to discover. It was a farewell party for the stoker and his wife: it was a bitterly cold winter and the stoker was responsible for most of the village's heating. The villagers paraded up and down to a band playing Sousa marches. The children, in honour of their English visitors, sang 'I've got sixpence' over and over again. Finally they all gathered round Stephen and Heather and shouted: 'We want to hear John Bull speak!' Stephen had somehow formed the impression that the departing stoker was the headmaster of the village school; so he delivered, to a largely uneducated audience, an off-the-cuff talk on 'the benefits of education'. No matter: it was rapturously received. To this day the villagers probably believe that in March 1957 John Bull came down, as from heaven, to be among them.

Back to California for lectures at the State colleges of San Diego and Long Beach; self-indulgence at Romanoff's and the Beverley Hills Hotel; and a routine visit to Forest Lawns cemetery to see if it was as bad as Evelyn Waugh had said it was, only to discover that it was worse. Looking up old acquaintances, they lunched with Cary Grant, Christopher Isherwood and Deborah Kerr, with Franchot Tone and Benita Hume and George Sanders. Stephen had not seen Benita Hume for thirty years since he had taken her to the 1917 Club. Cary Grant still wanted to make a comedy picture out of the *Lifemanship* books but somehow the project never got off the ground. It was too English in conception, it needed to be Anglo-Americanized. . . .

The power of Hollywood was demonstrated memorably on their last evening there. Dining with Sam Goldwyn's son and his wife they found they had not left enough time to get to the airport. Goldwyn Junior went calmly to the telephone and requested, in a manner that was as persuasive as an order, that the plane be held for his VIP guests.

In New York there were broadcasts and interviews, some of which Heather gave in her own right; Eddie Condon's, Commander (Schweppes) Whitehead, Toots Shor; a flying visit to Pittsburgh, and so, after five weeks away, home.

The Pittsburgh visit was to meet and interview Jack Heinz, of the famous canning firm, whose company history Stephen had been asked to write. Company histories are something which almost all authors of any versatility are asked to tackle at some stage of their careers. They are, however, fraught with difficulty, as we shall see.

In Aldeburgh Att was painting with total absorption. Her closest friends were now Benjamin Britten and Peter Pears in whose old house on the sea front she was now living. Britten, seeing how totally inconvenient Crag House was for a painter, generously offered her a piece of land next to the Red House. He would build a studio for her on it if she liked; it was about a mile out of the town, reached by a track known as Golf Lane. She accepted joyfully and was soon installed there.

The long American journey had its usual effects on Stephen's thinking. He must buckle down to it and produce the 'great Lit. works' which were a standing joke with Rupert Hart-Davis. What should he do next? The urge to autobiography, coupled with doubts about how to treat it, in how many volumes, with what prospects of sales, was ever present. He sent Muriel drafts and scraps of ideas, spasms of diary. She was the eternal witness of his fears that he would not, in the long run, make out as a professional writer. There were germs of another -*manship* book in his mind, however, and in various published articles which could be woven into it. Meanwhile, there was broadcasting: he was still in demand for various 'panel games' and 'The Critics', and his unmistakable voice was on the air roughly every three weeks.

One of these panel games was 'Call the Tune': more than twenty years later we know it on BBC Television as 'Face The Music'. Invented and produced by Walter Todds, its question master was Joseph Cooper. There was, as there is today, a Guest Musician who was supposed to know all the answers; and towards the end Joseph Cooper exercised his playful talent for improvising on the piano in the style of any given composer. The questions, asked in 1957 of a panel consisting of personalities such as Joyce Grenfell, Christopher Hassall and Stephen, today seem astonishingly unsophisticated; but part of the appeal of the show was, and is, the listener's feeling of superiority when he can identify something the panel cannot guess. Stephen's own performances revealed the limitations of his musical taste and experience: perhaps he had worshipped Beethoven too long and had not experimented far enough in the directions shown by 'Tom and D.' in the 1920s.

The 'house history' of Heinz was not easy to research and

Stephen was greatly helped by Colin Mann, then public relations officer for the company. Theoretically, in a task of this kind, the author has a free hand; but the fact remains that the object of the exercise is to present the company in what its management consider a positive light. No company founded in 1869, in the days of the American Robber Barons, can boast a past of spotless purity, and the Heinz company had come out of it, over the years, with an enviably good reputation. But Stephen was touchy about suggested alterations.

He was much consoled by the personality of Jack Heinz who turned out to be a natural Gamesman. He was able to admire Heinz's Gamesmanship tactics in appearing on the squash court in an off-putting loud-patterned shirt and swimming shorts. Nevertheless Stephen won.

Heinz had his annihilating revenge over luncheon at Claridges. Stephen, choosing the wine (which happened to be a Margaux), tasted it, rolled it round his palate, and criticized it in words which have not been recorded but seem to have been something like 'too many tramlines'.

Heinz looked at him with deadpan seriousness. 'Really? I'm most interested to hear your opinion. I happen to own the vineyard.'

In January 1958 Stephen wrote to Rupert Hart-Davis about his future plans. The Heinz book had not yet found a London publisher though the New York end had already been fixed up. It was hardly the sort of book that Rupert, a fastidious and, on the whole, 'literary' publisher, would have wanted for his list.

'I hope to have four books out or in proof by this time next year,' Stephen wrote,

and I hope you will be able to publish two of them.

1. My House History of Heinz. I hoped to finish this by the end of last month but as so often happens the last quarter is being very difficult. . . . This is being done by long-standing agreement with Putnams, though of course I would rather it was you, nice as that young fellow is.

2. My little short-story autobiographical essays on myself up to leaving school which I haven't touched for 6 months and I am longing to get back to. Half done. This for you of course. (This eventually became *Steps to Immaturity*.)

3. I have got material and quite a lot written for a new *Lifemanship*.

4. . . . A collection of the Schweppshire illustrated page advertisements done by myself and George Him. . . . I rather fancy you did not care for this

idea when I mentioned it a couple of years ago. . . . Out of all this there should be at least one Potter–Rupert book for this autumn.

A month later an awkwardness fell between author and publisher because Stephen, for once examining his royalty sheets, queried certain deductions; there was some disagreement about who should pay Lt.-Col. Frank Wilson the Queen's Messenger, greyhound-tied illustrator, for 'work returned as unsatisfactory', which Stephen had agreed to do. He was above all unwilling to lose Rupert's friendship and hastens to add: 'None of this excuses my moment of irritability to my glorious old pal. . . . Apologies. . . . "Manship 58" [which became *Supermanship*] is going well I think and you should have a fairly complete book early in March.'

In March he wrote to Rupert: 'Heather has I think had a really good idea for the title of Gameslife No. 4 – SUPERMANSHIP. . . . Frankie is already working on an idea for the cover of me as Superman. . . . A touch of food poisoning and an SOS from millstone Heinz has put me back on the finishing of your book. Also it is awfully difficult to be funny with gripes. . . . What is the genuine deadline?'

Rupert had been urging him not to stretch the Gameslife idea too far: would it really bear a fourth book? Stephen to Rupert, 21 April 1958:

Cheer up, Rupert, about this new vol. Dissolve, black clouds and gloomy prophecies, and remember that there was one sentence, on page one, which you thought was funny. Re-reading it after your comments, of course, I couldn't find even that. But I have shortened and put in footnotes. . . . The first chapter and Memoirs are intended as more serious satire and should remain so. But, on your good suggestion, I have added a Prelude and an Envoi.

It had been six years since *One-Upmanship* and the reading public's memory is short. They would have to be reminded what Games/Lifemanship was all about. 'I don't want you to take this unless you are reasonably enthusiastic. . . . By the time this is typed I will be in Spain. Perhaps this will revive my wits.'

There was much relief in 'glorious golf'. From Guadalmina, a postcard: 'Andalusia at last. . . . I managed to ace the difficult 3rd hole at Torremolinos in a birdie. Love Potski.'

Supermanship ('How to Continue to Stay Top without Actually Falling Apart'), despite both author's and publisher's misgivings, had been edited into shape. Its publication (in October) had been timed to anticipate, not to get swamped by, the Christmas list. Lt.-Col. Frank Wilson had excelled himself with imaginative realizations of the goings-on at Station Road, Yeovil, and there was a portrait of Potter in the cloak of Superman. In a prelude Stephen recapitulates the history of Games/Lifemanship, now celebrating the twenty-fifth anniversary of Joad's Gambit; and, emphasizing Yeovil's hatred of 'pernicious educational strangleholds' like examinations, points out that Yeovil's diplomas are 'by no means expensive to buy'. True, there have been changes: Odoreida now takes private pupils in his 'hateful little study at "Wendyways"', and a staff-member we have not met before, called Wert, has been cleared of Unlifemanship Activities and allowed to rejoin. This was topical at the time as were references to Angry Young Men. There are a number of new Yeovil Jubilee Pamphlets, among them Superbaby: the Baby as Lifeman ('babies are by nature one-up . . . whatever they do is *your* fault'); and a note on Odoreida's golf ploy of putting an opponent off his game by continually returning to the clubhouse to 'ring home' during his wife's pregnancy. There is a note, gracefully acknowledged to J. Bryan III, on 'When to Use Thin Spidery Handwriting', as in the case of Miss Sally Lou Buffington when protesting against a notice DO NOT BLOCK THIS DRIVEWAY, pointing out that, despite her crippled hip, she has gladly defied this uncouth admonition in order (with many italics) to carry some *jelly* to an *invalid*; Miss Sally Lou Buffington was an invention of Lifeman's own.

Reviewmanship – deadly true of so many reviewers – shows how to deflate the specialist ('It is surprising that so eminent a scholar as Dr. Preissberger . . .'); warns of the difficulties of reviewing novels, which 'may even entail actual reading of the first and last chapters', though it is wise to quote something from the middle pages too; and advises against pitching into poets lest you lose your status as a Friend of Literature. Some further observations on Carmanship include Accident Behaviour, especially the Continental approach: 'Well, eet is good? There are no corpse?' As for Christmas, full of good-old-Uncle-Arthur-ship, do not forget the Office Party – 'taking the opportunity to get one-up on your rivals, at that very time when . . . all thoughts of self-promotion . . . shall and must be in abeyance'.

In the *envoi*, making it clear that the Games/Life game is now

over, 'Superman says farewell. . . . . International Lifemanship has
enlisted his services' for Counter-Marxmanship to combat 'the
perpetual one-up-ness of Marxmanship' which ensured that 'the
Suez incident occupied five times the space of the Hungarian
massacre when the UN met to register moral disapproval'. The last
sentence, commenting on the Brinkmanship of Krushchev (three
years before Kennedy), and ascribed to one R. Abernethy, defines
International Lifemanship as 'the art of winning the world without
actually blowing it up'.

The book was dedicated to 'US 1' (Joe Bryan III) and Stephen's
inscribed copy to Joe Bryan reads: 'US 1. The loathing, deep but
difficult to express, which one must always feel for any book
dedicated to one, puts one in a difficult position, particularly if the
motive of the dedication includes a touch of friendliness, even the
faintest suggestion of gratitude. But it is all right, No. 1 has a way
out: acknowledge instantly, almost telephonically, but NEVER
READ.' The parcel in which it arrived was carefully addressed to J.
Brown III. Joe Bryan retaliated by addressing letters to 'S.P. Otter'.
Joe, whose name-ploy was to ask 'What was your name *originally?*',
had noticed, as many autograph hunters had noticed, that Stephen,
when signing anything, always stopped dead after the P as if striving
to remember how his name ended.

Relations with Rupert Hart-Davis were clearly now more
relaxed: his copy was inscribed, 'To Rupert, the one and only
Superpublisher'.

Reviews were mostly good and kind as if saluting once again a
national institution. Marghanita Laski, in the *Observer*, was in a
minority when she asked plaintively: 'Please may we have a new
joke now?' America was not yet tired of the joke: after a long,
quotation-filled review, *Newsweek* summed up: 'The hand of the
Potter, still steady.' The book sold 20,500 copies in Britain (less
than one third of the sales of *One-Upmanship*) and a little over
10,000 in America (less than one fifth of the sales of *One-
Upmanship*). It was by no means a failure, but not really producing
as much as a year's income. Had there been a change of fashion?
Was the joke worn out? Had there been a coarsening of satire as
commercial television took its toll? He had been a best-seller; he was
now in danger of becoming a cult figure amid a small Anglo-
American band of faithful admirers.

One of these admirers was James Thurber. There were elements of both men – in most ways so different – which, when they met, gave them a kind of mirror-image of each other. The link was Walter Mitty-ism. There were some of Stephen's critics who saw him as Harold Skimpole in *Bleak House*: 'All he said was free from effort and spontaneous, and was said with such a captivating gaiety, that it was fascinating to hear him talk. . . . There was an easy negligence in his manner and even in his dress . . . which I could not separate from the idea of a romantic who had undergone some unique process of depreciation.'

Stephen thought the brief ten pages of *The Secret Life of Walter Mitty* the funniest story he had ever read. Mitty is sent out by his wife to buy puppy biscuits – will he remember to do so? Mitty at the wheel of his car instantly falls into a day-dream, just as Stephen did, sometimes automatically driving to the Savile Club even when his original destination was in the opposite direction. He shared with Thurber the ability to invent felicitously convincing technical jargon. When, in *Mitty*, the Commander shouts, 'Throw on the power lights! Rev her up to 8,500 – we're going through! Switch on No. 8 auxiliary! Full strength in No. 3 turret!' and the crew murmur, 'The Old Man'll get us through!' – and the Surgeon barks, 'Ostreosis of the ductal tract – tertiary! . . . Coreopsis has set in . . .' it is very like Stephen spreading confusion among botanists by inventing new species complete with bogus Latin names.

When, therefore, on Christmas Eve 1958, Stephen, together with Honor Tracy and Michael Ayrton, interviewed James Thurber in 'Frankly Speaking' on radio, he was facing one of his heroes. The programme covered Thurber's early life and was full of his own wisecracks. One of the gaps in Stephen's own literary upbringing was that he had never been a newspaper reporter. Thurber's early days had been spent, in company with Nunnally Johnson the screenwriter and Laura Z. Hobson the novelist, on the old *New York Post* which, in the 1920s, had somehow survived on a circulation of only 65,000. He had sent twenty stories to the *New Yorker* – all rejected. Thurber's wife's advice contains a lesson for all writers. 'You write too carefully,' she said. 'Write faster.' So he set his alarm clock for forty-five minutes and stopped writing when the bell went. The story was immediately accepted by the *New Yorker* and he never looked back.

Towards the end of the interview Thurber thanked Stephen for coining the word 'Rilking' – scoring over others who have not the advantage of your knowledge of German poetry. He had used the word often himself: 'Don't start to *rilk*, just because you're with people who've never heard of Kierkegaard or whoever.'

To all outward appearances an aggressively healthy man, Stephen, increasingly bronchitic, had just come out of hospital after a sharp bout of pneumonia. To Muriel he wrote: 'I am quite sad at the thought that I am really now well enough to do a little work. One has never realized chemical medicine, or whatever it is called, working until one has observed penicillin taking charge of one's diseased self. Melodramatic.' Muriel has been sending him ideas for his autobiography and illness has jogged his memory: 'I only met Paul Robeson once and that was with a few people round a piano on an evening in 1925. . . . I think a man had just sung some drawing-room, though good, Vaughan Williams song. . . . Then Robeson started to sing, sitting on the floor where he was. Sort of moment one remembers.'

There were also vague aches and stiffnesses suggesting arthritis, but Stephen never used the word. He had done something to his hip while looking at a Picasso exhibition in a picture gallery in Antibes three years before: 'My old peace wound, you know.' A *Daily Express* reporter, Diana Gillon, describes him about this time as 'a tall thin man with a stoop'. This was not the 'scholar's stoop' cultivated at Merton College in the 1920s but a new development in a man who normally stood straight as a ramrod. Typically, he had forgotten the time of the interview, came home two hours late, and side-stepped the interview by making the interviewer play piano duets with him (Bach organ music, of course).

His letters to Muriel now nearly always contained news of Luke, rising two years old:

Luke, needless to say, combines the gifts of John Stuart Mill and an Olympic champion. He is large for his age with enormous legs (seriously) and is exploding into language in a general way, repeating any word he hears whether he understands it or not. . . . 'Fashionable' at once becomes 'fash-nobble' and 'helicopter' becomes 'hecopper'. I ought to know when a child of that age starts lessons and what they should be. I remember starting off Julian at a very early age, chiefly with numbers.

The Magic Number, his company history of Heinz, came out in May 1959, published by Max Reinhardt. It had been a 'millstone', but he acknowledges 'the great pleasure . . . of attacking and trying to grasp a subject entirely new to me'. There are genuine bits of Potter all the way through, beginning with a vivid description (from his diary) of the flight and arrival in Pittsburgh; a number of linguistic digressions on American usage, such as 'the dog wants out', 'cigar-store' for tobacconist, footnotes on the derivation of 'tin' and 'can', and the use of 'sample' as a verb which he traces back to the sixteenth century. He even managed to bring in botany: the slow growth of Heinz in England is compared to the life of the Burnt Orchid. The early history of the company, founded in 1869, the year in which Gould and Fisk tried to corner gold, and the story of the Bavarian family Heinz, are set against Upton Sinclair's grisly account of the meat-packing industry in its unreformed days. His greatest pleasure from the whole exercise was his friendship with Jack Heinz: 'Ed Murrow has the look of a reformed Humphrey Bogart: H.J.Heinz has the look of a reformed Ed Murrow.'

It had now been decided that the first volume of Stephen's autobiography, which would have 'Immaturity' in the title, would cover only the first nineteen years of his life, up to his father's decision to send him to Oxford. He was already collecting material, with Muriel's help, for a second volume which would take his youth up to 1929. This, though synopsized and recast several times, never got beyond the sketch-book stage. Autobiography obsessed him: writing to Muriel on her birthday he says how much he prefers it to 'piddling about with rather badly-paid articles, time-wasting, for *Punch*'. He had not really understood the new, younger *Punch*, which dates from Malcolm Muggeridge's editorship, 1953–7. Nor had he been very clever in handling Muggeridge's successors. There had been a joke which had gone wrong. He had been invited to lunch at the *Punch* Round Table, a signal honour which few have refused. Obviously he had, as so often, muddled his dates; and at the last moment *Punch* received a telephone message from his secretary: 'Mr Potter is very sorry, but he is hunting today.' The full nonsense of this can only be appreciated by those who have ever witnessed the extreme unease of Potter confronted by Equus. But the Round Table was offended.

There was, too, in his letters to Muriel, an increasing tendency to look back on their youth, not only for the sake of the autobiography. He was approaching his sixtieth birthday: 'I have long given up trying to be the oldest young man in London and am a little past, alas, now being the youngest old one.'

Chapter 14
Into the sixties

Steps to Immaturity, published in December 1959, did not sell well. Rupert Hart-Davis's inscribed copy from Stephen reads: 'Once again, you have been my "but-for-whom".' Rupert had done a lot of editing: 'Stephen had got into the habit of Lifemanship style,' he says, 'and couldn't get out of it. He found it a fearful effort to write naturally.' The result, nevertheless, was a picture of a south-west London suburban childhood of considerable charm and observation, though the observation is nearly all of his own reactions to people and events, rather than the more objective, Dickensian observation that attracts readers. Only thus can we be interested in other people's ordinary families who go monotonously to Swanage and Worthing for their holidays and have maiden aunts and uncles of insufficient eccentricity. Withal, *Steps to Immaturity* has humour and charm. Reviews were mixed, all, however, paying tribute to his writing.

Rupert Hart-Davis thought it Stephen's best book. The quirky spirit of *The Times Literary Supplement* did not quite know what to make of Potter taking himself seriously: 'Mr Potter's works have been so discrepant and so unpredictable that one may be forgiven for wondering if there are not several Mr Potters. . . .' There have been 'persistent rumours that he was really J. Middleton Murry, Miss Kathleen Raine or Mr Paul Jennings'. The lack of oneupness 'will cause consternation in Station Road, Yeovil'. Indeed, there is 'a certain flatness'. However, Mr Potter is good on smells (such as the 'major-key smells of the grocery department at the Army & Navy Stores'), and good at recalling the euphoria of being young. If there is a moral it is that children were happier in the opening years of the twentieth century because they had fewer treats.

In the same month a very different kind of autobiography had been published. This was Frank Norman's *Stand on Me*, an account of life in the Soho underworld. Frank Norman, a Barnardo boy gone wrong, had, a year before, published an extraordinary book, *Bang to Rights*, about his life in prison after five convictions. It was one of those freaks of publishing, a genuine social document, unedited, with even the author's appalling spelling left unaltered; and it carried a serious introduction by Raymond Chandler. Frank Norman had come to authorship by way of jail; Stephen by way of Westminster, Oxford, BBC and literary criticism. The two men faced each other in a BBC television programme, 'The Book Man', in the company of Jack Lambert, the introducer; Hammond Innes, best-selling novelist; Arthur Waley, translator from Chinese and Japanese; and Margaret Lane, biographer and journalist.

The Lifeman in Stephen might have been expected to hog the limelight; but, as nearly always when discussing other people's books, he was scrupulously fair and in this case enthusiastic. He and Frank Norman talked about autobiography. 'Two writers with such different backgrounds could hardly have been more difficult to find,' Frank recalls. 'Stephen spent the whole of our short discussion praising my book to high heaven and did not once mention his own.'

After the programme Stephen took Jack Lambert and Frank Norman back to Hamilton Terrace and produced several bottles of champagne. They were in Stephen's study, 'a room of spectacular untidiness', Jack remembers,

a kind of quintessential upper-class Bohemian room full of pictures, shelves and piles of books – and the unexpected grand piano, at which Stephen was soon seated, and by which I was soon standing; we worked our possibly tipsy way through several Schubert songs while Frank sat in semi-darkness among the books and magazines at the other end of the room, looking pleased but bemused. 'Gosh!' he said, 'I've never heard anything like that *live* before!'

Frank's own version of this evening is: 'I lounged on a sofa, guzzling champagne, an audience of one, wondering what on earth it was I was listening to – Wagner, I suppose.' Eventually a woman came to the front door in a dressing-gown and asked them to keep the noise down. 'It must now have been two in the morning,' Frank continues. 'We left the house, piled into Jack Lambert's car and drove to his house in Hampstead where Stephen accompanied him on the piano once more, the drink continuing to flow. The party did not break up until almost dawn. For a young man with my background it was a very strange experience, to say the least.'

Nineteen sixty began greyly. Luke was suffering from a mysterious fever which turned out to be pneumonia: there was talk with doctors about a temporarily collapsed lung which, Stephen wrote to Muriel, 'may infect the whole E.N.T. system'. The boy recovered, however, but his health was always to give anxiety.

Stephen continued to worry about his age: 'I've been rather depressed lately,' he wrote to Jack Collis, '– Luke ill, among other things; and I was certain you hadn't communicated because you'd found *Steps* so unsympathetic. . . . 60 on Monday – first time I have been really depressed by an age year.' To Andrew he said: 'I'm a young 60 who will quickly become an old 70.'

The film rights of all the Games/Life/One-upmanship books had been acquired by Carl Foreman. All efforts to create a Hollywood film, with Cary Grant or Rex Harrison starring, had come to nothing; Foreman eventually sold most of his interest to a British company which had, at no great expense, produced an Ealing-type comedy, directed by Robert Hamer and starring Ian Carmichael, Terry-Thomas, Alastair Sim and Janette Scott, supported by a reliable team of character actors ranging from Peter Jones and Hattie Jacques to Edward Chapman and Irene Handl. The cast-list ended with the name of Anita Sharp-Bolster which sounded so exactly like a Potter invention that nobody would believe it wasn't.

Manners were never more middle-class than in June that year when Stephen went back to Westminster School for the fourteenth annual cricket match between the Authors and the National Book League. There was a luncheon beforehand at which Sir William Haley, President of the NBL, proposed a toast to 'Cricket and Literature'. Stephen, replying to it on behalf of the Authors, said that he had come to love the game in spite of his school record which showed that he had used every conceivable subterfuge to get out of playing it. What he liked about it was the 'village cricket atmosphere', with the scoreboards never quite up to the minute: this made it particularly delightful to hear E.W. Swanton's commentaries on the radio while simultaneously watching the game on television. Swanton was in fact in the Authors' very strong team with Bernard Hollowood, Denis Compton, Godfrey Evans, Vivian Jenkins, Aidan Crawley, Ian Peebles, Jon Cleary, Michael Meyer,

Richard Hough, and Ian Scott-Kilvert, under the captaincy of Laurence Meynell. The Authors won. For Stephen the great thrill was meeting Jack Hobbs, a veteran guest of honour, and being photographed with him.

Volume II of his autobiography made slow progress, hindered by his inability to remember dates and so get things into chronological order. In letters to Muriel, making great demands on her memory, he blamed 'keep-going and hand-to-mouth jobs . . . largely radio and T.V.' which were 'enjoyable but unsatisfactory and rather nerve-racking'. In October there came an interruption which could hardly have been foreseen: he was required to attend the Old Bailey as an expert witness in the historic trial of Penguin Books Ltd who were charged with 'publishing an obscene article which is, in effect, the book *Lady Chatterley's Lover*, written by D.H.Lawrence and now published, or proposed to be published, for the first time in this country'.

The trial, which lasted two weeks, produced a most distinguished array of witnesses, including Dame Rebecca West, Richard Hoggart, E.M.Forster, Veronica Wedgwood, Norman St John Stevas, Janet Adam Smith, Cecil Day Lewis, Noël Annan, and the Bishop of Woolwich. Stephen, flattered that he should have been remembered for his very first book, *D.H.Lawrence: A First Study*, thirty years after its publication, was examined on the penultimate day by Jeremy Hutchinson, QC for the defence. C.H.Rolph, author of many books on crime and the police, reporting the trial, noted that, in addition to his academic and broadcasting work, Stephen admitted 'with a wide and deprecating smile' that he had written the Lifemanship books.

Mr Hutchinson: 'What was your view when you *first* read Lady Chatterley as regards its literary merit?'

SP: 'I thought that, in the whole cycle of Lawrence's novels, it was not the most successful. I thought also that he was perhaps using it too much as a pamphlet, although all his novels were written with a purpose. . . .'

Mr Hutchinson: 'What would you say as to its literary merit?'

SP: 'In general, Lawrence seemed to me then, and seems to me now, one of the greatest writers in a decade of giants. He made a great difference to me, and I owe a great debt to him. . . .'

Mr Hutchinson: 'Do you find the use of the four-letter words in the book valid?'

SP: 'I think Lawrence was trying to do something very difficult and very courageous there. . . . What he was trying to do was to take these words out of what you may call the context of the lavatory wall and give them back a dignity and meaning, away from the context of obscenity and of the swear-word. . . .'

The trial had its moments of comedy as when Richard Hoggart, in his sturdy Yorkshire voice, recalled the number of times he had heard the word 'fuck' used on a building site; or when Mervyn Griffith-Jones, for the prosecution, asked a very ordinary-looking jury: 'Is it a book you would wish your *servants* to read?' This led to the revival of an old joke: 'Would you mind your daughter reading Lady Chatterley? – No, but I should try to hide it from my gamekeeper.'

'It was a fifteenth-century trial for adultery,' wrote C.H.Rolph. 'Constance Chatterley was there in Court, the Scarlet Letter must somewhere be ready. She was distinguished culpably from Cleopatra and Madame Bovary by her lover's four-letter words.' She was, overwhelmingly, not guilty.

The trial was watched by notable people from all over the country, among them Vyvyan Holland, the son of Oscar Wilde, whom Stephen had last seen at a dinner of the Saintsbury Club. It was said of Holland that he made only one ponderous joke a year, and his joke for 1960 was directed at Stephen: 'Hello, Potter – what are you doing here? Gathering material for Fuckmanship?'

A fortnight later Gilbert Harding died. He had been chairman of 'Round Britain Quiz', one of the many radio shows he was so good at but which he despised; in the emergency Stephen was asked to take his place. Gilbert had been a fellow member of the Savile Club for many years. With Compton Mackenzie, Michael Ayrton, John Davenport, Robert Henriques and Peter Rennell Rodd, he had been one of a band of Johnsonian 'great talkers' at the Savile; Stephen, in his early days of membership, had hovered diffidently around them before being admitted to the inner circle. Roman Catholic convert and homosexual, ex-schoolmaster, ex-BBC announcer, ex-lecturer, ex-policeman, brilliant raconteur in several accents, a profoundly unhappy man, Harding had been reduced to tears on television, at the memory of his mother, under the probing questions of John Freeman in 'Face to Face'. Privately he used to say: 'Psychiatrists say it's all because of mother-domination. Rubbish! I just – like – *boys*.' Terribly rude in his cups, and terribly sorry afterwards, he had frightened new members of the club by going up to them and glaring at them: 'You say you're an author? What have you *written*? Never *heard* of it.' Or: 'You look an arrogant fellow. What have you got to say for yourself?' Taking Gilbert, drunk, in a taxi back to his flat in Weymouth Street had been the kindly task of several Savile friends in recent years. His *Who's Who* entry listed one of his hobbies as 'waiting'. The missing words were '. . . for death'.

After one's sixtieth birthday the death of friends grows frequent and one scans the newspaper with mingled gloom and triumph at one's own survival. There was one kind of death Stephen was determined to prevent and that was capital punishment. He had belonged to the anti-hanging lobby for a number of years and the fearful anomalies of the Bentley–Craig case were fresh in his mind. In the last weeks of 1960 he added his name to 106 others – bishops, artists and writers, including his old friend Francis Meynell – in support of a letter to *The Times* protesting against the sentence of death on two wretched youths under twenty, Francis Forsyth and Norman Harris, for kicking to death a man on a footpath. Other *Times* correspondents criticized the 'roping in of TV personalities' to sway public judgement. The petition failed but the cause ultimately triumphed.

Heather was, for the time being, the writer of the family: she was doing three articles a week for the *Evening News* as well as running her marriage bureau. Stephen was appearing less frequently on 'The Critics' now, but often enough to enjoy paying a tribute to an old friend. In May 1961 Harold Scott, the character actor and singer, published his memoirs. At once Stephen succumbed to a nostalgia for the twenties. Harold Scott had begun, long before the First World War, in end-of-the-pier concert parties. He had been part of Stephen's Cave of Harmony and 1917 Club life; had been among the original singers of Herbert Farjeon's songs, from 'I've Danced with a Man Who's Danced with a Girl Who's Danced with the Prince of Wales' to the first Freudian lyric, Farjeon's 'My Libido Baby' ('my very complex kid . . . come and sub-sub-sublimate with me'). Ivor Brown, who was on the programme with Stephen, remembered Arnold Bennett slapping his knees with delight at Scott's songs. 'He could do three different kinds of Cockney accent,' Stephen recalled, and praised him for his gentleness of character.

Much time was spent at home with Luke, now four and a half. 'Luke is bright, beautiful (it seems to us), amusing and highly intelligent, extremely quick on words and he can sing in perfect tune. Thank God, thank God! One of the *most* important things to me. He can add and subtract and knows his letters and can write words like "go" and "dog" if I tell him they are military messages standing respectively for "charge" and a code-word for "enemy".' Luke was obsessed with soldiers about this time. 'You know,' Stephen told him, '*I* was a soldier once.' The boy looked puzzled. 'And were you killed?' he asked.

Stephen had been corresponding with Alistair Cooke ever since his first visit to America and they often met in London when Cooke came over to stay with his friends the John Metcalfs. Early in 1962 came a chance of paying a tribute. As radio critic Stephen decided to review 'Letter from America' which, since 1946, had done so much to explain America to Britain and would help to earn for Cooke his rare distinction of KBE. Cooke's New Year 'Letter' came up for discussion on 'The Critics' the following week. Stephen sensed a movement round the table to debunk it. He began by calling the broadcast 'very good–average Alistair Cooke', and went on to praise his qualities of 'topicality, human touch, and serious comment on a recent American event'. These were the invariable ingredients of Cooke's fifteen-minute weekly talk which had been coming across the Atlantic for sixteen years. For example, he had made fun of New York astrology almanacs prophesying the end of the world on 4 February, something nasty happening to Chairman Khrushchev on 9 May, and an unfavourable constellation of planets in November for Richard Nixon, then contesting the governorship of California. Suddenly, in an imperceptible transition, we learn that President Kennedy is a high-70s golfer, and Eisenhower nearly ninety. 'Is the goodness in the writing or the speaking?' Stephen asked.

One critic thought Cooke 'not astringent enough'. Another, Roger Manvell, leapt to Cooke's defence, praising his lifelong love of America and his unique ability as one born in Blackpool, England, to see both British and American viewpoints simultaneously. At this point the chairman, Walter Allen, tried to whip up the argument by suggesting that Cooke was simply a 'sort of public relations officer for the United States'. It was too much for Stephen. 'That's unfair!' he burst out: 'Remember, it was New Year's Eve, when you're allowed to pick up emotionalism.

Remember that Cooke actually read American history and American folk-song at Yale, after he'd taken a first in English at Cambridge. Remember, above all, how objectively he reported the presidential election, and how violently anti-McCarthy he was at a time when it was pretty risky to be so!' Cooke's style might be light and casual but he was ruthless about injustice. . . .

The BBC sent a copy of the script to Cooke in New York. 'It showed a side of Stephen – a serious devotion to principle – which I frankly hadn't known existed,' Cooke says. 'My affection for him was, to say the least, massaged by this.'

Stephen's old interest in wild life – always renewed whenever he met James Fisher (who was responsible for some of the Bird-manship gambits in *One-Upmanship*) – was stimulated about this time by Sir Peter Scott, yet another Savile Club friend; and the Potters were guests one year at the Wildfowl Trust dinner at the Guildhall. 'Everything we ate, except the pudding, had been caught or shot,' Heather remembers. In return, Stephen did some research into place-names and bird-names associated with wild life. It had all begun in a Lifemanship ploy of Peter Scott's:

One evening when we had been dining together at the Savile Club, Stephen got out a cigarette. I leant across to light it with one of the then quite new gas-filled lighters. 'I say, that's rather a good lighter,' he said. I handed it to him and he tried it a few times. 'D'you like it? Well, then it's yours,' I said. 'By all means keep it.' Stephen was clearly delighted. What he did *not* know was that I had that week given up smoking. I was not going to water down the Oneupmanship of my apparent generosity by telling him.

Stephen had temporarily abandoned volume II of his auto-biography for 'a long book on English Natural History Words, their background, etymology, etc.'. In this he would boldly challenge established authorities such as the *Oxford English Dictionary*. In letters to Sir Peter Scott he derived 'Slimbridge', centre of the Wildfowl Trust in Gloucestershire, from 'Heslinbruga', in the Domesday Book, meaning 'hazel bridge'; and 'duck' from an old German verb meaning 'dive', through a chain of words stretching back to an Aryan root by way of Latin, and aside to a Dutch word meaning 'decoy'. The name 'Scott' once may have meant 'wanderer', and may be related to Old French *escote* = a spy. 'That would mean,' Stephen concludes, 'that you were originally a tremendous hero or a frightful rotter, according to which side you were on'.

Social life was increasing, it seemed, in inverse ratio to his literary output. Muriel, in hospital, recovering from a major abdominal operation (she was now sixty-nine) had heard him on early-morning radio in November. It had been recorded

at 1 am at Grosvenor House . . . just after I had rowed in a race, Old Crocks against Oxford, on rowing machines on the dance floor, 1,000 guests, John Snagge stroking, in aid of the Lords Taverners Playing Fields Association. Prince Philip was umpire, in imitation exaggerated Leander clothes. He clowned brilliantly for half an hour and gave us each a miniature oar at the finish . . . last night we heard this same hero talk cogently about the preservation of Wild Life – another hero of mine, Peter Scott, asked us.

In New York, *Gamesmanship*, *Lifemanship* and *One-Upmanship* had been reprinted by Holt, Rinehart and Winston in one volume under the title *Threeupmanship*, with a new introduction by Stephen claiming that 'Lifemanship not only *is*, Lifemanship *does*. . . . I want [Americans] to think of me as each and every American's humble mouthpiece only, of a movement *which existed here before my name became known*. . . . Every State and many Counties of the Union has its own Number 1 Lifeman. It was indeed Mr Adlai Stevenson who first brilliantly added "brink" to "manship".' Rupert Hart-Davis's copy, sent to him for Christmas, was inscribed 'To Rupert – for reviving glorious memories.' Stephen flew over to New York for the launching and wrote back to Jack Collis: 'Every now and then, a fortunate break! I write an article for *The Sunday Times*, England, and after a pause comes £10. Fine. But here they ask – the magazine asks – for a series, and will I come over for a week and bring my wife too, all expenses paid . . . the only trouble is (a) I can't afford to tip the lift man, and (b) what I want most at this moment is a tennis single with you.'

Another 'fortunate break' – the interest on a considerable investment – was the publication, in 1963, of a Penguin edition of all the -*manship* books (except *Gamesmanship*) in separate paperbacks, each selling about 70,000 copies. This was not exactly bringing Potter to the masses, nor great wealth to Potter, but it was useful pocket-money to one whose pocket frequently had a hole in it.

His correspondence with Jack Collis, his great link with youth and the twenties – always intermittent, with long silences, yet picking up wherever it had left off – now revived. Collis had just published *Marriage and Genius*, a study of Strindberg and Tolstoy as husbands. Stephen had always felt that Collis's work had been neglected and undervalued and was glad of the opportunity, in a 'World of Books' broadcast, to give his old friend a few minutes of warm praise. He had telephoned the *Sunday Telegraph* to find out whether they were going to review the book (they were), and then dashed off a postcard to Collis: 'I meant to say, on the telephone yesterday, that the grip of your book was keeping my interest completely. I am as you know a very slow reader; but coming home at 3.15 am last night I still could not refrain from 40 minutes of Collis meat.'

In August 1963 Stephen appeared as chairman or compère of a television programme, 'The British at Play', produced by Sid Colin. In a series of gently mocking, sub-Farjeon sketches about holidays at home and abroad, Terry-Thomas played half a dozen different roles, assisted by Wendy Craig and Tony Tanner. It was the sort of show Stephen ought to have written himself but somehow never did. What distracted everyone's attention, however, was that Stephen walked on to the set with a limp, supported by a stick: '. . . whether as a ploy, or because of a disability it was not explained', wrote the *Daily Telegraph*, which described him as 'donnish'. The mysterious complaint, never given a precise name, had already shortened his drive at golf. He looked arthritic but it was unwise to use the word in his presence: he would have brushed it aside with something about 'my old peace wound'.

In November Stephen, perhaps belatedly, received radio's accolade for those who have truly arrived: he was invited by Roy Plomley to choose his eight records, his favourite book other than the Bible or Shakespeare, and his one luxury in that thirty-seven-year-old fantasy which only Bernard Shaw ever refused to appear in, 'Desert Island Discs'. This uncannily revealing programme, which instantly detects a false note or betrays a pose, showed Stephen at his best. It began with a routine bit of Lifesmanship:
Plomley: 'Stephen Potter, I've known you so long – may I call you Stephen?'
Potter: 'Why not, Plomley?'
How would Stephen react to life on a desert island? 'I'd be afraid of going mad. To prevent this, I would choose records associated with different times in my life, records I remember not only as

music but as *places*.' He remembered his 'wonderful cousins' at
Warlingham when he was nine, and their loft where there was a
model railway and an old phonograph with only three cylinders, one
of *Tannhäuser*, another of the March from Elgar's *Wand of Youth*
suite, and a third of Harry Lauder.

The Elgar was record no. 1. 'There's an extraordinary change of
tempo and key in the middle, and this opened a door to me, I think,
of a new kind of music. Different from hymn tunes, anyhow.' His
second choice, from the same period, was the trio from Act I of
HMS Pinafore which he had seen at the Kennington Theatre when
he was ten: 'A British tar is a soaring soul.' He remembered 'the
intense excitement of hearing an opera for the first time, which I
already perhaps partly knew from Father and Mother playing and
singing bits of it.' Under Roy's gentle interrogation he retraced
schooldays at Westminster, the London of before 1914: 'In those
days I wasn't sure whether I wanted to be a writer or a musician.'
The conversation turned on joining the Army, going up to Oxford,
teaching at Birkbeck, 'writing an unreadable novel under the
influence of Virginia Woolf', beginning to write for the BBC in
Schools Broadcasting. . . .

Record no. 3: Beethoven Quartet Op. 18, No. 4: 'After school I
used to thump slowly through the Beethoven piano sonatas – like
Bernard Shaw, I was educated by them – but this Quartet was the
first thing that made me realize there was more to Beethoven than
sonatas.' Potter's progress in music had been hampered because the
Potter family, although theatre-going and church-going, had not
been concert-going. After a short look back to the BBC and 'How'
there was record no. 4 – Stravinsky's *Petrouchka*, 'my gate to
modern music'. Times and places were to be the basis of his choice,
he had said; but he did not further explain this choice to Roy
Plomley: we shall see, from our knowledge of Stephen's life, that it
can be linked with record no. 8.

Plomley asked the inevitable questions about the *-manship* books
and then there was record no. 5 – the Bach Double Violin Concerto
– 'and that means the Proms' – and no. 6, Fred Astaire's 'Top Hat,
White Tie and Tails' (his only concession to popular music, which
is odd in a man who, in his youth at least, could not bear not to know
the latest tune and the latest dance-step). This, he said, is 'to remind
me of my dancing days and especially of the thirties'. No. 7 was
more Bach (odd in a man who always saluted Beethoven as the

greatest): the Busoni piano arrangement of the Toccata from the Toccata, Adagio and Fugue. And lastly, the finale of Poulenc's ballet suite, *Les Biches*, was played, 'a reminder of the great pleasures of modern music and the ballet in the twenties under the Diaghilev regime. I learnt so much music then. . . .' (Yes, but from whom? Surely from 'Tom and D.', the guitarist and his lutenist wife, who laughed at Wagner, loved the Dolmetsch revival of old music, yet welcomed the moderns and introduced Stephen to the ballet. Was not Poulenc his Vinteuil, *Les Biches* his *petite phrase* that brought memory flooding back? Stephen, sturdily English in most of his tastes, was not over-fond of Proust and would probably have pooh-poohed the idea.)

Stephen moved back to simplicity in his luxury and his book choice: a pair of field-glasses, and 'a good book on sea birds and waders so that I could try to identify them'.

Another, more domestic, kind of bird was in his mind and would be the subject of his next book. It is strange, perhaps, that Stephen, so good at amusing children, who had brought up two sons by his first wife and was now in a sort of father-grandfatherly relationship with Luke, nearly eight, should never have written a children's book until now. Taking Andrew and Julian to school in the thirties he had told them stories of a rather tiresomely one-up parrot called Squawky. He had told Luke stories of the same bird who, it must be admitted, had some remarkably Potterish qualities. He lived in the Zoo and amused himself by putting up spurious notices everywhere, such as 'Professors and Chief Keepers Only' in the children's playground, and changing the labels on the animals' cages so that the tigers were called camels.

This was because Squawky was a Clasperchoice and Clasperchoices are only born once every hundred years. (Anyone who notices a resemblance between this and E. Nesbit's *The Phoenix and the Carpet* should look the other way.) Squawky was multilingual; he could both talk and write; he 'could not only imitate, he could make his voice seem to be coming from different places, even out of different people's mouths. . . . Squawky didn't mean to be bad. It was like sneezing; he couldn't help it.'

Eventually Squawky is dismissed from the Zoo; but all comes right in the end when, to please his friend Bolo, a puffin, he clears the puffin island of marauding gulls and wins a hero's medal.

It is clear that Stephen intended this to be the first of a series of children's books and that Squawky was meant to be a kind of James Bond among parrots. But the book sold only 5355 in Britain and just under 5000 in America. It was translated into Polish and published in Warsaw in 1980. George Him, who did the pictures – he had also illustrated the whole Schweppshire advertisement series – carried out his task supremely well, considering that the whole Potter world was 'alien' to him ('that Savile Club terrified me'); his explanation of the comparative failure of *Squawky* was taken from a New York publishing friend who said: 'A boid on the cover *never* sells.' Or, as a trade press reviewer put it: 'Jokes packed too hard for young readers.'

The Lifemanship game had long begun to pall, but Stephen was stuck with the label and any newspaper story about him mentioned it. In April 1964, joining Heather for a holiday in southern Spain, he managed to remember his passport but found, on arriving at London Airport, that it was out-of-date. Headlines everywhere: 'One *Down*.' But there were other games, especially word games. With John Metcalf, head of an advertising agency, he always played the 'If Only' game, invented by both of them. It consisted of creating a set of circumstances which would enable a Great Wit to utter a Great Witticism. It irritated Stephen that personalities like Noël Coward, Sydney Smith, Oscar Wilde and Dorothy Parker had the reputation of Great Wits although only about six *bons mots* of each are actually known and remembered by the majority of people – Dorothy Parker on Katharine Hepburn: 'the gamut of emotion from A to B'. Noël Coward at the Coronation: 'Who's that little man beside Queen Salote?' – 'Her lunch, I expect.' The secret of being a Great Wit was to be able to say, at exactly the right moment, exactly the right thing to encapsulate the situation, if necessary making an unpardonable pun. (There are similarities to Muir and Norden's radio panel game 'My Word!' in which an involved story about Eskimos ends with 'You can't have your kayak and heat it'.) Thus a long story involving the Gulf of Mexico and Gertrude Stein is contrived so that the Great Wit can say at the end, 'A niche in time saves Stein'; and an equally long story about Leopold Bloom and James Joyce's brother ends with 'There's many a Jew word spoken in Trieste'. In cold print it looks terrible but with a few drinks on board it is hysterically funny to its originators. Similarly, an exhibition of vintage motor-cars is entitled, 'These you have shoved. . . .'

He had met John Metcalf in Cambridge in 1946. Metcalf was reading English with Dr Leavis. As secretary of a literary society at King's College, he had invited Stephen to give a talk on D.H.Lawrence. His first impression of Stephen was the cautious, Lifemanlike comment he made on an abstract painting in someone's rooms: 'I say, that's rather fun!' This perfectly OK thing to say gave rise to one of Stephen's nicknames – That's-Rather-Fun Potter. The two men had met again on Metcalf's election to the Savile Club three years later. Stephen, in the last decade of his life, had become devoted to his grandchildren, among whom he somehow included John Metcalf's children. He would arrive, uninvited, at their birthday parties and invent games for them. His entrance was always made in the same way: at the front door – 'A chap doesn't come unannounced to other chaps' houses – but *I* do'; and then, a clown's face appearing round the door of the room where the party was going on.

Christmas 1964 was spent at Graffham, Sussex, at the home of Jack and Joan, Lord and Lady Bethell, whom Stephen and Heather had met in Spain. It was a Christmas of worries. Heather was imperfectly recovered from bronchial asthma; Luke had been rushed to Queen Mary's Hospital for Children at Carshalton with acute nephritis; Stephen had been so worried that he had forgotten to go to a business luncheon 'where I was due to speak for a large fee'. Stephen to Muriel: 'I so often wish my work was anything else but writing, which needs a reasonable ability to concentrate equably. . . . The daily journey to Carshalton is ruining us in time and nerve strain.'

A Christmas of conflicting interests as between grown-ups (bridge) and children (television), 'tremendous meals' and the need for exercise. On Boxing Day they went to a meet near Midhurst – 'a hopeless quest', Stephen tells his diary. So why not revisit Heyshott, only two miles from Graffham, where D., his 1925 girl, had lived? He had heard, some years ago, that D. was dead. The village pub, the Unicorn, was just as he remembered it. He inquired after the family – yes, D.'s children and grandchildren were still in the neighbourhood. He knocked at the door of D.'s old house: no reply. He went back next day and there they all were, gathered together for Christmas,

and D., her looks miraculously preserved – it was *Tom,* the brilliant eccentric, who had died – huge talk about old times, grandchildren and

neighbours listening in. . . . Extraordinary flashbacks to 1925! . . . That soft
alluring femininity, the infectious, uncontainable laugh (which made her
neck flush) – that most excellently classical profile – that self-possession and
pale skin – that thick hair, just pre-1925 in an Eton crop. . . .

It so happened that he was now writing *Anti-Woo*, originally
titled 'How to Lose a Woman'. He had recently changed both his
literary agent and his publisher. His agent had been A.D.Peters,
one of the 'Big Four'. Authors tend to blame their fluctuating
earnings on the failure of agents to create opportunities for them,
and Stephen believed he had disposed of his film rights too cheaply.
He had accordingly transferred his custom to a new agency headed
by his old friend Sir Gerald Barry. His publisher was now
Heinemann; no longer 'my one and only superpublisher, Rupert'.

Anti-Woo begins, like *Supermanship*, with a recapitulation of the
whole history of Games/Lifemanship, as if the author were afraid
that in two years he had been forgotten. He is offering the world 'the
Lifeman's improved primer for non-lovers', embodying 'Coad-
Sanderson's scale of progressive rifts', and 'how not to be in love
without actually thwarting'. Pyramus discourages Thisbe by
closing the hole in the wall. Hostesses, by forcing men to meet
women, create anti-woo situations. Remember escape-ploys at
parties, like saying 'let me get you a drink' and then disappearing; or
remarking 'my wife is longing to meet you'. Reflect that a woman's
eyes are *not* like stars, they are more like jellyfish; her neck is *not* like
a swan's, but more like 'the southern entry to the Doncaster By-
Pass'. The way to lose Potter is to hover behind him with an ash-
tray, saying 'Mind the carpet. . . .' Yes, the invention is beginning
to flag. Some of the gambits leading to 'love-freeness' are too true
for comfort, such as 'losing any desire to show that you are a happy
couple', because there are 'no more reserve tanks of affection'.
There are bits of Stephen's own life everywhere: the case of Harold
Doe of Wembley who, 'after reading Samuel Butler's *Way of All
Flesh* . . . broke away and took a bedsitter in Frognal'; and the signs
of boredom – the deep voice, small smile and the steady gaze that
mean he isn't listening.

The book, published in August 1965, was tepidly reviewed; *The
Times Literary Supplement* bestirred itself so far as to call its author
the 'all-time champion in the art of making the same joke in the
same way without any sense of strain or sign of diffidence'. It was

very nearly the kind of book People Give Each Other for Christmas without Actually Reading.

There was again an escape by travel, however, this time to Canada and Mexico on another lecture tour. In Canada he visited the new Simon Fraser University at Vancouver which had just been opened by the head of the Fraser clan, Lord Lovat. 'We were in chaos,' says Professor R.J.Baker (now Vice-Chancellor of the University of Prince Edward Island), then head of the Department of English:

I took him round the university, showing him *Gamesmanship* classified in the Library as 'physical education', but also showing him that we had *The Muse in Chains*. He seemed particularly pleased that we had it and that I knew it.

Simon Fraser is on top of Burnaby Mountain, rising from the sea to 1200 feet. Potter suggested a number of ploys for our athletic teams. 'You could put a cylinder of oxygen in the opponents' dressing-room, saying: "Now don't worry about the height. We always have oxygen – and doctors – available. You may feel a little dizzy and breathless – with a few chest pains – but it's never permanent; well, rarely." '

He also told a few stories of attempts to play Gamesmanship on him, especially in the US, and of the strain of playing the role all the time.

Stephen apparently told Professor Baker he was working on a 'scholarly dictionary' (this was presumably the 'etymology of words from Nature' which was eventually published as *Pedigree*). 'I told him what was happening in English language studies, in particular the work of Chomsky. . . . He seemed very tired. . . . He still regretted not having had an academic career.'

Stephen did not enjoy this trip. He was not used to travelling without Heather. He came south to Mexico, feeling desperately lonely. To his diary: 'Something about that tenth-floor bedroom in Mexico City. Alone . . . beating heart – my desperately unattractive old guide waiting to get me going next morning . . . feeling of being alone in the *Universe*, not just the world.' And to his brother-in-D.H.Lawrence, Jack Collis, a letter from Acapulco, hot, humid and full of tourists:

I think very often of you. 3 days ago I was staring at the mysterious carvings of the Quexalcoatl pyramids – bang in the middle of Plumed Serpent land. The strange thing about this place is that it is in continual decay. The modern Mexican is less sophisticated than the 'Revolution' Mexican of 1910 – he less than the Spanish Colonial Mexican, he less so than Aztec,

Aztec less so than Maya, and so on back through eras – a sort of pocket edition of Spengler.

All this is free, but I am very lonely, rather unhappy, inclined to moan, and, in Mexico, hampered by a feckless, charming, unpunctual, but nevertheless offical (part of the bargain) guide. Let's meet when I'm back in early October – I'm dying for tennis – but *how* is your arthritis-shoulder? If you can't serve I shall have a chance. Hooray! Stephen.

Chapter 15
Diminuendo

His depression had physical causes: he was about to enter 'the worst year of my life', a year of fear and courage, his spirits going up and down, but more often down, as work and health interfered with one another. To Muriel, his stern critic, thanking her for a birthday fiver, he wrote in February 1966: 'You always seemed to approve of me more when I was a flibbertigibbet pleasure seeker, rushing round. Now that I am steady, unextravagant, family-supporting and "good", you sometimes approve less. . . . I prefer the young Potter.'

On 2 March he woke up at 5 am with 'my bloody little complaint, paroxysmal tachycardia'. It went on for six hours: 'That horrid grey feeling of imminent dissolution – not so much that I was going to die, but that death itself was going to be colourless and dreary and the absolute end of everything.' Two months before, he had gone to his doctor, 'the immortal Morgan', with a number of symptoms he did not understand. 'Immortal Morgan' had told him that he hadn't got 'it' (presumably cancer), that he should stop worrying, above all stop reading medical books; he gave him some tranquillizers. 'I seem to be getting it now every ten days,' Stephen told his diary, 'and something tells me the heart won't stand it much longer. Damn – I shall have to go to a specialist.' What were his most harmful habits? He wrote them down: 'Cigarettes 40%, drink 30%, too much food (H. says starch) 50%.' This makes a total of 120% but no matter: 'This boils down to a slightly misused stomach – surely rather a severe payment?'

Consolation – a soothing escape into the past: 'I'm transcribing my diary for 1948, and note the constant lunches with . . . [he names three girls] etc. – not long before THE one came to put a stop to all that kind of nonsense.'

His illness must be kept, as far as possible, from editors, publishers and the BBC. He must remain employable. On 21 April, just before a 'Critics' recording session, an alarming urinary symptom:

After dinner Morgan, for once, doesn't smile at me and tell me it's nothing ... rings up the John and Lizzy genito-urinary man, whom I'm to see tomorrow. He pretty well told me I might have cancer, the chances were against it, but I must prepare for some sort of exploratory hospitalization; walked home with me and gave me a couple of sleeping tablets which I was thinking of taking in bed, but fell asleep instantly – my usual reaction to serious trouble.

Crash: when hopes collapse, Stephen writes *crash* in his diary. He was having to undergo exploratory tests, perhaps even surgery, just when some writing assignments and radio and television engagements were coming in again. On 22 April: 'Effect on me of first real chance of terminals must be observed. Wave of depression is intense. Not particularly long-lasting though. Rather a good thing that Heather regards it, not of course understanding because I haven't told her, as another household nuisance like the meat not arriving. I don't want sympathy – I remember Uncle Josh in a similar situation shutting me up when I tried it.'

Many daily entries now end with the admonition to himself: 'Courage, Potter!' He manages to cut down on tobacco and alcohol and cheers up enough to write a letter to *The Times* in June. The paper had carried one of its famous fourth leaders about a big tailoring company's poll of 10,000 women on how they thought men should be dressed. The anonymous author (who may have been Stephen's friend Peter Fleming) quoted Lifeman's recommendation of 'Break-Phast shoelaces for the man who wants, in a hurry, to look carelessly dressed'. Stephen replied:

In your leading article today (June 2) you suggest that the wearing of odd socks or broken shoelaces, advocated by me, is not the best way to gain favour with women, who prefer their escorts to be well-groomed. *Lifemanship has always admitted this.* We do maintain however that in face of the extraordinary difficulties of self-grooming, it is better not to make a half-shot at it. Positive untidiness is in every way preferable to the merely neat.

John Curtis of Weidenfeld & Nicolson had been trying to get him to write a book on some aspect of games but, in a fit of depression, Stephen wrote saying that 'recent hints of serious illness' had drained him of energy. It was an unusual admission.

'Pompity-pompity-pomp ... the small puppy in my chest struggling for freedom. .... I daren't tell anybody, because they'll all start giving me advice – "see a good doctor".' He did take a second opinion, however, and in November entered St Mary's Hospital for tests. Among several complaints was a new heart condition with another frightening name, auricular fibrillation, in which the heart beats with a completely irregular rhythm unless it is controlled by digitalis. 'My water is not only red-brown, it has a head on it like Guinness. My only doubt is whether I have cancer of the liver, lungs, stomach, or pericardium, or chronic glomulero-nephritis.' (Oh, those medical books!) Next day he has cheered up: 'Two bright spots. (a) That this hospital is outrageously comfortable and the nursing first-class and even the food highly reasonable. (b) If I am really ill, and have been for some time, then I am not so much to blame for my work failure of recent weeks or months.' The day after this: 'Joy! the pulse, though 90, is *regular*. It is possible to relax. Yet do I feel waves of returning health? Far from it . . . something is said to be holding me back and the secret seems to be locked in the chest X-ray. . . . This little mark in the chest. Interesting.'

Ten days later he was home again, writing symptoms and fears and doubts in his diary – can he believe the doctors 100 per cent? – why is he so drained of energy? He who had once walked at a speed of five miles an hour, who could not let any day pass without a round of golf or its equivalent: 'I don't *want* to walk out of doors. I feel lazy, armchair-bound. . . . When I see the concealed worry of glorious H. I realize that the one thing I mustn't do . . . is to pass out slowly, *diminuendo*. In 1936, the year Edgar died, I saw this in close-up, and its effect on Moyna. . . . A quick exit, if exit it must be, would help Heather and Luke to make a new life.'

He turned with pleasure to completing a review of a bird book, which he had left unfinished before going into hospital, and to television, 'the last of the Sherlock Holmes repeats, *The Illustrious Client*. I can only say I watched this transfixed with pleasure. Douglas Wilmer – just the right looks (but not quite the ascetic introspection) of Holmes. Nigel Stock the Dr. Watson for all time – and Peter Wyngarde the perfect villain, with lots of fog. Oh, joy!

Much more entertaining than a glimpse of Cassius Clay knocking out his 5th victim.'

Crash. Not health this time so much as money. On 7 December: a slight uplifting of spirits as the *Sunday Telegraph* invites him to write 100 words on 'my book choice of the year': he chooses Harold Nicolson's *Diaries and Letters, 1930–39*, and the *Oxford Etymological Dictionary*. There were no other commissions, no answers from publishers to ideas submitted. Twelfth December is full of disappointments: a letter which looks as if it contains a cheque turns out to be a statement of royalties already paid; negative telephone calls to publishers; and a tachycardia. 'I don't think I've had a worse day since school, about 1915.' Deepest of all worries is one which has been pushed out of sight: '... my approaching £800 overdraft and £1,000 debts due January 1st'. He has not yet told Heather.

Three days later he awoke from a nightmare: in his dream he was saying goodbye to dinner guests after midnight, among them Doyne Bell, his doctor friend. 'The top light in the hall looked dim and eerie. The hall looked larger, with darkness at the edges, and a high roof. Then suddenly the front door blew open. . . . I gave a mock ghostly laugh as if to say "Bogey, Bogey!" Doyne echoed me; and then it seemed to me that the laugh was echoed again, immense but very distant. . . . I was too hot. But how's that for a premonition?'

As Christmas approached he grew reckless: 'Because I am, according to all common sense and probability almost ruined, I am particularly extravagant, by the standards of my monstrous overdraft, in getting presents for everybody. I have a "last time" feeling about it, and want to, if I can, please everybody.'

Andrew knew about his finances. At Christmas Stephen shrugged it off with 'something always turns up', and lost himself in his family and grandchildren; it was a Christmas organized by Heather who 'does it all with matchless charity and humour'. '*How I would die for H.*,' Stephen told his diary on Christmas Day, 'if it could do any good. With quite a cheerful cheer.'

Something did turn up: on the day after Boxing Day his literary agent telephoned: 'He said that McGraw-Hill had made an offer for *Golf Gamesmanship* with an advance only slightly below that for *Anti-Woo*. This has the precise shape of the "last-minute save" which I've always lived on. . . . All quite jolly!'

Taking stock on New Year's Day, as he had done every year since his sixtieth birthday, he wrote, looking back on 1966, 'in mind, character and health I am completely different from myself 9 months ago . . . in April last, I began to lose confidence; to feel an intermittent irascibility, which I now realize was pathological; I failed to get on with interesting commissioned books. . . . I began to lose friends; even e.g. Ralph Richardson, and, unbelievably, Muriel; I put up the backs of some members of the Savile. . . .' But he has a book, or books, to do; he must discipline himself to write 1000 words a day. . . . As he writes Heather comes into the room: 'H., my utter standby: loyal in all the important ways . . . going off to Berkshire to play golf. . . . I am so glad she *is* doing this. She must redevelop her games, probably now without me. (Now then, Potter. No tears of self-pity. Down with the one dry sob dept. And it helps no one to say I wish I was dead.)'

There had been little golf for Stephen for a long time. Arthritis had shortened his drive though his approach shots were still cunning up to the crisis of April 1966. Golf was the love of his life and it cheered him now to be working on a book about the game, helped from afar by friends such as Alistair Cooke who did not yet know how ill he had been.

Sunshine was always good for him and, in January 1967, he and Heather went to stay with friends in Jamaica. Here, surprisingly, he played tennis and drove a car. Driving had never been forbidden by his doctors but there had been some near-disasters. 'From Jamaica, 84°,' he wrote to Muriel, 'we flew 3 hours North to New York, 4°, and full of snow ploughs and abandoned cars. We had 4 days of this.' In Jamaica,

in spite of thrilling flora, and extraordinarily charming lizards who remain stock-still, clasping the middle of a white ceiling with tiny hands, because evolution has taught them that stillness is the best hiding place; in spite of charming birds, to which nature, because of their extreme smallness, has given a fierce expression as a defence; in spite of clear gentle crystalline seas and white sands, in spite of amusingly humorous West Indians and an astonishing absence of colour bar . . . I am glad to get back, because England is much the nicest place.

He thanked Muriel, in the same letter, for her birthday fiver. He was sixty-seven. To his diary: 'I must say my age gives a tremendous Zing to the reading of the *Times* obituaries. Most of them seem to be a little one side or the other of 66 – with a slight preponderance of the less. It keeps one on one's toes. My heart sinks a little when I see a 64 or 5. These mid-sixties seem quite vulnerable.' For about twelve years Stephen had been clipping obituaries from *The Times* and annotating them – people he had either known or admired from a distance.

In much better health and spirits he threw himself into a new interest, the St John's Wood Preservation Society, which usually met at 23 Hamilton Terrace. 'They really are a delightful lot. They are completely transformed by their second drink. Old Councillor — starts off: "Can we get started, I've got an appointment," and then stays to the non-bitter end – an hour later: "I always enjoy it here." . . .' The Society's principal aim at this time was to prevent the demolition of some early Victorian houses in Loudoun Road (where Bertie Farjeon had once lived); Stephen's name helped to give it publicity in the press ('One-Up Man Opposes Building Scheme').

Heather was also writing. She had published two books on marriage, from the experience of her bureau, and in this year published *Royal Wives*, an unusual study of the Queens of England – as wives. She and Stephen could not work in the same room because they both thought aloud as they wrote. Almost daily, immediately after lunch, Stephen went to the Savile – generally to the snooker table. The tachycardia, for the time being, seemed to be under control. It needed to be, for Stephen was still occasionally appearing on television in programmes like 'Call My Bluff', the word-guessing game; once Heather appeared with him, both as members of Frank Muir's team.

Alistair Cooke was a regular visitor to London. Stephen had got to know him in New York in 1951, in the flush of his *Lifemanship* success, when Cooke had recently published a book on Alger Hiss, *A Generation on Trial*. 'The first time he came up to my apartment,' Alistair Cooke remembers, 'he brought me a copy of *Lifemanship* inscribed "To Alistair Cooke – Piles of love from S.T.Coleridge (for delightful Hissmanship from Stephen Potter)". "Delightful",' Cooke comments, 'is a gruesome choice.'

The two men met again at John Metcalf's in London. One evening, Cooke says,

Stephen was sitting on a sofa talking to my wife with that desperate seriousness which was the vehicle of his best humour. Still thrashing away at his theme he reached into his breast pocket and pulled out a case of pencil-slim cheroots. He put one in his mouth and, just as he was putting the case back, retrieved it and flashed it in front of my wife. As her hand went forward, he said: 'Would you care for one? Frightfully expensive.' Although she pulled away for only a split second, before breaking into a great grin, it was the only time I have ever seen Jane blush with embarrassment – over anything in life.

Stephen managed to make Alistair join the Savile Club slightly against his will – 'best club in London, old boy': it was done in a typically oblique Potter manner:

He made a tremendous phoney conspiracy of the whole procedure of putting me up, protecting me from 'a little cabal that I think is forming against you'. I was having a drink in the Sand Pit before the committee was to pass judgement on me. I was going back to America the next day. He took me aside and hissed: 'Have you got a good doctor in America? Good, because on the twenty-fifth they sit to decide. May I suggest that on the twenty-fourth you get your man to give you something – a sedation, a mild tranquillizer? Mind you, I don't think there'll be any serious trouble, I think we've managed to scotch this opposition clique. Still. . . .'

Alistair Cooke took a very personal interest in *Golf Gamesmanship*, the book Stephen was now working on. John Metcalf thought that the book would do much better in America if Alistair wrote a preface to it, and this Alistair enthusiastically promised to do. He also feared that Stephen wasn't getting on with it fast enough. Over Christmas 1967 he bombarded Stephen with letters and suggestions. What about certain ploys used by Bob Hope and Bing Crosby, Lynch and Cameron, Ike Hardy and Bobby Jones and Herbert Warren Wind? 'Meanwhile,' Alistair concluded, 'I pray you will keep the right elbow in, the right knee braced, the pressure on the inside of the left sole, the club held so as to hold but not hurt a bird, the left hip out of the way as soon as possible, and the faith, baby. . . . God save you from the Klangles.' (Klangles, according to a definition attributed to Bob Hope, is 'a rush of cold shit to the heart'.)

Three days later, another letter: is Potter's *Golf Gamesmanship* really being written or is it only a rumour? If Stephen doesn't get on with it he, Alistair, will fly over to London himself and pick up the manuscript for McGraw-Hill. Another idea: how about Cameron's ploy of taking photographs of your opponent's swing, stance etc. and sending them, annotated with corrective advice, to your

opponent just before the match? Stephen *must* come over to the next
Masters' tournament; Alistair promises him a game with himself,
Pat Ward-Thomas of the *Guardian* and Herbert Warren Wind. . . .

New Year's Day, 1968: Stephen taking stock – usual gloom:
'Looks as if it's going to be a really bad year. Only saving grace is
that I've still got *this* object around' (here he glues in a photograph
of Heather). A week later:

Starting the day, at the moment, with something I really enjoy –
transcribing my diary. 1946 is the current choice. I would have to get out
my *New Statesman* criticisms to snip out the odd paragraphs, if they seem
any good.

Chief thoughts on above: Then and Now. One doesn't realize, when one
is in the middle of it, the happiness of being overworked, of being praised,
of being wanted (work-wise), of being regarded as good at one's job, of
never really having made a major blob – even if one *had* no money and no
car – and all those lunches, after all, were on the B.B.C. Yet I was often
moaning – complaining!

How is he, work-wise, today? He is, or has been, working on three
books; *Golf Gamesmanship* progresses at the expense of the other
two. 'Now to perform the balancing act . . . I've got a 6-month
respite for *Pedigree*. Now I've got to placate John Curtis [of
Weidenfeld] (lunch Monday).' The Weidenfeld book, always
nebulous in concept, was to have been about golf: the lunch took
place at the Savile but most of the time was spent at the snooker
table. *Pedigree* ('essays in the Etymology of Words for Nature') was
for Collins: it was, in aim, slightly beyond Stephen's scholarship
but he had the encouragement of James Fisher to lean on. He had hit
on the title when taking Luke to the Zoo: observing the crane's foot
(*pied de grue* = pedigree), he suddenly saw why it had been used, in
old genealogical tables, as a symbol of succession. The idea took him
back to boyhood, to his early botanical explorations with Muriel,
the romance of finding henbane on the walls of Corfe Castle, bee-
orchids on the path above Folkestone Warren; and later, on an
expedition with James Fisher, love-in-the-mist on the shore of a
loch in Easter Ross.

It was fatally easy to escape into the past or to tackle any task that
postponed the slog of a thousand words a day: 'Meanwhile, I'm
doing my first deep tidy for years. At the end of today I've got
through the wire baskets. Very little visible difference.' There was
escape into snooker, too: in 1968 the Savile Club celebrated its

centenary and it was thought proper to take this opportunity of codifying the rules. The task fell to Stephen, both as the Oldest Regular Player, and as the nephew of William Reynolds (Uncle Willie/Josh), 'a great student and devoted spectator of the game' and the inventor of the Reynolds System of Scoring. The resulting document is a model of clarity and good organization. 'The rules of Savile Snooker,' we are told, 'have never been written down. They represent the accumulation of civilized custom and word of mouth agreement. . . . Savile Snooker is basically "Volunteer" – i.e. a colour may be attempted without first potting a red. . . . It is uniquely typical of the Savile that certain rules have been accepted because they make things more, not less, agreeable for the player.' Thus the 'push shot is allowed, partly because it seldom helps, and partly to avoid long wrangling arguments'. The document goes on to such refinements as the 'Lawrence Gilliam treble', and the evils of Slow Play – 'Not more than 45 minutes for a game if other members want to play . . . the phrase "I retire" involves *no loss of face whatever.*'

Stephen's own ploy was very deliberate: he demanded absolute silence while planning a stroke: 'Your conversation is so riveting that it's putting me off. Can you please talk a little less loudly.' Another member who played with him noticed what seemed to him a Gamesmanship ploy: 'When the balls were lying promisingly he would announce his score after every stroke – (pot the red) ONE, (pot the black) EIGHT, (another red) NINE, and so on. I said: "I see you're going to make a big break," and explained why. Of course it put him off and he missed the next shot. One up to me!'

Stephen even had a special pair of glasses made for snooker: the sidepieces were attached to the *bottom* of the lenses so that he could see *all* distances on the table. To the Savile Centenary Brochure, 1968 (a year in which, incidentally, the Club had an American President, Herbert Agar), Stephen contributed an article on 'Ghosts of the Billiard Room', with anecdotes about William and Ben Nicholson, Orpen, Howard Marshall and Eric Linklater.

He was thinking obsessionally about the past now, sometimes chiding himself for doing so:

24 January 1968: Rang up P. (Poppy = Att) at Aldeburgh. I usually do this in a rush of feeling she must be lonely – or is it old affection that makes me want to talk to her? Next month she goes to stay with Ben [Britten] in Venice for a fortnight, all paid for. She's just as 'lonely' as she wants to be now.

'You come back to an empty house – no sound – except one or two mosquitoes. Quite harmless – but that is the sound which makes the house seem empty,' she once said.

On 1 February he was sixty-eight. 'Perhaps the best present is a small – tiny – watercolour from Att – which she knows I like and which is packed with enormous paddings and wedges of straw and tissue paper so that it looks like an incredibly valuable egg in a nest.' Next day, a birthday party, at which Att and the grandchildren were present: 'I enjoyed one of the pleasures usually prevented by the Great Dichotomy – seeing our grandchildren together. . . . Att . . . is so completely right with children. . . . Have deep talk with Att – who could be more simpatico?' Later that evening: 'But H. and me have such a good time at Stella's cocktail party!'

His health and spirits went up and down. Sometimes he was well enough to shout: 'Peardrops!' which meant that everyone had to drop everything else they were doing, even if they were in the middle of an acrimonious argument, and execute the wild dance, half reel, half hopscotch, which he had invented with Gordon Hamilton Gay nearly fifty years ago at Oxford. In May Heather took him to the healing sunshine – this time to Cyprus.

Alistair Cooke came over from New York, as usual staying with the Metcalfs in Charles Street; he was still anxiously awaiting the publication of *Golf Gamesmanship* and had written articles on Stephen in various golfing magazines. Stephen's last recorded game of golf was in July 1968 at Worplesdon but he was often fit enough to walk round a golf-course; one day he met Alistair unexpectedly.

'I went off to play golf at Swinley Forest,' Cooke recalls,

with Pat Ward-Thomas, the *Guardian*'s man, and Rita Hayworth, who was visiting London and had been my favourite golf partner at Riviera, one of the great golf courses in Los Angeles. When we'd finished our round, the three of us ambled over to Wentworth to watch the end of a tournament in which a young whiz-kid, Warren Humphrey, was beating the veteran Max Faulkner, once a fine golfer and always a dandy on the course. Walking down one fairway we ran into the Potters.

Suddenly a photographer appeared from nowhere and took a picture of Ward-Thomas, Rita and me. Nothing was said at the time, but Stephen didn't forget it. Next time I saw him, I'd forgotten all about it; but he came up to me, peered over both shoulders in his well-known Secret Agent pose, and whispered: 'Masterly ploy, that Rita Hayworth bit. Absolutely shattered Faulkner. Not a prayer of winning after that. Must have been pretty expensive to arrange, though – jet flight from Los Angeles, hotel suite and all that. Well done!'

In *Golf Gamesmanship* Stephen celebrated twenty-one years of Gamesmanship and dedicated the book *in memoriam* Edgar Lansbury (9) and Ronald Simpson (11), the figures representing their handicaps. Several informants and researchers are thanked in the acknowledgements, among them Bernard Darwin, Pat Ward-Thomas, Alistair Cooke, Geoff Paine, Henry Longhurst and Herbert Warren Wind. On page one there was a strangely uncomfortable sentence for anyone who knew the state of his health: 'The Great Handicapper calls: my debts to a great game must be paid, the small monument must be completed.'

Golf is susceptible to Gamesmanship, he says, because it is a *still ball* game whose players are in close contact: 'The less violent physically, the more vulnerable psychologically.' In an historical outline he notes that Scotland began the game and America took it over. The British, ruined by 'faulty warm-hearted play', are now permanently one-down and waste time on trying to choose one of the twelve different ways of pronouncing the word 'golf', from 'goff' to 'gerlf'. The great one-downness of British golf, we are given to understand, dates from the 1913 American Open at Brookline when Vardon and Ray were beaten by Francis Ouimet, 'an unconscious gamesman'. Hagen, by contrast, was a spectacular Gamesman, driving golf balls from the deck of the *Mauretania* into the sea and from the Savoy Hotel roof into the Thames.

Hagen, too, was unnervingly well dressed, with two-tone shoes and plus-fours. He also carried a special left-handed club for getting out of the rough (this was in the happy days when you could carry up to thirty clubs). Alistair Cooke contributes the information that Doug Saunders (USA) wears off-putting puce shoes and magnolia trousers.

There follows an ingenious speculation about pre-golf golfers and their putative handicaps. Julius Caesar was probably 11; Mark Antony posed as 6 but was really 16; Mozart 'a bare 13'; Aeneas? difficult to assess; Dido would have made an 'unpopular President of Sunningdale Women'.

Odoreida reappears as the originator of Oafish Remarks likely to upset an opponent. Several incidents of Stephen's 1951 golf tour of America reappear (such as the non-appearance of President

Eisenhower at Burning Tree, and the President of Pine Valley who gave Stephen a game because he thought he was Stephen Spender); and so do the stories of C. Joad gatecrashing a golf club where he was not a member and bathing nude in a stream in the middle of a game. The book ends, again uncomfortably, with an Ave Atque Vale: now that Gamesmanship has come of age, 'I am glad to leave it (with a touch of regret) in the hands of my successors as long as they refer to me for a final decision'.

There is something about golf which inspires good writing, even poetry. Reviewers of the book were divided equally between professionals like Henry Longhurst and laymen for whom golf was a spectator sport. The back of the dustcover bore a photograph of Stephen demonstrating a ploy to Ronald Simpson who wore a suitably comic expression of bafflement. One of the most enthusiastic reviews was by W.A.Darlington, veteran theatre critic of the London *Evening News*: 'My feelings, in reading this collection of the Master's writings on gamesmanship in golf, which are now world-renowned and have added a most valuable word to the language, are like meeting a V.I.P. whom you first knew as a small boy. Apart from all that, it is a reminder of how very beautifully Potter does write.'

Among the many signed copies he sent to friends was one to Joe Bryan III, inscribed: 'To Joe (who knows, better than me, that life *is* golf, if on a smaller scale) warmest Christmas greetings and general affection from Heather and Stephen.'

His correspondence with his sister Muriel, who was now seventy-four, had become intermittent since 1966; she seemed not to understand how ill he had been, probably because he had told her only bits and pieces of what was happening to him so as not to worry her. In the autumn of 1967 he had begun a letter to her but had thought better of it. Now, a year later, he dug it out, finished and sent it to her: 'What has happened to that fine old Stephen/Muriel axis?' Has he offended her? Has she heard something bad about him? She had been over-critical of him since his year of illness in 1966: was there some misunderstanding?

We do not know what Muriel wrote in reply but in his next letter to her he unburdens himself of his acute financial worries. He has small speaking engagements, he and Heather are both speaking at a luncheon in Southport for the Lord Roberts Fund. He has been asked to open an exhibition at Hatchards in Piccadilly for the launching of Margaret Lane's life of his namesake Beatrix Potter. . . . But, in general, owing to 'diminished work power', he is not earning enough. He has done that fatal Scott Fitzgerald thing, borrowed money from his literary agent. Heather does not know. 'I have ONE asset – something I could use as security – my Gamesmanship Books MSS. Some American University? But the placing of these takes time, and depends on luck.'

On 8 November 1968 he wrote Muriel the longest letter he had ever written anyone. It was a kind of 'General Confession of S.M.Potter'. To Muriel, 'my oldest and dearest friend', he admits

a huge fault in my life. If you were ever seriously to criticize me, it should be for this – but you don't. . . . I am to a pathological extent a head-in-the-sand man about profit and loss. I have seldom been able to contemplate the idea of building up a sound position. . . . After 2 days hard work I give myself treats and a holiday. From '25 to '36 I was (except for *Coleridge*) giving myself a happy time, playing some game almost every day, at the expense of work.

He feels guilty about Att, who also loved games and social life, but had had to bring up the boys at the expense of her painting; yet she had somehow, as the boys grew up, worked harder than ever. 'I worked very well, for me, from '36 to '49 – but I let up again, terribly, after that when the money came in for *Lifemanship*. . . . Most of my life I have been behind with bills – something I hate happening, in reverse, to me. . . . Above all, I didn't take advantage, when I had it, of the blessing of marvellous health and strength.'

He counts other blessings – his children and grandchildren, his peacefully happy first marriage after 'two years' platonic friendship with the corduroy Slade student'. He reviews his 'many flirtations' which could not, he claims, become full-scale affairs while he was still married to Att because of 'the Buried Nonconformist Conscience'.

'I seemed destined, though a young and strong 45, to settle down on the outside of someone else's circle, as a wispy sort of Mr. Chips. Then came my last flirtation, and it was no flirtation. I fell in love with Heather and she with me. . . . Yet parting with Att was fraught with agony.' Heather, miraculously, had given up 'financial security of the most permanent sort . . . to live with the muddle and inefficiency and financial sickness of the Potter world – *my* world I mean.'

Yet he can look back on some successes, 'beyond my dreams, and

I think beyond my talents'. His first ambition, at twenty, had been 'to amuse people, to become a comic writer'. Yet his first novel, *The Young Man*, had been entirely humourless and he had given up hope. 'The big novel or the moving play – I never completely give up hope here. I wanted next to be a great critic or literary Professor. To be the man, for instance, who, when G.B.S. died, would write the definitive obituary. But when Shaw died I was given 7 minutes on an Overseas broadcast.'

He had perhaps an illusory view of the rewards of authorship. He complained that he 'never got the weekly column in a Sunday paper I hoped for', but there is a suggestion that he expected too much money – on the American scale, not the British.

'The comic trick developed later, into a sort of gift for affectionate satirical observations of human behaviour.' *The Muse in Chains* had shown the germ of such a gift; keeping diaries had helped it along; then the BBC sketches and finally *Gamesmanship*. 'This is something I am very proud of,' he tells Muriel, who had never thought much of it:

I am the only non-scientific writer of this century to introduce at least four words into the English and American Dictionaries. It made me loads of new friends just when I wanted them. It introduced me to a wonderfully amused America, and friends there.

On two successive weeks only *last month* I was sent a long thesis from the Department of Anthropology and Sociology in the University of Victoria on *Strategic Rhetorics in Face-to-Face Interaction : the Sociology of Stephen Potter*. No. 2 was a textbook on comic writing with a long extract from *Lifemanship* and *examination questions on the style*. It makes me feel I've sort of come full circle.

Stephen was being taken seriously about books which had been purely comic in intention. That Victoria thesis was the very kind of jargon-ridden 'educationalism' which he had mocked during his lecture tours of America.

His letter to Muriel ends in gloom, thinking of the death of old friends: this time it is Gerald Barry, 'a sort of model of mine for forty years. . . . About a month to live, as he well knows.' And a postscript: 'Can *you* do the *Times* crossword as it is now?'

He had now, to a great extent, learnt to live with constant illness, except for the inability to work which it imposed. He wrote quite clinically to his doctor about symptoms of increasing deterioration.

There was his tachycardia, attacks of which were usually marked in his diary with the abbreviation 'a/t'; a tachycardia now complicated by auricular fibrillation. He lamented the length of time it took to accomplish small tasks. He could walk only with a stick. The word 'cripple' appeared frequently in his diary. What he thought of as rheumatism or arthritis or even arterio-sclerosis was now complicated by something new which eventually would be identified as myelomatosis, a malignant disease of the bone marrow. Knowing this he must also have known that, as the medical dictionary coldly observes, 'it runs an invariably fatal course'. He even felt a certain macabre satisfaction in having a *rare* disease.

Early in 1969 he made arrangements to sell some of his papers and manuscripts to an American university. It was emotionally painful, as if he were selling his youth and middle age irrevocably, but it seemed 'my only prospect of money to keep me going a few months longer'. This time there was no last-minute financial rescue. A projected holiday in Jamaica had to be cancelled for lack of funds. On his birthday, 1 February, he wrote in his diary: 'Am in my 70th year and have just been reading an article which says "the normal span" is still basically the same. Must buck up and get going with my writing. Officially my last year?' He made a great, partly successful, effort to conceal from friends the extent of his illness, especially those who lived abroad. Alistair Cooke was trying to arrange another visit to America, a journey he could not have made.

What Stephen had feared most was now happening: he was going out of life *diminuendo*. One of the symptoms of his mysterious new illness was pins and needles in his fingers: 'By the pricking of my thumbs, Something wicked this way comes!' he told visitors. Always a lean man, he was now ghostly thin; but, says John Metcalf, 'he played his role, the perkiness never broke down in public'. He struggled along to the Savile Club, wearing his Leander tie, or a pink woollen knitted version of it which, when challenged, he seriously called 'my *select* Leander'.

He was by now losing the grip of his right hand and had to have his food cut up for him. There were spells in and out of King Edward VII Hospital at Midhurst and other hospitals in London. He had always been spectacularly forgetful; now he sometimes forgot where he was. At a cocktail party he wandered out of the house into the street, did not know where he was or why he was there. He began to have blackouts and hallucinations: one of these was that Robert Morley was living on the top floor of 23 Hamilton Terrace: 'We must get *rid* of him,' he kept telling Heather. At other times his mind was clear, his wit as fresh as ever.

In August his son Andrew wrote to Stephen's doctor, trying to get some idea of the prognosis. He received a carefully worded reply which listed a great number of things wrong. The doctor had at first diagnosed 'lung cancer leading to brain damage'. There was also 'scattered arthritis' and, of course, the patient was 'depressed'. The bone-marrow disease was not actually named. In sum, 'the outlook cannot be good'.

Cheerfulness breaks in: 'Dearest Muriel, it was marvellous to see you. I wished one of my impressable friends had come in so that I could show you off. . . .' He had just come out of one of his times in hospital. Soon he is writing about the Test Match and tennis: 'Wasn't the penultimate match in the Davis Cup superb?' Back to the remote past: 'Talking of links, there is nothing like the Old School' – and he does not mean Westminster. 'A charming lady who lives near here heard that I needed secretarial help. . . . Her name is Josephine Parr – a name which even I well remember, not only because she was at Clapham High School and knew you, but because she was a member of that enviably large family of Parrs, five girls and a boy, who lived at 2 and 4 Old Park Avenue.' How much did Muriel know about his illness? A year before he had said to her in a letter: 'I am reasonably certain that you will outlive me.' Now he minimized everything: 'It is a slow business, but I am getting on, in spite of one or two side effects of my drug, e.g. difficulty in gripping a pen (?psychological).'

To Andrew, he gave another explanation:

You wanted to know how I got on in Harley Street yesterday. A 40-minute session. Well, basically I was relieved. . . . My hand – or hands, very especially the right, are partially paralyzed. But this is not due, as I frankly feared, to a growth block in the brain, but to a lack of blood which naturally follows the original brain symptoms. It and I will adapt to the disability and pain involved. Most interesting. I am warmly assured, in answers to my most searching questions, that there is no malignancy.

Later that month he received a postcard from Jack Collis. Their friendship had always continued afresh at each intermittent meeting but there had been long lapses in their correspondence and they had seemed to be drifting apart. 'Nothing was going right for me,' Collis says in his autobiography, 'and I did not confide in him: I was too proud.' The postcard showed a picture of Killiney, Jack's home in Ireland, where he and Stephen had had (for Stephen) such an unforgettable holiday nearly fifty years ago. Stephen wrote back a dictated letter with handwritten additions: 'Your KILLINEY card gave me a big nostalgic pang. Two ends of one's life. Slight melancholy because I am slowly recovering from disease originally diagnosed as fatal. Marks? Huge meaty story when we meet. Please ring.' With difficulty he signed his name, adding: 'Note partially paralyzed hand.' Ironically the pain of holding a pen made his writing more, not less legible.

They met, and Stephen gave him an inscribed copy of *Golf Gamesmanship*. 'I had seen death in his face,' Collis says. For years Stephen had been telling him that he ought to write his autobiography. Collis was now ready to do it. Just after he had begun he telephoned Stephen again and was told he was 'away'. He assumed that this meant 'away for the weekend' and concluded that he must be getting better. In fact, Stephen was in hospital – for the last time. He now had pneumonia.

Visitors were admitted carefully for he was easily exhausted. They were mostly family, with one or two very old friends. Heather, knowing that she had seen him for the last time, came out of the hospital and on the steps met Gordon Hamilton Gay, cox of the 1921 Merton Boat and part-inventor of the 'peardrops' dance. He was the last of Stephen's friends to see him alive. 'I was expecting to find him confused, unknowing and distressful,' he afterwards wrote to Muriel; but 'he knew me immediately I walked in, with quite a cheery "Hello, Gordon!"' . . . When I reminded him of our old-time special whistle, which we always whistled on meeting, and was always rather a joke . . . he laughed quite clearly – tried to whistle it, but gave it up and laughed again.' Gordon mentioned that he had been reading *Golf Gamesmanship* with enjoyment. With an effort Stephen managed to say: 'I – liked – golf.' Then, with a last summoning up of defiance: 'I'll be out of this place in a week.'

He died early next morning, 2 December. The conventional obituaries appeared, all dutifully summarizing his *-manship* books, his works of criticism, the radio features, his Clubmanship; all ending with phrases like 'by his first marriage he leaves two sons, and one by his second'. By a macabre slip-up at Independent Television on 3 December Bill Grundy's 'Today' current affairs

programme contained a recorded interview with Stephen on
'Gamesmanship in golf'. That his last television appearance should
have been about golf would certainly have pleased him.

Then the unconventional obituaries appeared. 'Rare among
people who can talk so well,' wrote David Holloway in the *Daily
Telegraph*, 'he could, and willingly did, listen too. But then,
courtesy was always at the root of even his most outrageous comic
inventions.' Lord Horder added a footnote in *The Times* on the
unforgettable experience of playing piano duets with him:

There were certain rules you had to observe. 'Remember!' he would
suddenly cry in the middle of nowhere, 'we're coming to the bit *I* like to
play' – and then, whatever the printed score said, it was best to give way to
him, since his hands were large and rough. Or carried away by some
specially well-loved piece of embroidery – during which it was wise to
reduce the tempo so that he could savour it to the full: 'Come on, we must
have those bars again, *now*.' . . . It was perhaps Bach/Potter we used to play,
rather than Bach; but we enjoyed ourselves.

'British humour,' thought *Time* magazine, 'can be highly perish-
able, and its point is often so obscure as to defy detection – except
perhaps by the British themselves. But Stephen Potter's wry and
understated advice on how to win games, including the game of life,
with losing hands endeared him to readers on both sides of the
Atlantic.' The article occupied most of a page which, under the
heading 'Modern Living', it shared with a story about the Japanese
fashion for play-beds, including one that moved up eight feet to a
'mirror-covered nook in the ceiling'.

Bernard Levin devoted a whole article to him in the *Daily Mail*
and found him 'firmly in the tradition of English humorists that
includes Lear and Carroll, the Grossmiths and Pont'. Boldly
contradicting the *Oxford English Dictionary* he credited Potter with
the invention of the word 'ploy'. But the tribute that would have
pleased Stephen most came from Henry Longhurst who devoted
the whole of his golf article in *The Sunday Times* to golf
Gamesmanship. Potter's terminology had 'become part of the
currency of the language all over the English-speaking world.
Sherlock Holmes, Robinson Crusoe, Fifth Column, Quisling,
Blimp and the Old School Tie are examples that come readily to
mind.' He quoted examples of Gamesmanship from his own golfing
life, especially the importance of 'breaking the opponent's flow' and

wearing intimidating clothes. Why, Hagen and Sarazen had done this consistently! As his own drive shortened with age Longhurst devised a ploy of his own. To an opponent with an enormous drive, as he approached his second shot, he would say 'and to think that Nicklaus would *drive* this green with a 3-wood'. No doubt the Founder would have approved.

The BBC memorial programme for Stephen, broadcast just after Christmas, was one of those hastily-put-together features at a time of the year when you cannot get hold of anyone at short notice. Joyce Grenfell narrated and, with Carleton Hobbs and Betty Hardy, heroically bore the brunt of the script and of reading extracts from his books and radio scripts with Stephen's own voice from an earlier broadcast.

Stephen, a hoarder of personal memories, had few material possessions, but one of them he left to Joe Bryan III. It was his old Brigade tie. He seldom wore it, preferring the Leander but, when he did, it was in order to upset young Guards officers whom he met occasionally at parties and who could not reconcile his appearance and style of dress with that of a Guards officer in mufti. The brasher of them sometimes challenged him: 'I say, er, are you aware that the tie you're wearing, er, is . . .?'

'Perfectly aware. Second-Lieutenant S.M.Potter, Coldstream Guards. World War One, you know.' Collapse of young Guardee.

In May 1970 four people met for luncheon at the Dorchester Hotel. They were Raymond ('Canada One') and Dorothy Massey, and Edward and Norah Lydall. Edward Lydall had met the Masseys in New England and afterwards in his Albany chambers where they had all been filmed with Stephen for American television 'playing bridge in a gamesmanlike way', such as Edward's 'pushing a burning cigarette in an ashtray towards Ray so that the smoke went up his nose just when he was considering what card to play'. There was no bridge at the Dorchester that evening; just a solemn memorial toast to the Founder; and perhaps to the happy immaturity of all who have failed to carry out their life's designs for the sake of 'laughter and the love of friends'.

Acknowledgements

My thanks are due to many people who have helped me in the preparation
of this book. Above all to Lady James (Heather Jenner), Mrs Mary [Att]
Potter and Messrs Andrew and Julian Potter, for placing at my disposal
family letters, diary extracts, a draft and notes for Stephen Potter's
unpublished second volume of autobiography, and for much information
and help generally. To Sir Rupert Hart-Davis for information, the loan of
correspondence, and much kindness. To Mr John Stewart Collis, FRSL,
for the loan of correspondence. To Mr Alistair Cooke, KBE, for his long
letter about Golfmanship. To Mrs Ellen Dunlap, librarian, and Miss
Cathy Henderson, research assistant, of the Humanities Research Center,
University of Texas at Austin, Texas, for their help and guidance through
the Potter Archives. To Mr Keith Piercy for his account of Potter's
adventures as an amateur naturalist; and to Mr Lionel Millard for many
anecdotes about Potter at Oxford and the 1917 Club. To Miss Challice
Reed and the staff of the BBC Drama Script and Programme Information
Libraries. To the committee and manager of the Savile Club for
information (including the Rules of Savile Snooker), and to the secretary
of the Garrick Club. And to all those readers of the *Sunday Telegraph*,
Observer and *Guardian* (too many to list individually) who so kindly
replied to my letter to the editor asking for personal reminiscences.

The following, however, were especially helpful: Mary Hope Allen
(Mrs Merrington), Doone Beal (Lady Marley), Captain Jack Broome,
DSC, RN, Maurice Brown, Joe Bryan III, Mrs Elaine Brunner, Norman
Claridge, Douglas Cleverdon, Judge Cyril Conner, Dr Robert Gittings,
Mrs Jeanette Grenfell, Mrs Joyce Grenfell, OBE, Betty Hardy, Jack
Hargreaves, Lady Herbert, Lord Horder, Elizabeth Jane Howard (Mrs
Kingsley Amis), Lord Jacobson, Mrs Betty Johnstone, Dame Alix Kilroy
(Lady Meynell), J.W.Lambert, CBE, DSC, Edward Lydall, John and
Shelagh Metcalf, Gerald Moore, CBE, Professor Geoffrey Mure, Frank
Norman, Roy Plomley, OBE, Max Raison, Sir Peter Scott, CBE, DSC,

Margaret Stevens (of A.D.Peters & Co Ltd), Leslie Stokes and Professor
James Sutherland.

Among books consulted were Fowler's *Modern English Usage*; *Roget's
Thesaurus*; *The Life and Letters of Henry Arthur Jones*, Doris Arthur
Jones, Gollancz 1930; *Island of Skomer*, John Buxton and R.M.Lockley,
Staples 1950; *The Trial of Lady Chatterley*, ed. C.H.Rolph, Penguin
1961; *Am I Too Loud?*, Gerald Moore, Hamish Hamilton 1962; *Men and
Marriage*, Heather Jenner, Michael Joseph 1970; *An Eye for a Bird*, Eric
Hosking, Hutchinson 1970; *Ariel and Prospero*, D.G.Bridson, Gollancz
1971; *Bound Upon a Course*, J.S.Collis, Sidgwick & Jackson 1971; *My
Lives*, Sir Francis Meynell, The Bodley Head 1971; *Desert Island Discs*,
Roy Plomley, William Kimber 1975; *Oxford in the Twenties*, Christopher
Hollis, Heinemann 1976; *Joyce Grenfell Requests the Pleasure*, Joyce
Grenfell, Macmillan 1976; and *Fair Play: Ethics in Sport and Education*,
Peter McIntosh, Heinemann 1979.

The works of Stephen Potter

The Young Man, Jonathan Cape, 1929
D.H.Lawrence: a First Study, Jonathan Cape, 1930
Minnow among Tritons, Nonesuch Press, 1934
The Nonesuch Coleridge, Nonesuch Press, 1934
Coleridge and S.T.C., Jonathan Cape, 1935
The Muse in Chains, Jonathan Cape, 1937
The Theory and Practice of Gamesmanship, Rupert Hart-Davis, 1947
Lifemanship, Rupert Hart-Davis, 1950
One-Upmanship, Rupert Hart-Davis, 1952
Sense of Humour, Max Reinhardt, 1954
Potter on America, Rupert Hart-Davis, 1956
Supermanship, Rupert Hart-Davis, 1958
Steps to Immaturity, Rupert Hart-Davis, 1959
The Magic Number, Max Reinhardt, 1959
Anti-Woo, Heinemann, 1965
Squawky, the One-up Parrot, Heinemann, 1965
The Complete Golf Gamesmanship, Heinemann, 1968
Pedigree, Stephen Potter & Laurens Sargeant, Collins 1973

Index

weakness regarding financial
investments, 23; musical
accomplishments, 29; death of, 110
Potter, Gillie, 114
Potter, Heather, *see* Jenner, Heather
Potter, James, uncle of S.P., 22
Potter, Julian, 5q.: birth of, 95; to
Burgess Hill school, 98; evacuated to
Scotland, 110; attends schools, 117;
at Westminster School, 131; wins
'pancake greaze' at Westminster
School, 146; in Korea on national
service, 151, 156
Potter, Luke, 210, 218; birth of, 197;
suffers from pneumonia, 214;
contracts acute nephritis 225
Potter, Mary ('Att') first wife of S.P.,
3q., 16, 65, 77, 79; a good tennis
player, 79–80; a scholar of the Slade
School, 80; marriage to S.P., 83–4;
has first one-man exhibition, 95; has
exhibition of paintings, 158; divorces
S.P., 186; painting at Aldeburgh, 204
Potter, Muriel, sister of S.P., 23–4: at
St. Hugh's College, Oxford, 27;
teaches English at St. Paul's Girls'
School, 34, 55; headmistress of
South Hampstead High School, 98;
gives financial assistance to S.P.,
131–2; sends S.P. ideas for
autobiography, 210; illness of, 220;
receives 'confession' from S.P., 241
Potter, Stephen Meredith, 4q., 5q.: his
appearance, 7; as inventor of
Gamesmanship and Lifemanship, 7;
conceives first outline of
Games/Lifemanship science, 9;
invents *word* 'Gamesmanship', 11;
writes *Gamesmanship*, 16ff.; birth of,
20; boyhood, 21, 23ff.; his reading in
early years, 24; holiday venues with
family, 25; a 'mother's boy', 26;
education, 26; to Westminster
School, 26; starts keeping diary, 26;
as day-boy at Westminster School,
28; not very successful at school, 28;
interest in certain subjects at school,

29; minor talents apparent, 29; music
as chief outlet for sensibilities, 29; his
interest in sport, 30; volunteers to
join school rowing club, 30; desire to
join Army, 31; joins Brigade of
Guards in World War 1, 32; with
Jack Collis invents word-game
Atrocious Juxtaposition, 33;
commissioned in Coldstream
Guards, 33; in father's firm as
accountant, 34; offered opportunity
to go to Oxford, 34; enters Merton
College, Oxford, 36; first experiences
of Merton College, 37–8; in many
Oxford 'sets', 41; joins Merton
dramatic society, 41; his main
friendships, 41; develops song-and-
dance act with Gordon Hamilton
Gay, 42; with Jack Collis devises
system of Life Scoring, 43; non-
committal regarding politics, 43–4;
offered captaincy of Merton Boat
Club, 44; on vacation, 44–5; tells
mother of engagement to Tropical,
45; shares lodgings with Cyril
Conner, 46; begins practising
flirtation, 47; introduced to string
quartets, 48; joins Bach Choir, 48;
divides friends into 'sets' and
'specialists', 49; invited to dine at
High Table, 49; his theatrical debut
at Alvescot, 50; role as Claudio in
Much Ado About Nothing, 50–1;
nears Final examinations, 51; a cycle
tour of Cotswolds with Lionel
Millard, 52; second in Class Lists,
52; is recommended to Otto
Jespersen, 53; interest in 'wireless
broadcasting', 53; interviewed for job
with BBC but rejects offer, 53; vague
desire to be writer, 53–4;
indetermination of, 55ff.; books read
by, 56; inserts advertisement in *The
Times* to cure Cockney accents, 56;
resolves to take up violent physical
exercise, 56; decides to go on long
walk, 56–7; on holiday with Jack

258 Stephen Potter

Potter, Stephen Meredith (*contd.*)
Collis, 57; 'freelancing' in London,
58; attends Fabian meetings, 58; is
taken to 1917 Club, 58ff.; first
conversation with H.G. Wells, 58;
determination to write with purpose,
60; a passionate desire to conform,
60; plays tennis with Professor Joad,
60; in Professor Joad's company, 61;
meets Jack Collis again, 61; G.B.
Edwards as new friend, 61–2; enjoys
company of Meinertzhagens, 62–3;
applies for scholastic employment,
63–4; as housemaster at McNalty's
school for boys, 64; taught dancing
by Mary McNalty, 64; taken dining
and dancing by McNaltys, 65;
introduced to notabilities by
McNaltys, 65; first meeting with
Mary Attenborough, 65; meets
celebrities at Sir Alan Herbert's
house, 67; resigns housemastership,
67; coaches Sir L.M.'s son, 67–8; his
experiences during week-ends off,
68–9; becomes 'secretary' to Henry
Arthur Jones, 69; taken by Henry
Jones to Reform Club, 70; resigns
job with Henry Arthur Jones, 71; as
junior assistant lecturer in English at
Birkbeck College, 71; life at Birkbeck
College, 73; reads much English
literature, 73; his propensity for
'waffling', 73–4; pupils' impression
of, 74; list of books read by, 75; his
popularity with colleagues, 75;
uncertainty as to whom he is
addressing, 76; propounds his
method of dating a girl, 76; attempts
to convert others to own
enthusiasms, 76; introduction to
Elizabethan music and Russian
ballet, 77; partakes of long walks, 78;
his interest in botany, 79, 135;
holiday in Normandy, 79; again
meets Mary Attenborough, 79; Mary
as a good tennis player, 79–80; his
feelings towards Mary, 80; his

easiness when with Mary, 81;
courtship of Mary, 81; his
admiration for Sir Francis Meynell
and Herbert Farjeon, 81–2; to
Wychwood with Mary to meet
parents, 82–3; meets Mary's parents,
83; engagement to Mary, 83;
marriage to Mary, 83–4;
honeymooning at Chesil Beach, 84;
takes up residence at Chiswick Mall,
85; obtains car, 86; working on novel,
86; birth of son Andrew to Mary,
86–7; favourable reviews of first
book, 88–9; working on next book,
89; involvement in parties and sport,
90–1; playing word games, 91;
decides to write book on D.H.
Lawrence, 91; second book
published, 92; mixed reviews of
book, 93; book establishes S.P. as
'authority on Lawrence', 94; a new
party piece and 'cod lecture' act, 94;
birth of son Julian to Mary, 95;
cogitates on next subject for writing,
96; writes about Coleridges, 96;
favourable reviews, 97; holidays in
England and France, 97–8; children
sent to Burgess Hill School, 98;
disposition as father, 98; abhors
ignorance in sons, 98–9; established
as authority on Coleridge, 99;
opinions of writing in *The Times
Literary Supplement*, 100; writes
freelance scripts for BBC, 100–1; as
godfather and unofficial uncle to
Angela Lansbury, 102; his friendship
with Edgar Lansbury, 102; leads an
extremely busy life, 103; writing
criticism of English Literature
establishment, 103; his admiration
for George Saintsbury, 104; opinions
on literature and reviewers, 105–6;
criticism of his book on English
literature, 107; 1937 as an
outstanding year for S.P., 107;
elected to Savile Club, 107–8; his
improvement in golf, 108; offered

permanency as writer–producer in
BBC, 108–9; 'Guide to the Thames'
broadcast, 109; sends children to
Scotland during Munich crisis, 110;
meeting with Joyce Grenfell, 110;
move to larger house following
father's death, 111; fondness for
gardening, 111; devises 'Air Raid'
programme, 111–12; last notable pre-
war programme, 113; to Manchester
working for BBC, 115; billeted in
Rusholme, 115ff.; family together in
Manchester, 117–18; his liking for
J.B. Priestley, 118; acquires car,
118–19; losses at sports, 119;
produces documentaries, 119–20;
move to Hale, 120; plays croquet,
120; entertained by Sir Osbert and
Edith Sitwell, 121; his involvement
in producing plays, 122ff.; praise for
S.P. as producer, 123; enjoys War
Effort programmes, 125; move back
to London, 125; resides at Berwick
Hall, 125; his reliance on Betty
Johnstone, 126; improvises
'How . . .', 127ff.; extensive dealings
with Army, 130; physical fitness of,
130; collaborates in dramatized
documentary on extinction of Great
Auk, 130–1; has money worries,
131–2; augmenting salary by
reviewing, 132; criticism of Sir
Donald Wolfit, 133–4; move back to
London, 134; joins expedition to
Skomer, 135–6; presents satirical
programme on BBC, 137–8; spends
weekends with Sir Francis Meynell,
138–9; indulges in 'cod philology',
139; produces Chaucer's *Canterbury
Tales*, 140; special 'How' programme
at Christmas, 1946, 140; writes
Gamesmanship, 141–2; continues
'How' programmes, 142; produces
plays, 142–3; first meeting with
Royalty, 143; on scientific expedition
to Scotland, 143ff.; friendly reviews
for *Gamesmanship*, 145–6; broadcast

of 'How' programme at peak
listening hour, Christmas Day, 1947,
146; first meeting with Heather
Jenner (Cox), 147; engaged as editor
of *The Leader*, 148; on another
expedition to Sutherland, 148–9;
freelancing for BBC and book-
reviewing, 150; resigns editorship of
The Leader, 151; courtship of
Heather Jenner, 152; fascinated by
peers, 152; invited to fishing
weekend at Mull, 152; writing
Lifemanship, 153–4; has heart
condition, 155; *Lifemanship*
published, 155; invited to review
own book, 155; praise for book,
155–6; involvements after writing
Lifemanship, 157–8; house-hunting
in Hampstead and Thames Valley,
158–9; plans visit to America, 159; in
United States, 160ff.; on American
television, 162; hospitality by
Raymond Masseys, 162; meeting
with Joe Bryan III, 163ff.; his interest
in books and pictures whilst guest of
Joe Bryan III, 165; sails home, 165;
buys house in Aldeburgh, 166; at
height of fame, 166; in regular
correspondence with Joe Bryan III,
167; on all-male holiday to Spain,
167–8; enters into life of Aldeburgh
Festival, 169; entertains Edward
Lydall, 169ff.; a frequent visitor to
Lydall at Albany Chambers, 171;
social life interfering with work, 172;
writing *One-Upmanship*, 172;
synopsis of book after publication,
172ff.; lifelong fascination with
doctors and diseases, 173; success of
One-Upmanship, 174–5; suggests
writing novel, 175; enlists help of
Lionel Millard for editing anthology
of humour, 175; split in private life,
175–6; upstaged by Jack Broome in
golf game, 176–7; his 'flirtations',
177–8; makes many 'public
appearances', 179; gives lectures,